Moto Guzzi
THE RACING STORY

Other Titles in the Crowood MotoClassic Series

Aprilia	Mick Walker
Ariel	Mick Walker
BMW Motorcycles	Bruce Preston
BMW – The Racing Story	Mick Walker
BSA	Owen Wright
BSA Bantam	Owen Wright
BSA Unit Twins	Matthew Vale
Ducati 4-Valve V-Twins	Mick Walker
Gilera	Mick Walker
Honda Gold Wing	Phil West
Laverda Twins & Triples	Mick Walker
Matchless	Mick Walker
MV Agusta Fours	Mick Walker
Norton – The Racing Story	Mick Walker
Royal Enfield	Mick Walker
Triumph and BSA Triples	Mick Duckworth
Triumph Bonneville	Paul Hazeldine
Triumph – The Racing Story	Mick Walker
Vincent	David Wright

Moto Guzzi
THE RACING STORY

Mick Walker

THE CROWOOD PRESS

First published in 2005 by
The Crowood Press Ltd
Ramsbury, Marlborough
Wiltshire SN8 2HR

www.crowood.com

© Mick Walker 2005

All rights reserved. No part of this publication may be reproduced or transmitted in any form or by any means, electronic or mechanical, including photocopy, recording, or any information storage and retrieval system, without permission in writing from the publishers.

British Library Cataloguing-in-Publication Data
A catalogue record for this book is available from the British Library.

ISBN 1 86126 735 5

Dedication
This book is dedicated to my great friend Arthur Wheeler, one of the truly legendary names in Moto Guzzi racing. Although Arthur is no longer with us, his memory and exploits will live on forever.

Mortons Motorcycle Media are market-leading publishers of classic and vintage titles, and own one of the largest photographic archives of its kind in the world. It is a treasure trove of millions of motorcycle and motorcycle-related images, many of which have not seen the light of day since they were filed away almost 100 years ago. In particular, the collection of glass plate negatives – a collection weighing almost two tons – is a priceless resource for anyone interested in the heyday of the motorcycle.

Mick Walker and The Crowood Press are grateful to Mortons Motorcycle Media for their co-operation in the production of this book and the use of their archive photographs.

Designed and edited by Focus Publishing
11a St Botolph's Road, Sevenoaks,
Kent TN13 3AJ

Printed and bound in Great Britain by CPI Bath

Contents

Preface		7
1	Early Days	9
2	TT – The Italian Armada	22
3	Gentleman Racers	32
4	In-Line V-Twin Development	42
5	Three Cylinders	54
6	The Albatros	59
7	The 250 Parallel Twin	73
8	The 500 In-Line Four	79
9	The Golden Era	85
10	The V8	123
11	Record Breaking	133
12	Early Transverse V-Twin Development	148
13	The Le Mans Series	163
14	The Modern Era	175
Index		189

Preface

For more than four decades I have been deeply involved with Italian motorcycles, having at first ridden them on the road, followed by racing them. I've been a dealer, importer, spares specialist, and over the last two decades I have written many books about them.

Not only this, but I have formed close and lasting friendships with staff in the Moto Guzzi factory, Mandello del Lario; the former British importers, Coburn & Hughes and later Three Cross Motorcycles. Having been a Moto Guzzi dealer and the official UK spares importer for much of the 1970s was an added bonus.

To Italian bike enthusiasts all over the world, Moto Guzzi is very special indeed. Founded in 1921, it has gone on to produce just about every conceivable engine type and configuration, from humble small-capacity two-strokes, through to the V8 of the 1950s and, more recently, its vast range of transverse V-twins.

Moto Guzzi – The Racing Story is very much about the motorcycles themselves, their designers and the great riders who helped create the legend.

The list of people who have helped me with the story is large and includes: Jim Blomley, Amadeo Castellani, Roy Armstrong, Chris Clarke, John Sear, the late Arthur Wheeler, Trevor Barnes, Bill Lomas, Brian Fox (Italia Classics), Keith Davies (Three Cross Motorcycles) and, of course, the staff of Moto Guzzi, in particular Gemma Pedretta.

Many of the photographs came from my own camera and Italian sources, including the factory. But others have helped including Vic Bates, Will Nash, Jack H Smith, George Schofield and N Gamberini. And last but not least, the Morton's Motorcycle Archives.

I have dedicated this book to my old friend Arthur Wheeler, who I was lucky to know for some forty years.

Mick Walker
Wisbech,
Cambridgeshire

ABOVE: The very first Moto Guzzi production model, the Normale, a 498.4cc single with a horizontal cylinder, set a trend that the company followed for many years.

LEFT: The Moto Guzzi factory as it was in 1921, with the railway line and little else at Mandello del Lario.

1 Early Days

In terms of Italian racing motorcycles, one marque stands above all others in the history of the sport – the legendary Moto Guzzi. Of course there are other famous brand names: Gilera, MV Agusta, Ducati, Benelli and FB Mondial to name but a few. But none could match Moto Guzzi in terms of the sheer breadth of their machinery: horizontal singles, parallel twins, in-line and transverse V-twins, triples, in-line fours and the amazing V8.

Origins

The First World War of 1914–18 was instrumental in the birth of Moto Guzzi. A youthful Carlo Guzzi had been recruited, like the majority of his generation, to serve his country. He joined the Italian army in 1914, but was eventually transferred to the fledgling air force where he came into contact with two flying officers, Giorgio Parodi and Giovanni Ravelli, both young men from wealthy and influential families. Parodi's was an old-established dynasty of shipping owners from the port of Genoa, whilst Ravelli, whose home was in Brescia, was already well-known in sporting motorcycling spheres, having successfully competed in a number of pre-war races.

The three men soon became friends, thanks to their mutual love of motorcycling, and found relief from the dark days of war by planning a business association for when the conflict ended. Sharing the task was easy – Parodi would organize the finance, Guzzi would design the machines, whilst Ravelli would ride them to fame on the race circuit.

But before these dreams could become a reality, fate intervened. A few short days prior to war's end in November 1918, Ravelli lost his life in a flying accident – the winged emblem carried by virtually all Guzzi bikes, even to the present day, was to be a constant reminder of the two surviving friends' loss.

Lesser men might have given up at this point but Guzzi and Parodi set about their task with a renewed purpose. First they needed finance to enable a prototype to be constructed. The money for the project came from Parodi's father, Emanuele. The now well-known letter dated 3 January 1919 in which Emanuele Parodi granted his approval to the project, is still kept in the Moto Guzzi museum within the factory at Mandello del Lario. Translated, the letter reads:

> So the answer you should give your companions is that on the whole I am in favour of the idea, that 1,500 or 2,000 liras [this being in a period when the lira was of much greater value than in later times] for the experiment are at your disposal provided this figure is absolutely not exceeded, but that I reserve the right to personally examine the design before giving my final support for seriously launching the product, because in the fortunate event that I like the design, I am ready to go much further with no limitation on the figure.

Besides being the supplier of finances, Emanuele Parodi was also to prove a

Early Days

The Tipo Sport, 1923–28, with its ioe (inlet over exhaust) valve system, was typical of many early Guzzi models.

stabilizing influence through the testing early years of the enterprise. No two men could have been more different, both in background and temperament, than Guzzi and Parodi. Guzzi, who came from a relatively poor family in Milan, was a reserved, quiet individual. Averse to taking unnecessary risks, he would always favour the safe and prudent course. Parodi, on the other hand, was both flamboyant and impulsive.

However, the combination of their respective natures, their strengths and weaknesses provided just the right ingredients for success. There is no doubt that if Guzzi had been left wholly to his own devices, his design genius would never have reached a larger audience. However, if Parodi had taken total control of the company, it would have risen and fallen in a spectacular fashion. But together the two men formed a successful partnership that was to last for some thirty-five years; and ensured that Moto Guzzi itself was able to continue after the founding fathers' passing.

The GP Prototype

Work on the first prototype bike was not completed until late 1920. When it was finally shown to Emanuele Parodi it not only received his approval, but he was forced to confess that it exceeded his wildest expectations. And so the promised additional funding facilities were forthcoming. Named simply GP (Guzzi and Parodi) the prototype was, for its era, an extremely advanced design with notable technical innovations.

The engine, which owed much to aeronautical design practices of the day, featured four parallel valves that were operated by a single overhead camshaft (sohc) driven by bevel gears. There was also a dual ignition system with twin spark plugs fired by a single German Bosch magneto. But perhaps the most interesting feature was the adoption of a layout that was to characterize the Italian company's products for many years – that of a single horizontal cylinder with unit construction of the engine and transmission. A prominent characteristic of the design was the 'bacon slicer' external flywheel (this also allowed a much smaller crankcase than would otherwise have been possible). Another was a positive gear-type oil pump that was driven from the nearside end of the crankshaft.

Guzzi's design also included unusual (for the time) oversquare bore and stroke dimensions of 88 × 82mm – in other words the engine was short stroke, in an era when long stroke was very much in vogue. Clearly, Guzzi was thinking ahead to the future, when engines would need to be higher revving to extract ever more power.

Not only was there chain final drive when several manufacturers were still using the ancient belt, but Guzzi had also given his design geared primary drive.

The frame was a sturdy affair featuring front downtubes that passed either side of the cylinder head. At the front was a pair of girder front forks with dual springs placed centrally just forward of the steering head, square-section mudguards, a sprung single saddle, and a single brake that operated on the rear wheel. The front wheel carried a massive gear (like a sprocket) that drove the speedometer. The three-speed gearbox was operated via a massive hand lever mounted on the offside of the flat, box-like fuel tank.

The Tipo Normale

The first word the general public had of the newcomer, now re-named Moto Guzzi, came in the 15 December 1920 issue of *Motociclismo*. The name change had come about because Parodi had not wanted 'GP' to be taken as coming from his initials and he suggested instead that it should be named Moto Guzzi, meaning simply Guzzi Motorcycle.

For its time, the prototype was simply too advanced for its own good. Therefore Guzzi made changes to the design to make it suitable (and financially viable) for series production.

The overhead camshaft (ohc) was replaced by the simpler pushrod operated valves, whilst the cylinder head of the 498.4cc (the bore and stroke dimensions remained unchanged) now sported two instead of four valves.

The first production version, known as the Tipo Normale produced 8bhp at 3,200rpm; the three-speed gearbox, geared primary and

---

Series Production

As far as series production street bikes are concerned, over the years, many variations of the basic 88 × 82mm horizontal single appeared, including the Tipo Sport (1923–28); GT and GT16 (1928–34); Tipo Sport 14 (1929–30); Tipo Sport 15 (1931–39); V, GTV, GTW and GTC (1934–48); Tipo S and GTS (1934–40); Astore (1949–53) and finally, perhaps the best known of them all – the Falcone. The original version was built from 1950 through to 1967, with a heavily revised version, the Nuova Falcone, being offered from 1970 through to 1976. Besides this, the series production 500 horizontal single was also widely manufactured in military and police versions.

Apart from this wide range of half-litre models, the horizontal single-cylinder layout was also available in other capacity sizes. The first of these arrived in 1932, with the introduction of the 174cc (59 × 63.7mm) P175; followed by the P250, a derivative displacing 238cc (68 × 64mm), which first appeared in 1934. Production of both these machines ceased with Italy's entry into the Second World War in June 1940, but in any case, an improved 250, the Airone (heron), had débuted in 1939, and this model remained in production until as late as 1957. The Airone, with its 247cc (70 × 64mm) engine, was available in both touring and sport guises, and proved an extremely successful model in the domestic Italian sales charts during the boom years of the immediate post-war period.

Early Days

chain final drives remained, as did the cylinder layout.

Guzzi Go Racing

Moto Guzzi went racing thanks to Parodi not Guzzi, even though it was Guzzi who designed the bikes!

This was because as a publicist, or at least someone who understood the importance of publicity to achieving sales, Parodi realized that the quickest way for Moto Guzzi to become an accepted part of the motorcycle industry was to go racing and that in any case, racing had been the spur behind the enthusiasm shared by all three of the original partners, before Ravelli's unfortunate death.

The marque's first race – the Milano–Napoli – was only entered after Guzzi had very reluctantly agreed to allow the two racing prototypes thus far built to be ridden by Aldo Finzi and Mario Cavendini.

The race got underway in the early evening. Travelling through the night, Cavendini reached Bologna shortly after 10am the next morning, followed shortly afterwards by Finzi, who had broken the headlight on his machine in a fall just outside Modena and was forced to continue the remainder of the journey by moonlight!

By the time the finish in Naples was reached, Cavendini was in twentieth place with an average speed of 27.3mph (44km/h), with Finzi two places lower.

One month later, Finzi's brother Gino provided Moto Guzzi with their first taste of victory in no less an event than the legendary Targa Florio, held in Sicily. Events such as this in the pioneering days of motor sport were often far more about the endurance of the competitors and reliability of the machinery than the outright speed of the machine. In fact, just completing the course was an achievement in itself.

1922 saw a concentration of resources into standard production models, followed, in 1923, by the first real Guzzi racing motorcycles. This time the effort had Guzzi's full approval, as by now he had accepted the value of taking part in competitive events.

The Corsa 2V engine, showing exposed pushrods and hairpin valve springs.

12

The Corsa 2V

The Corsa 2V followed the basic formula of the horizontal cylinder. It was the design of the valve gear that displayed the most radical departure from the marque's standard practice, for it featured overhead valves (ohv) operated by exposed pushrods and rocker arms. Bore and stroke dimensions at 88 × 82mm followed the standard design, but with increased power – 17bhp at 4,200rpm – maximum speed had risen to 75mph (121km/h). The 2V was also notable as the first Moto Guzzi of any description to feature the classical Italian Racing Red paint finish that was to characterize many of the factory's single-cylinder models.

The racing début of the Corsa 2V came during the Giro d'Italia (tour of Italy) in the spring of 1923. Ridden by Valentino Gatti (Guzzi's brother-in-law), the newcomer averaged 37.8mph (60.8km/h).

Circuito del Lario

1923 was also the first year in which Moto Guzzi contested its local event, the Circuito

The C2V following its victory at the local Lario circuit in spring 1923. From left to right: Mario Cavendini, Carlo Guzzi, Giorgio Parodi, Guido Mentasi, Valentino Gatti and Pietro Ghersi.

del Lario, which is best described as the Italian equivalent of the Isle of Man TT circuit. Staged over a 24.8-mile (40km) lap over public roads, the Lario took in, like the Isle of Man, some breathtaking scenery and some torturous going around the hills above Lake Como near the factory. Running through the eastern section bordering the lake, it swept through the demanding bends of the Valbrona

Corsa 2V 1923

Engine	Air-cooled, ohv, single with two valves, horizontal cylinder, iron head and barrel, exposed pushrods, hairpin valve springs, parallel valves, vertically split crankcases
Bore	88mm
Stroke	82mm
Displacement	498.4cc
Compression ratio	5.25:1
Lubrication	Gear pump, dry sump
Ignition	Bosch magneto
Carburation	Amac
Gearbox	Three-speed, hand-change
Clutch	Multi-plate, wet
Final drive	Chain
Frame	Full cradle, steel tubing
Suspension	Front, girder forks; rear, rigid
Brakes	Rear drum★
Tyres	3.00 × 26 front and rear

General specification

Wheelbase	1410mm (55.5in)
Dry weight	130kg (287lb)
Fuel capacity	11ltr (2.4gal)
Maximum power output	17bhp at 4,200rpm
Top speed	75mph (120km/h)

★Later machines had drums front and rear

Early Days

The 4V (4-valve) 498.4cc sohc horizontal single; winner of the European Championship, 1924.

Valley, and in those early days another hazard was that it was run over dirt roads.

Beginning in 1921, the Italian Tourist Trophy, as it was widely known, soon became famous throughout Italy, being won at various times not only by Guzzi but also by most of its rivals, too. Perhaps the most famous record was by the legendary Tazio Nuvolari, who swept the board in the 350cc class with four successive victories on factory Bianchi overhead cam vertical singles between 1927 and 1930. The final Lario event was staged in 1939, and it saw future World Champion Nello Pagani win on one of Guzzi's Condor models, averaging 52mph (83km/h).

A large monument was erected alongside the old course and dedicated to its memory by the FMI (Italy's governing body for motorcycle sport) on 9 December 1961.

The Corsa 4V

The C4V (racing 4-valve) made a sensational début in 1924 where first time out it was ridden to victory in the Lario event by Pietro Ghersi, who averaged 42.2mph (67.8km/h); Guzzi also came second and fourth in what can only be described as an impressive performance.

That same year, the new 4-valve single was also victorious at several other venues throughout Europe, including the German Grand Prix held over the Avus circuit in Berlin. But the undoubted highlight came in September 1924 when Moto Guzzi won the European Championship (forerunner of today's World Championship). Run as a single event at Monza autodrome on the outskirts of Milan, Guido Mentasi averaged 80.6mph (130km/h) when taking his C4V to victory; with second and fifth places falling to Erminio Visioli and Pietro Ghersi respectively, both riding the new 4-valve Guzzis.

The huge success of the Corsa 4V prompted the factory to put a customer version on sale towards the end of 1924. This was sold to privateers until 1927 when it was superseded by the 4VTT (1927–29), and finally the 4VSS (1928–33).

Technically, besides having four instead of two valves, the C4V series differed from its predecessor by having ohc rather than ohv. Like the original GP prototype, the new racer had its drive to the single ohc by bevel gears and a shaft running up the offside of the cylinder.

Features of the original 1924 version included a compression ratio of 6:1, a three-speed, hand-change gearbox, a Bosch magneto, a dry weight of 287lb (130kg), a twin-port cylinder head (with dual exhaust pipes), an Amac 28.5mm carburettor, and a separate 4ltr (0.8gal) oil tank mounted above the 10ltr (2.2gal) fuel tank. Official Guzzi sources quoted maximum power as 22bhp at 5,500rpm and a top speed of 94mph (150km/h).

Each year saw a round of small updates to the design as lessons were learned in the heat of combat. This not only resulted in ever-improving power output figures, but also changes to the cycle parts.

The Grand Prix of Nations, 18 September 1924 at Monza. Guido Mentasi was the 500cc race winner, on a Guzzi 4-valve single.

Corsa 4V 1924

Engine	Air-cooled, sohc, single with four valves, horizontal cylinder, iron head and barrel, drive to camshaft by shaft and bevel gears, hairpin valve springs, inclined valves, vertically split crankcases
Bore	88mm
Stroke	82mm
Displacement	498.4cc
Compression ratio	6:1
Lubrication	Gear pump, dry sump
Ignition	Bosch magneto
Carburation	Amac 28.5mm
Gearbox	Three-speed, hand-change
Clutch	Multi-plate, wet
Final drive	Chain
Frame	Full cradle, steel tubing
Suspension	Front, girder forks; rear, rigid
Brakes	Rear drum*
Tyres	2.75 × 27 front and rear

General specification

Wheelbase	1380mm (54in)
Dry weight	106kg (234lb)
Fuel capacity	10ltr (2.2gal)
Maximum power output	30bhp at 6,000rpm
Top speed	93mph (150km/h)

*Front, at various times none, caliper type or drum

Early Days

LEFT: *The 1930 works team with the 4-valve ohc single. Left to right: Amilcare Moretti, Alfredo Panella, Terzo Bandini, Riccardo Brusi and Ugo Prini.*

BELOW: *The C4V engine made a return to the original GP (Guzzi Parodi) prototype of 1920.*

Early Days

Salzburgring 1983; a 1929 Moto Guzzi 2VT being put through its paces.

The engine was slowly improved, not by any major change to the design, rather by tuning. The results speak for themselves, with a leap from the original figure of 22bhp to 32bhp over some nine years. The frame, forks and most notably the brakes also came in for considerable attention; as did cosmetic components, notably the oil and fuel tank changes.

The final version put out enough power to reach 105.4mph (170km/h). Its last race in factory colours was the 1932 Milano–Napoli, where Carlo Fumagalli rode to victory, averaging 57.7mph (93km/h) – almost double the speed of the original version.

The 2VT and GT2V

Thereafter, in the 500cc division, Moto Guzzi chose to campaign, at works level, the wide-angle in-line V-twin that made its début in 1933 (see Chapter 4). However, there were two other early 500 singles worthy of mention, the 2VT and GT2VT. Both were limited-production versions of the successful 4CV, but with only two valves.

Conceived towards the end of the 1920s, around eighty 2VTs were built as pukka race bikes, but intended exclusively for long-distance events where reliability counted for more than speed and power output. The GT2V was a fully equipped road-going version with lighting equipment, comprehensive mudguarding and most notably a sprung frame based on the series production roadster GT model that had débuted in 1928.

A Scaled-Down 500

An entirely new design, as described in the following chapter, had made its début back in 1926. This was to have a considerable significance for the future of the single-cylinder Moto Guzzi family. Displacing 246.8cc (68 × 68mm), the machine retained the horizontal cylinder and bevel-driven ohc but used two valves instead of four. At the time, Guzzi's offi-

17

Early Days

Swiss rider Alix Aeberhard photographed by the author at Cadwell Park in 1984, with his nicely restored 1929 2VT.

cial explanation was that: 'the smaller engine has a smaller head area', and although the 2CV/4CV 500 series had been relatively successful, this was nothing compared to that enjoyed by the smaller-engined bike. For example, in 1927, fifty of the sixty-two races won by the factory were with the 250, whilst in if it took no less than thirty-six of the thirty-nine wins. Not only that, but a specially prepared version run at Monza gained a number of new world speed records. Like the larger machines, the 250 was also offered for sale to the public in two versions – the TT (1926–29), with a maximum speed of 74.4mph (119.7km/h), and the improved SS variant (1928–33) which could reach 77.5mph (124.6km/h).

As the 1930s dawned, with the world facing the worst economic depression it has ever known, Moto Guzzi were still able to develop racing machinery, thanks to continuing strong sales of its series production, road-going models.

This continuous programme enabled the Italian marque to rule the roost (in Italy at least) in the 250cc class for much of the early–mid 1930s. By 1935, the works 250 was putting out a class-leading 20bhp. It was the very success of the smaller machine that led Guzzi to produce the 500 V-twin racing series – essentially a pair of 250 cylinder heads and barrels angled at 120 degrees on a common crankcase and fitted into sturdier running gear to cope with the increased power.

The final pre-war development of the factory 250 came towards the end of the 1930s. This version, equipped with a Cozette blower, was the first supercharged four-stroke single in the world. With the supercharger attached, power shot up to the then amazing figure of 38bhp at 7,800rpm, giving the little Guzzi a speed in excess of 130mph (209km/h).

In 1939, in the hands of Raffaele Alberti, one of the supercharged bikes broke the world speed record for the 250cc category at 132.2mph (212.7km/h), whilst Guglielmo Sandri set a new standing-start kilometer figure of 25.45 seconds – equivalent to 88.18mph (142km/h).

However, with the longer distances involved in racing, the vast increase in power led to reliability glitches. Even so, the 1939 German Grand Prix saw Moto Guzzi triumph over home favourites DKW, when Sandri and Nello Pagani humbled the Germans in their backyard.

Fuel Injection

Besides supercharging, Guzzi were also working on a fuel-injected version of their 250, as was reported in the 31 May 1939 issue of *Motor Cycling*:

> The so-called 'carburettor-less' Guzzi's supercharger pumped in air alone, whilst the fuel was provided by an electromagnetic injector built under Caproni-Fuscal patents and similar in principle to a diesel type. The system was claimed to give greater power output and improved accelera-

Early Days

1930 Four-Cylinder

One of the least known, but most technically interesting racing motorcycles of its era was the 1930 Quattra Cilindri (four-cylinder).

It was an air-cooled, across-the-frame four-cylinder, with pushrod operated valves; the cylinders, in traditional Guzzi style were horizontal. The heads and barrel were manufactured in iron, whilst the inclined valves (two per cylinder) featured hairpin springs.

But perhaps of most interest was the supercharged four-cylinder 500; then a relatively new invention. Guzzi believed that the arrival of the supercharger would mean his existing single-cylinder racers would come under increasing pressure. So he countered this by designing the supercharged four-cylinder 500. The design also included extensive use of specialist light alloys for both the engine and the cycle parts.

Displacing 492.2cc (56 × 60mm) and running on a compression ratio of 5:1, the supercharged four power output was a most impressive 45bhp at 7,800rpm with a dry weight of 165kg (363.4lb), maximum speed was almost 110mph (177km/h). Other features of the unit construction engine included a three-speed, hand-operated gearbox, multi-plate wet clutch, gear-type oil pump and a Bosch magneto.

The frame was a mixture – part steel and part aluminium; even though the first Guzzi featuring rear suspension had been built in 1928, the 1930 four's frame was rigid, whilst at the front were a set of period girder forks, with a central, single spring. There were also drum brakes front and rear, gear primary and chain final drives.

On paper, the four looked impressive, but unfortunately even after extensive testing for several months, its overall performance, notably in the areas of road holding, handling and braking was unsatisfactory. Guzzi was finally forced to accept that as a competitive racing motorcycle, the four was no better than his singles, and the entire project was abandoned.

It has to be said that this was probably the first serious failure of the fledgling Guzzi organization. And one together with the equally impressive looking Tre Cilindri (three-cylinder) deluxe road bike of 1932 and 1933, meant that the Italian marque largely stuck to its line of single-cylinder machines (and the 120 degree V-twin – virtually a pair of singles in a common crankcase) during the 1930s and 1940s for both series production and racing.

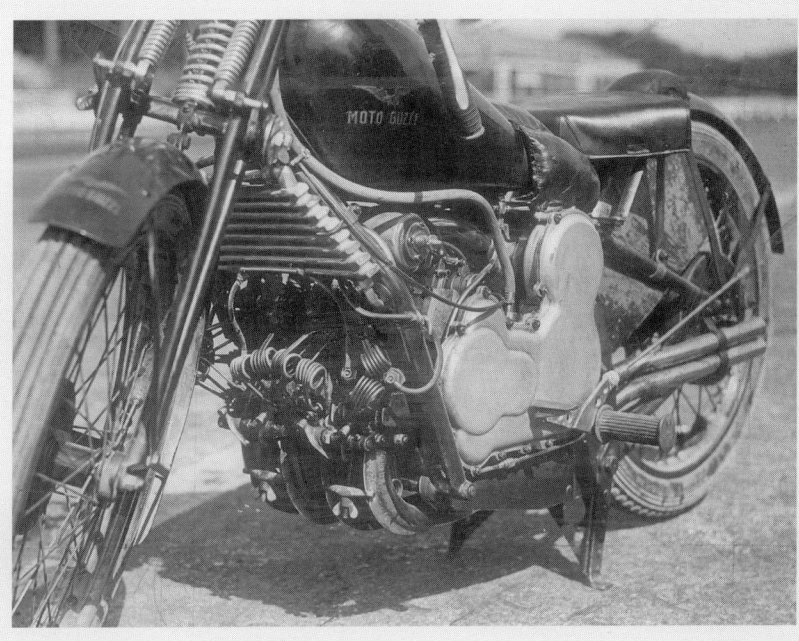

Supercharged 492.2cc four-cylinder racer of 1930. Interesting technically, but not a success.

500 Across-the-Frame Four 1930

Engine	Air-cooled, supercharged, ohv, across-the-frame four-cylinder with horizontal cylinders
Bore	56mm
Stroke	60mm
Displacement	492.2cc
Compression ratio	5:1
Lubrication	Gear-type pump
Ignition	Bosch magneto
Carburation	Cozette supercharger
Gearbox	Three-speed, hand-change
Clutch	Multi-plate, wet
Final drive	Chain
Frame	All-steel construction, rigid
Suspension	Front, sprung girder forks; rear, none
Brakes	Drum, front and rear
Tyres	N/A

General specification

Wheelbase	N/A
Dry weight	165kg (363.4lb)
Fuel capacity	12ltr (2.6gal)
Maximum power output	45bhp at 7,500rpm
Top speed	109mph (175km/h)

ABOVE LEFT: *Supercharged Quattro with its creator, Carlo Guzzi (standing) at Monza in the summer of 1931.*

LEFT: *Air-cooled, supercharged, ohv, across-the-frame four-cylinder engine; 45bhp at 7,800rpm.*

tion, allowing the engine to rev to 8,000rpm, as well as providing 30 per cent lower fuel consumption than with the supercharger alone.

The fuel-injected bike was first seen during the 1939 Milano–Taranto race. Omobono Tenni, Guzzi's top rider, put up a fine performance on a supercharged model, leading his class for some time at an average speed of 95mph (152km/h) before being slowed by poor weather. But the chief interest was focused on the bike ridden by Alberti: the top-secret injection machine.

Running on a mixture of 50/50 petrol and benzene, the fuel-injection Guzzi was the only factory-entered machine to last the entire distance and showed its excellent fuel economy by stopping only four times to refuel, whereas more conventional machinery needed no less than seven!

War Stops Play

If the war hadn't intervened to put a stop to development, not only would the various experiments with supercharging and fuel injection have paid off on a wider scale, but there would, no doubt, have been much wider use of the supercharged 500 three-cylinder racer on which Guzzi were working when war broke out.

The full story of this potentially sensational machine is described in Chapter 5, but suffice to say that much could have been expected, had not the FIM banned supercharging in 1946. As it was, Guzzi did use one of the pre-war works supercharged 250s again in 1948, but only for record-breaking purposes (*see* Chapter 11).

A Double Fatality

Although Guzzi had some tremendous victories during the post-war era, it also suffered several tragic fatalities. In July 1948, Tenni and Achille Varzi were both killed whilst practising

Guzzi Factory-Supported Riders 1920–1957

Carlo Agostini	Pietro Ghersi
Duiglio Agostini	Ken Kavanagh
Luigi Agostini	Gianni Leoni
Leon Alberti	Guido Leoni
Raffaele Alberti	Bill Lomas
Giordano Aldrighetti	Enrico Lorenzetti
Fergus Anderson	Count Giovanni
Ferdinando Balzarotti	Lurani
Terzo Bandini	Adelmo Mandolini
Manliff Barrington	Guido Mentasi
Bruno Bertacchini	Alano Montanari
Bernardo Bertolucci	Amilcare Moretti
Ricardo Brusi	Giovanni Moretti
Keith Bryant	Primo Moretti
George Burney	Biagio Nocchi
Keith Campbell	Alfredo Panella
Maurice Cann	Aldo Pigorini
Gino Cavanna	Ugo Prini
Mario Cavendini	Bruno Ruffo
Guido Corti	Amedeo Ruggeri
Dickie Dale	Luigi Ruggeri
Derek Ennett	Guglielmo Sandri
Bob Foster	Piero Taruffi
Bruno Francisci	Omobono Tenni
Carlo Fumagalli	Achille Varzi
Valentino Gatti	Stanley Woods

for the Swiss Grand Prix at Berne, one of the most potentially dangerous circuits on the Grand Prix calendar at the time. Not only were sections of it cobbled, but also much of the course was tree lined. Certainly, the danger aspect would preclude such a circuit from being used today. But of course, in those far-off days, safety was not a word often used in conjunction with motorcycle racing.

It was the end of an era – and the beginning of a new age. The following year, 1949, the first full-status World Championship would be held, and with it Moto Guzzi's star was to rise even higher. The golden age of Grand Prix racing was about to unfold as the new decade approached.

2 TT – The Italian Armada

1926 was an important year for Guzzi – as well as making their first foray into producing something other than their existing half-litre (500cc) engine size, by entering the Isle of Man TT races for the first time they would be challenging the British on their home ground.

The TT250

The new motorcycle was still very much in the Guzzi mould of a single cylinder with a horizontally placed cylinder. Its 246.8cc (68 × 68mm) engine featured a bevel and shaft drive on the offside (right) to the overhead camshaft (ohc).

Producing a class-leading 15bhp at 6,000rpm, things looked good – a specific power output of 60bhp per litre was virtually unheard of in the mid-1920s, and then only in the automobile racing world. Coupled with a dry weight of 105kg (231.5lb), factory testers were soon singing the newcomer's praise, both in terms of outright speed and acceleration. Handling was another major plus, it being on a par with anything in Europe at that time.

There is absolutely no doubt that the TT250 was a masterpiece of design and a real trendsetter from the moment it first appeared. As a result of continuous development, it was to remain at the very peak of motorcycle racing until the early 1950s, which shows just what an advanced design it really was. During this time it won several European Champi-

250 TT 1926

Engine	Air-cooled, sohc, single with two valves, horizontal cylinder, iron head and barrel, drive to camshaft by shaft and bevel gears, hairpin valve springs, inclined valves, vertically split crankcases
Bore	68mm
Stroke	68mm
Displacement	246.8mm
Compression ratio	8:1
Lubrication	Gear pump, dry sump
Ignition	Bosch magneto
Carburation	Binks 25mm
Gearbox	Three-speed, hand-change
Clutch	Multi-plate, wet
Final drive	Chain
Frame	Full cradle, steel tubing
Suspension	Front, girder forks; rear, rigid
Brakes	Drums front and rear
Tyres	2.75 × 27 front and rear

General specification

Wheelbase	1360mm (53.5in)
Dry weight	105kg (231.5lb)
Fuel capacity	12.5ltr (2.75gal)
Maximum power output	15bhp at 6,000rpm
Top speed	78mph (125km/h)

TT – The Italian Armada

1926 TT250 with ohc single cylinder and 'square' 68 × 68mm bore and stroke measurements.

onships (the forerunner of the post-war World Championship), sixteen Italian titles, three World Championships (introduced in 1949), and no less than eight TT victories in the 250cc class.

Isle of Man TT Races 1926

Carlo Guzzi and his partner Giorgio Parodi were so impressed with their new bike that they decided to give it the ultimate test – which in those days meant the Isle of Man TT races, held annually in June. This event stood head and shoulders above anything else in the motorcycling calendar at the time. Victory in one of these races, first held in 1907, was similar to winning the Moto Grand Prix series today; and having a TT winner gave the company involved immediate world-wide recognition.

It was a challenge that the young Guzzi team simply could not resist, and with their new 250 model, they believed that they had a machine capable of running near the front, possibly even winning. In fact, the challenge was made even more difficult, as only one machine and rider were sent to contest the TT. Pietro Ghersi had already proved himself on the larger singles after becoming a Guzzi works rider in 1923. However, this experience counted for little when pitted against the most demanding and dangerous circuit in the world that takes a tremendous toll upon machine and pilot alike with its fearsome 37.73-mile (60.7km) lap and numerous torturous climbs, descents, high-speed 'blind' sections, hairpin bends and everything in between.

The reader also has to remember that British bikes and riders totally dominated the event at the time. Because of this, many pundits considered Guzzi's lone entry (in the Lightweight event) of an Italian machine ridden by an Italian rider to be laughable, some even went as far as saying it was foolhardy.

Pietro Ghersi celebrates after finishing runner-up in the 1926 Lightweight (250cc) TT.

Most considered that Ghersi and Guzzi would simply be outclassed.

But this didn't happen. Ghersi not only came home second, but set the fastest lap of the race at an average speed of 63.12mph (101.5 km/h). But the end of the race was in fact only the beginning of the drama.

On his entry form, Ghersi had specified one particular make of spark plug, but had actually used a total of three plugs during the course of the race, all of which were of a different make from that stated on the entry form. Only when the machine was examined by officials of the ACU (Auto Cycle Union) in the post-race enclosure was the discovery made. In a sensational judgement, which *Motor Cycle* reported in their issue of 24 June 1926 and described as 'The Guzzi Incident', Ghersi was axed from the official results – but still credited with the fastest lap.

This came as a bitter blow to everyone connected with the Guzzi effort and created something of a public relations disaster for the over-zealous ACU officials. Guzzi had also entered Ghersi in the Senior race on a 500cc single and the mood cannot have been helped when he retired.

A Return to the Isle of Man

Although the team returned to Italy demoralized, it was nevertheless determined to return and fight again. So 1927 saw a hive of Guzzi activities with several entries in both the Lightweight (250cc) and Senior (500cc) TTs.

For the Lightweight, three riders were initially selected. The first of these was called Ghersi – this was not Pietro, but Mario, his younger brother. The latter had ridden for Bianchi in the 1926 Lightweight, finishing thirteenth. He was joined by Achille Varzi and Vitorio Prini, but in the race itself Archangeli replaced Prini. This proved a sound move, as Archangeli finished runner-up behind experienced race winner Wal Handley (Rex-Acme), while Varzi came fifth and Ghersi retired on lap 5.

Guzzi made three entries for the Senior, but with only two specified riders: Varzi, who retired on lap 1, and Archangeli, who finished fourteenth. The other entry was not fulfilled.

Pietro and Mario Ghersi

The team missed the TTs in 1928 and the following year Pietro Ghersi was the only entry for the Lightweight. Showing all his undoubted skill, he led the race only to retire when comfortably in the lead on the final lap. He also rode for Cotton in the 1929 Lightweight and Senior races, but with no success there either.

The Isle of Man was certainly not a happy hunting ground for Ghersi who then switched to cars for 1930, driving for Alfa Romeo.

He was back on two wheels again in 1931, piloting the little Guzzi single in the Lightweight TT, but again struck problems and retired. He then quit bikes entirely, driving cars for Bugatti and Maserati as well as Alfa Romeo, before finally calling it a day in 1938.

Meanwhile, his brother Mario had not been idle and in 1931, riding for the Birmingham-based New Imperial concern had finished sixth in the Lightweight and thirteenth in the Junior TTs. Although Guzzi were not officially represented the following year, in 1933 Mario was back on a Guzzi for the Lightweight, this time scoring a sixth for the Italian marque.

Success at Last

1935 was the year when everything at last fell into place for Moto Guzzi and the TTs. Their team consisted of Omobono Tenni and two Irishmen – the great Stanley Woods and his brother-in-law JG (Gordon) Burney. Years later in the 1950s, Fergus Anderson, then himself a works Guzzi star, revealed that the Italian

In 1935, Stanley Woods gave Moto Guzzi their first TT victory with this 2-valve single. It was the first time a foreign bike had won a TT since 1911.

factory had asked Woods by letter to 'name his own signing-on fee', such was Guzzi's desire to taste TT success.

The combination of an Italian machine and Irish rider might have seemed strange, but Guzzi and Woods were just about to become headline news. As the 26 June 1935 issue of *Motor Cycling* reported: 'For the first time in the history of the TT races an Italian machine has won the Lightweight. Never before has the "foreign menace" been so much to the fore'. And it was a race to remember, as despite poor weather conditions, Woods put in a magnificent performance to average 71.56mph (115km/h) in the 264-mile (425km) race.

The Race in Detail

This long-awaited success is worth recording in detail. Wednesday 19 June 1935 dawned with leaden skies. Nevertheless, the steady breeze gave a promise of mountain roads clear of mist. However, this promise was not to be fulfilled, as by the time the start drew near, reports of poor visibility were coming from some areas of the circuit.

In 1935, for the first time, TT regulations allowed machines to be 'warmed up', with the twenty-seven riders riding their bikes up and down the stretch of road between the start and Governor's Bridge. Besides various high-ranking officials from Germany, it was announced over the loudspeaker system that Guzzi and Parodi were in attendance to watch the contestants roar away from the start.

And the two were not to be disappointed. At the end of lap 1, Woods went past the spectators at the starting-line – first on the roads and first in the race. Team-mate Tenni came through in fourth position, just as a drizzling rain began to fall, heralding the onset of rain for the remainder of the race. As if this was not enough, an even more serious hazard for the riders to contend with came in the form of increasingly poor visibility over the mountain section from Ramsey onwards.

By the time that lap 2 was completed, Tenni had moved up to third. There were now only seventeen riders left in the race, including all three works Guzzis. It was then that Woods took a pit stop to refuel; this was completed in 23 seconds (an exceptionally quick time for the period).

On lap 4, Tenni overtook Tyrrell-Smith's

The Guzzi team for the 1935 Isle of Man Lightweight TT. Left to right: Ombono Tenni, Giorgio Parodi (team manager), Stanley Woods and JG (Gordon) Burney.

Italian Guzzi star Omobono Tenni after winning the Lightweight TT in June 1937; the first Italian to win in the Isle of Man.

Rudge to take second, but this success was to be short-lived – the pointer on the giant scoreboard recording the position of Tenni's bike stayed stationary at Creg-ny-Baa. Later, it was learned that the Italian had crashed there, fortunately with no more serious injury than a bruised back and a few grazes, but his motorcycle was too badly damaged to continue.

By then, only twelve riders were left. Over the final two laps, Woods slowed to win comfortably from Tyrell-Smith, with Ernie Nott third on another Rudge. The remaining Guzzi ridden by Burney came home eighth.

Trade Support

Although no advertising was permitted on machines or riders in those days, press and public alike attached much importance to the equipment used by the winner, with the various 'trade barons' vying bitterly for the honours. Below is listed the components used on Woods' 1935 winning 250 Moto Guzzi:

- Amal carburettor
- Andre steering damper
- Bosch magneto
- Bowdenex controls and cables
- Ferodo brake and clutch linings
- Lodge spark plug
- Moseley air cushion (seat padding)
- Pirelli tyres and tubes
- Renold chain
- Shell petrol
- Tecalemit greasing
- Vacuum oil
- Wellworthy piston rings

A Double Victory

Woods went on to win the Senior TT a few days later, again on a Guzzi, but this time on one of the wide-angle V-twin models (see Chapter 4). Unlike the Lightweight race, the Senior TT was no walkover. And this was to prove one of the most dramatic TT finishes ever. Norton star Jimmy Guthrie had already been hailed as the victor, when Woods came from behind with a record-breaking last lap to cross the line mere seconds in front – a feat that everyone had thought impossible.

The double TT victory effectively propelled Guzzi to the very top of the motorcycle racing league table. Although several major races had been won in Italy – winning the TT was the ultimate prize.

27

The 250cc supercharged model for long-distance races in 1938; based on the successful TT-winning normally aspirated flat single.

On the Eve of War

There was no Guzzi team for the 1938 races but, despite the gathering clouds of war, they were back again the following year. 1939 marked the entry of the new supercharged 250 plus the return of Woods to the Italian factory's ranks – this was to be his final TT – and Tenni was a late entry for the Lightweight.

There had been considerable speculation that Guzzi would be absent, but as *Motor Cycling* stated in the 14 June 1939 issue: 'Apparently the Guzzi people argued so loud and long that the Italian Government eventually agreed to let the firm take the money necessary to cover expenses out of the country'. The report suggested that they had been so insistent because of the run of success enjoyed by Ted Mellors on his Benelli, and also mentioned a rumour (ill-founded) that Cann would be present on a spare machine.

The race was staged in truly appalling weather conditions with visibility down to 25 yards on the mountain section. After a thrilling contest for the lead on the first lap, Tenni went out on the second with plug problems. Woods fared a little better and survived for two more laps, recording the fastest lap of the race at 78.16mph (125.7km/h) before he too dropped out, this time with engine glitches. Only thirteen riders completed the full distance, with the race eventually being won by Benelli-mounted Mellors, with an average speed of 74.25mph (119.4km/h).

TT Action Resumes

War was declared in September 1939, bringing an end to the Isle of Man TT races for eight long years but in 1947 TT action was able to get underway once more. However, it was to be without supercharging, which had been banned a few months earlier by the FIM (the governing body for motorcycle sport).

However, Guzzi were back on form – Woods might have hung up his leathers, but there was another Irish rider, Manliff Barrington, to follow in the wheel tracks of the maestro. It was Barrington who scored a confident and comfortable victory in the 1947 Lightweight race. In this he was ably supported by Cann, the latter finishing runner-up and setting the fastest lap at 74.78mph (120.3km/h). Barrington's average speed was 73.22mph (117.8km/h), completing the seven lap, 264.11-mile (424km) course in just over 3 hours, 36 minutes.

TT – The Italian Armada

Details of the 1938 supercharged Guzzi engine. With a Cozette blower it put out a class-leading 38bhp at 7,800rpm.

Offside (right) view of the supercharged engine, showing the carburettor, supercharger unit, magneto, external oil pump, bevel shaft tube and hairpin valve springs.

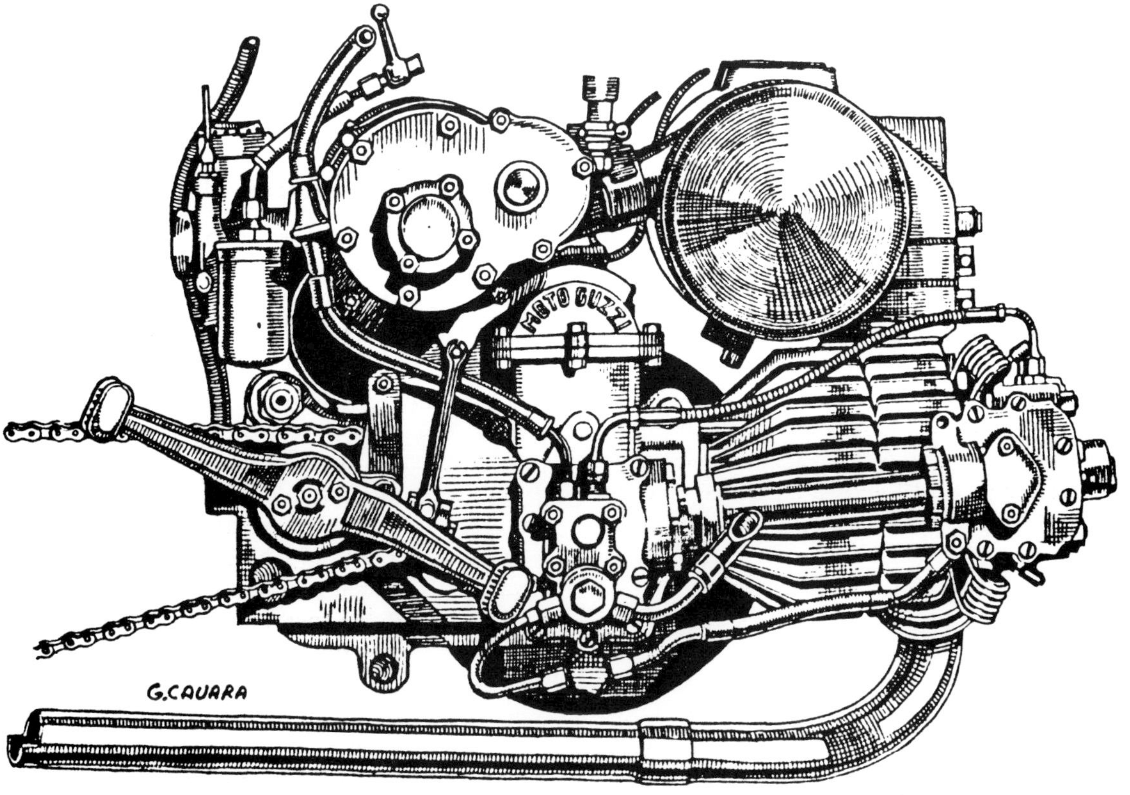

Period drawing of the supercharged Guzzi engine, 1939.

29

TT – The Italian Armada

ABOVE: *The fuel-injected works 250 used by Omobono Tenni in the 1939 Milano–Taranto race.*

BELOW: *Manliff Barrington won the 1947 Lightweight TT and is seen here crossing the Clady circuit start/finish line at the Ulster Grand Prix a couple of months later.*

The full finishing order is as follows:

1st   M. Barrington (Guzzi)
2nd   M. Cann (Guzzi)
3rd   B. Drinkwater (Excelsior)
4th   L.J. Archer (New Imperial)
5th   R. Pike (Rudge)
6th   G. Paterson (New Imperial)
7th   S. Sorensen (Excelsior)
8th   C.W. Johnson (CTS)
9th   L. Martin (Excelsior)
10th J. Brett (Excelsior)
11th W.M. Webster (Excelsior)

Cann's Turn for Victory

In 1948, once again Moto Guzzi made the Lightweight TT their own, with Cann winning in 3 hours, 30 minutes and 49 seconds, an average speed of 75.18mph (120.9km/h). This was some six minutes faster than Barrington's 1947 figures. And what of the 1947 winner himself? Well, Barrington was mounted on Guzzi's new twin-cylinder model (*see* Chapter 7) and had led for the first two laps, displaying an impressive turn of speed if not outright reliability. Meanwhile Cann was mounted on one of the trusty horizontal singles in its latest guise; interestingly the official dry weight of both motorcycles was declared at 265lb (584kg).

With Barrington in retirement, Cann took first place with Roland Pike on his home-tuned and very rapid Rudge as runner-up. Only six out of the original twenty-five finished, so it was a race of high attrition.

This was to be the last TT as an independent event. The Isle of Man joined the World Championship series in 1949, ushering in a new era for racing and for the Guzzi works effort.

The Guzzi works at Mandello del Lario in 1948. Compare to the 1921 picture on page 8.

3 Gentleman Racers

This breed of big single Moto Guzzi racers originated in the mid-1930s, when, with competition becoming ever fiercer, the factory's management attempted to satisfy a growing demand for customer racers, machines that the ordinary man in the street could afford. In Italy, Guzzi were not alone in this, several manufacturers were responding to the needs of the market – and so the era of the 'Gentleman racers' began.

The formula around which these bikes were built was governed by rules laid down by the Italian Federation. The customer racers were supposed to be 'production' and sold with a full set of road accessories including lighting equipment, a kick-starter, horn and silencer. However, in their bid to produce the most competitive machine, the majority of manufacturers soon began to produce bikes that were little different from pukka works racers except for the camouflage of road equipment.

This led to another problem because instead of providing these bikes at an affordable price as had been the original idea, the prices of these highly tuned specialist machines put them out of reach of all but the very well-off. In other words, hardly any aspiring racers could actually afford to buy a 'production' bike.

The GTC

Moto Guzzi had gone about things in its own particular way. Initially, it responded by producing the GTC – little more than a souped-up version of the standard 498.4cc (88 × 82mm) GTW sports roadster, itself a development of the Tipo V that had arrived for the 1934 model year.

Putting out 26bhp at 5,000rpm and featuring a specification that included a 28.5mm Dell'Orto carburettor, 17ltr (3.74gal) fuel tank, 19in wheels and a dry weight of 160kg (353lb) the GTC was extremely robust but it was neither sufficiently fast nor was its handling adequate to compete successfully as a racer.

It was in many ways an excellent layman's type of machine in the fashion of Britain's BSA Gold Star, but at the time of its production in late 1937, the GTC was judged a failure for its intended purpose, and that was all that mattered. This prompted Moto Guzzi to build something different, something more in tune with the racetrack than the street.

The Condor

The result was the Nuovo C, which soon became known simply as the Condor. Although it retained the general Guzzi horizontal single-cylinder configuration, including the same bore and stroke dimensions, the Condor was largely a new motorcycle.

The cylinder head and barrel were of aluminium instead of cast iron, whilst there was now a low-slung single exhaust pipe and silencer (the GTC featured a hi-level pipe branching into twin silencers, stacked one above the other). A larger 32mm carburettor

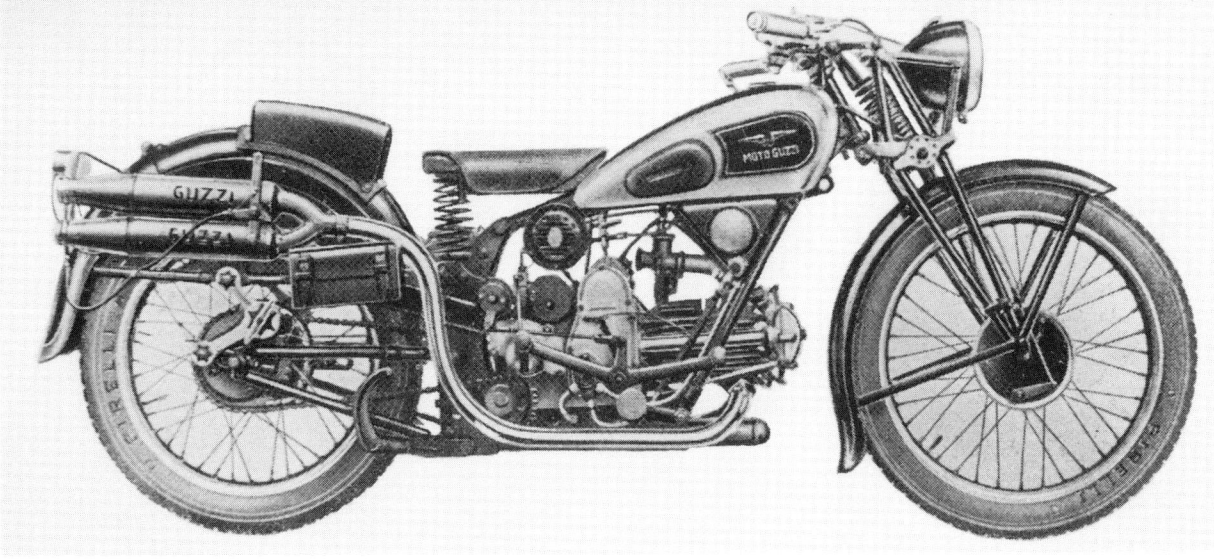

First of the breed, the 1937 GTC 500.

	GTC 1937
Engine	Air-cooled, ohv, single with two valves, horizontal cylinder, cast-iron head and barrel, enclosed pushrods, hairpin valve springs, inclined valves, vertically split crankcases
Bore	88mm
Stroke	82mm
Displacement	498.4cc
Compression ratio	5.5:1
Lubrication	Gear-type pump, dry sump
Ignition	Magneto
Carburation	Dell'Orto 28.5mm
Gearbox	Four-speed, foot-change
Clutch	Multi-plate, wet
Final drive	Chain
Frame	Full cradle, steel tubing
Suspension	Front, girder forks; rear, sprung
Brakes	Drums front and rear
Tyres	Front 3.00 × 20; rear 3.50 × 19

General specification

Wheelbase	1465mm (57.6in)
Dry weight	160kg (353lb)
Fuel capacity	17ltr (3.74gal)
Maximum power output	26bhp at 5,000rpm
Top speed	90mph (145km/h)

	Condor 1938
Engine	Air-cooled, ohv, single with two valves, horizontal cylinder, alloy head and barrel, enclosed pushrods, hairpin valve springs, inclined valves, vertically split crankcases
Bore	88mm
Stroke	82mm
Displacement	498.4mm
Compression ratio	6:1
Lubrication	Gear-type pump, dry sump
Ignition	Magneto
Carburation	Dell'Orto SS32M
Gearbox	Four-speed, foot-change
Clutch	Multi-plate, wet
Final drive	Chain
Frame	Full cradle, steel tubing
Suspension	Front girder forks; rear sprung
Brakes	Drums front and rear
Tyres	Front 2.75 × 21; rear 3.00 × 21

General specification

Wheelbase	1470mm (57in)
Dry weight	140kg (309lb)
Fuel capacity	18ltr (3.9gal)
Maximum power output	28bhp at 5,000rpm
Top speed	100mph (160km/h)

The second of Guzzi's 'Gentleman racers', the 500 Condor Sport, circa 1938.

was specified which, manufactured by Dell'Orto, was now a pukka racing SS32M instrument. Instead of the relatively wide-ratio gears of the GTC came a new set of close ratio components (still selected by the traditional Italian heel-and-toe pedal).

Part of the secret of its increased competitiveness was the frame, which was entirely new, with the rear section constructed from hydronalium, a special lightweight alloy of great strength, widely used in the aviation industry.

Other notable features included 21in alloy wheel rims, 220mm (8.6in) drum brakes, a tank-top oil container and the traditional Guzzi massive 'bacon slicer' outside flywheel with its chromed outer rim. Like the crankcases, the hubs and brake plates were cast in electron-magnesium alloy.

The Condor came complete with a dynamo (located above the crankcase, behind the magneto), a nearside (left) mounted kickstarter, full lighting equipment, separate rider (sprung) and pillion saddles and a centre stand. Because of the emphasis on weight saving, the Condor was already 20kg (44lb) lighter than the GTC. By removing these components, the weight could be reduced by a further 15kg (33lb).

An 18ltr (3.9gal) fuel tank with the aforementioned separate 3.5ltr (0.77gal) oil tank carried over it gave the machine almost a pioneer appearance. One big advantage enjoyed by the Condor over the majority of its rivals was its fuel consumption, which under racing conditions was around 45mpg, meaning it could cover longer distances then most of its rivals without the need to refuel.

When launched in Italy during 1938, the asking price of the Condor was 11,000 lira. For that the buyer got a power output of 28bhp (still at 5,000rpm), which was enough to propel the Condor to a maximum speed of a genuine 100mph (160km/h).

Racing Success

Guzzi's new 'Gentleman racer' got off to a flying start with a resounding success very soon after its launch, winning a competition at the prestigious local Lario circuit classic in spring 1938. The layout of this ultra-demanding course – Italy's equivalent of the Isle of Man TT – is described in Chapter 1. But suffice to say, winning at this event proved conclusively the reliability of the machine, its excellent handling and roadholding abilities.

Another famous victory came in one of the final events run prior to Italy's entry into the Second World War in June 1940. This was the Milano–Taranto long-distance road race, when a Condor ridden by Guido Cerato took the flag. Other renowned pre-war Condor riders included Alberto Ascari and Dorino Serafina.

A New Rival

Although main production did not begin until after 1945, 1940 had seen the arrival of the Gilera Saturno which, when racing resumed in Italy after the war, was to be the main antagonist of the big Guzzi flat singles in production-based events.

The Saturno was the work of the designer Ing. Giuseppe Salmaggi and gained its name from his love of astronomical names. It featured a 498.7cc ohv single-cylinder engine with a vertical cylinder and enclosed valve gear.

The Dondolino

With the arrival of the Saturno it was evident that Guzzi had a serious competitor. So, when civilian production resumed in 1946, it came as no surprise that the Mandello del Lario design team had not been resting on their laurels. The Condor had received a new lease of life and gained a new name – the Dondolino (rocking chair). The most important improvement was more speed – up to 106mph (170.5km/h) with a silencer and over 110mph (177 km/h) with an open pipe. Guzzi quoted official figures of 33bhp.

Unkind critics suggested that the name stemmed from the result the extra power had put on the handling, which was endowed with a rocking-like motion on fast corners. Despite this, the Dondolino was good enough for Enrico Lorenzetti to win the Swiss Grand Prix at Berne.

The following year, 1947, saw several

Enrico Lorenzetti en-route to victory with his Dondolino during the Swiss Grand Prix at Berne; summer 1946.

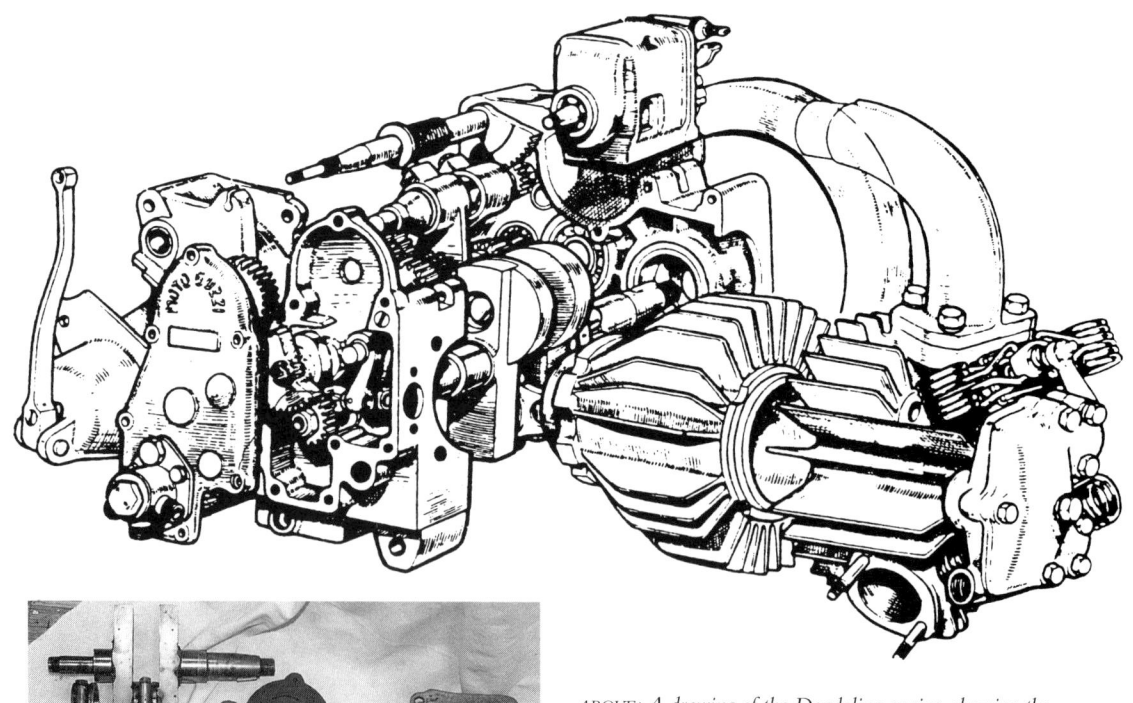

ABOVE: A drawing of the Dondolino engine, showing the main components.

LEFT: The crankcase and crankshaft from the Dondolino shows the differing lengths of the connecting-rods for the long- and short-stroke engines.

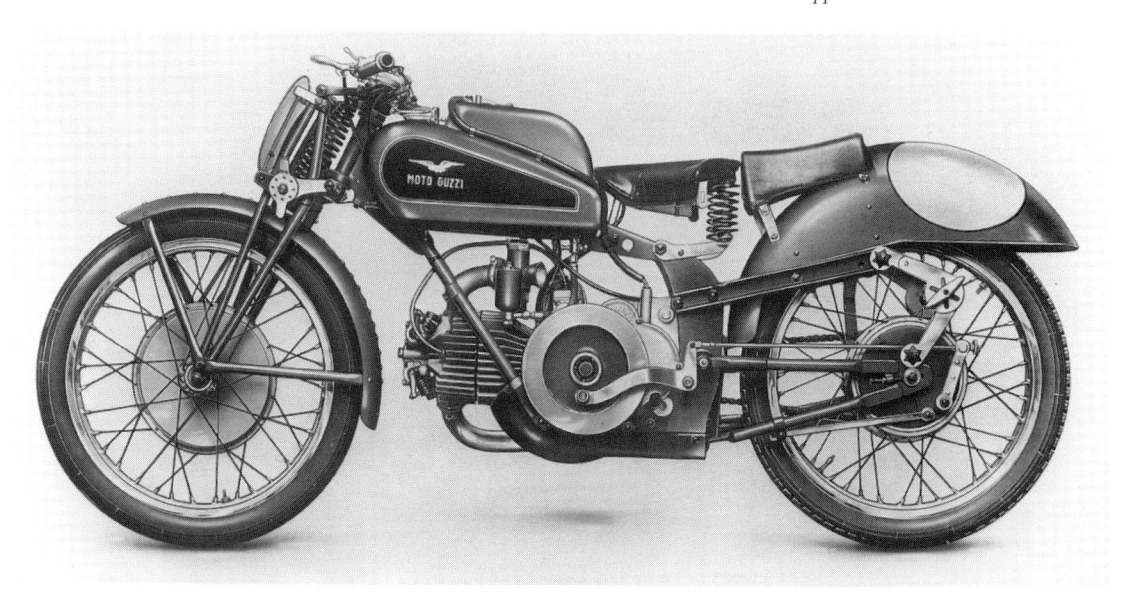

BELOW: The Dondolino as it appeared in 1945–47.

A Dondolino engine showing the aluminium head and barrel, widely splayed front frame downtubes, 'bacon slicer' outside flywheel and massive Dell'Orto SS carburettor.

improvements, including a larger front brake 260mm (10.2in) and a hand-beaten aluminium mounting for the rear mudguard/racing number plates. There were also minor changes including a front mudguard with a shortened front section and a stay at the base only, a larger 19ltr (4gal) fuel tank and a choice of either a street-legal silencer or a straight pipe (thus enabling customers to take part in either production-based events or open class racing). The Dondolino tipped the scales at 128kg (282lb) in racing trim.

The Dondolino continued its career well into the 1950s, thanks to events such as the

Dondolino 500 1946

Engine	Air-cooled, ohv, single with two valves, horizontal cylinder, alloy head and barrel, enclosed pushrods, hairpin valve springs, inclined valves, vertically split crankcases	Frame	Full cradle, tubular and sheet steel construction
		Suspension	Front, girder forks; rear, sprung
		Brakes	Drums front and rear
		Tyres	Front 2.75 × 21; rear 3.00 × 21
Bore	88mm		
Stroke	82mm		
Displacement	498.4cc	**General specification**	
Compression ratio	8.5:1	Wheelbase	1470mm (57.8in)
Lubrication	Gear-type pump, dry sump	Dry weight	128kg (282lb)
Ignition	Magneto	Fuel capacity	19ltr (4gal)
Carburation	Dell'Orto SS35M	Maximum power output	33bhp at 5,500rpm
Gearbox	Four-speed, foot-change		
Clutch	Multi-plate, wet	Top speed	105.5mph (170km/h)
Final drive	Chain		

Gentleman Racers

Grand Prix of Nations, September 1947. A Dondolino (169) leads a Manx Norton (44) at the Fiera street circuit in Milan.

Milano–Taranto race, which was to prove a happy hunting ground for Moto Guzzi. Bruno Francisci won in 1951 and 1952, Duilio Agostini (no relation to Giacomo) in 1953 and Sergio Pinza took the racing class in 1954.

The Gambalunga (Tipo Faenza)

Guzzi built another machine alongside the Dondolino – the Gambalunga (long leg). This was more highly tuned and specialized, as by this time Guzzi realized that they needed to offer the very best possible machine to not only garner publicity for themselves, but also to provide a potential winner for top line riders at national and international level.

Strangely, the Gambalunga came about almost by chance. Factory tester Ferdinando Balzarotti had begun to demonstrate in the years immediately before the war that he was

Bruno Francisci seen at the night start of the 1953 Milano–Taranto race. The Guzzi rider won the event on a Dondolino in both 1951 and 1952.

The more highly tuned Gambalunga arrived in 1946 and ran alongside the existing Dondolino.

likely to develop into a first-rate rider. When hostilities ended and racing resumed in Italy, Guzzi's famous racing designer Ing. Giulio Cesare Carcano was requested by the management to 'see if you can do something towards helping this young rider'. In 1946, that 'something' emerged as the Gambalunga, for which Guzzi quoted a maximum speed of 112.5mph (181km/h).

The Design

The Gambalunga's name came from the fact that, contrary to conventional Guzzi practice, the engine's 90mm stroke was considerably larger than the bore size of 84mm, making a 497.7cc 'long stroke'. Still an overhead valve (ohv) design, it was tuned to produce even more power than the Dondolino.

The valves were set at an angle of 60 degrees and were 46mm diameter inlet and 40mm for the sodium-filled exhaust valve. Both featured 11mm split valve guides in bronze and exposed hairpin valve springs manufactured in 4mm shot-peened wire. As on all such designs, this exposure contributed significantly to the wear suffered by the valve components.

The three-ring piston with its virtually flat top together with lavish ribbing under the

Gambalunga 1946–48

Engine	Air-cooled, ohv, single with two valves, horizontal cylinder, alloy head and barrel, enclosed pushrods, hairpin valve springs, inclined valves, vertically split crankcases
Bore	84mm★
Stroke	90mm★
Displacement	497.7cc★
Compression ratio	8:1
Lubrication	Gear-type pump, dry sump
Ignition	Magneto
Carburation	Dell'Orto SS35M
Gearbox	Four-speed, foot-change
Clutch	Multi-plate, wet
Final drive	Chain
Frame	Full cradle, tubular and sheet steel construction
Suspension	Front, leading-link forks; rear, sprung
Brakes	Drums front and rear
Tyres	Front 2.75 × 21; rear 3.00 × 21

General specification

Wheelbase	1470mm (58.7in)
Dry weight	125kg (275lb)
Fuel capacity	23ltr (5gal)
Maximum power output	35bhp at 5,800rpm
Top speed	112mph (180km/h)

★After 1948; 88 × 82mm; 498.4cc

39

Gentleman Racers

The 1950 version of the Gambalunga – compare differences with earlier versions such as the front brake and rear sub-frame.

crown, offered a normal compression ratio of 8:1. Its 20mm gudgeon pin ran on a bronze bush pressed into the eye of the connecting-rod, which was manufactured of chrome-nickel steel and featured a split big-end eye running on uncaged steel rollers, a system employed on the series production Guzzi 500cc street bikes, but considered impractical by most other manufacturers.

In practice this system worked well enough – and it had the additional advantage for a racing engine in the hands of a private rider that it was unnecessary to realign the crank flywheels during a rebuild – unlike the majority of contemporary high-performance racing singles, which used one-piece connecting-rods and caged roller bearings in built-up flywheels.

There was a further feature of the Gambalunga that marked it out from the Condor or Dondolino – it was fitted with Guzzi's own design of leading-link front fork instead of the ancient girder type used on earlier bikes. These forks, used on all future Gambalungas became a feature of the factory's full Grand Prix models of the 1950s.

Weaknesses

The most irritating feature of the Gambalunga was the need for constant adjustment of the pushrod length and rocker clearance. The variable quality of fuel available to the racing fraternity at this time made it necessary to change the compression ratio frequently by fitting compression plates, which upset pushrod adjustment. This was compounded by the differing coefficients of expansion of the barrel, valves and pushrods, which made it necessary to adjust for different engine temperatures as well.

The problem was so acute that when the correct racing clearances were set and the engine allowed to cool, both valves were lifted right off their seats! This led to a peculiar cold-starting drill: the tappet adjusting screws were slackened off, the engine was warmed, stopped, and then the tappets were re-set.

When one considers that most riders in those days went without the luxury of a mechanic and so had to perform this task perhaps as often as six times a day, it's easy to understand why it was such a major source of annoyance, testing even the most patient competitor.

A solution was eventually discovered, using 1 × 10mm steel pushrods from the three-wheel Guzzi Ercole Motocarri (light truck). The ends were of a different design to the racing components, and the total weight of these alternative pushrods was much lower.

Tipo Faenza

In 1948, the bore and stroke reverted to the firm's traditional 88 × 82mm and the usual displacement – this later design was referred to as the Tipo Faenza (Faenza being the Milan street circuit).

On the low 73-octane fuel of the era, the standard compression ratio on both types of engines produced 34bhp at the rear wheel. The Tipo Faenza peaked at around 5,500rpm compared to the original Gambalunga's 5,800rpm. Both were 'safe' to 6,000rpm, but if this ceiling was exceeded by a considerable margin, the result could be a cracked crankcase, which both on safety and cost grounds was something to avoid.

In performance terms there was little to choose between the two versions, although the Tipo Faenza developed its power at lower revs with consequently reduced engine stress. The original series engine featured a thick compression plate under the cylinder barrel to compensate for the extra stroke (and a much longer connecting-rod), but except for obvious compensating changes such as reworking the crankcase mouth, there were no structural differences between the two designs.

120mph Plus

In 1951 a specially tuned version built in the factory's race shop appeared prior to production of the Gambalunga later that year. For this bike, Guzzi claimed 37bhp at 6,000rpm and a maximum speed of over 120mph (193km/h).

When one considers that Guzzi also had motorcycles such as the 500 V-twin and various 250s, to say nothing of developing brand-new designs such as the 500 in-line four and 500 V8, it is a wonder that they ever managed to successfully develop the final versions of the 'Gentleman racer' to such good effect.

The Gambalunga's greatest success came with Lorenzetti in the saddle. Following several victories on a Dondolino, he had Grand Prix wins in Italy (1949), Switzerland and Ulster (1948) riding a Gambalumga.

Enrico Lorenzetti (7) leads a Norton (47) and a Gilera Saturno (17) at San Remo in 1947.

4 In-Line V-Twin Development

Bicilindrica

The Bicilindrica (twin-cylinder) V-twin 500 Grand Prix design made its début in 1933 and was still being raced as late as 1951.

At 120 degrees, the angle between the cylinders was exceptionally wide. The design utilized the 68 × 68mm 'square' bore and stroke dimensions of the company's existing 250 (*see* Chapter 2). The idea was that it would produce the power of two 250cc models. The exact engine size was 493.90cc, which would remain unchanged throughout its long life. As *Motor Cycle* commented at the time, the new wide-angle V-twin was of 'exceptional interest'. And compared with rival British single-cylinder machines, that statement was entirely true.

In an era when the engine, gearbox and clutch were usually assembled separately, the Bicilindrica boasted unit construction of the components. Each cylinder had its own camshaft situated in the head and driven by shaft and bevel gears. With such a wide angle the front cylinder was horizontal and the rear one laid back at an angle so that it was pointing directly underneath the rider's sprung saddle.

Each cylinder had a 28.5mm Dell'Orto remote float carburettor and a single exhaust port. The valves (two per cylinder) employed hairpin springs. Ignition was courtesy of a

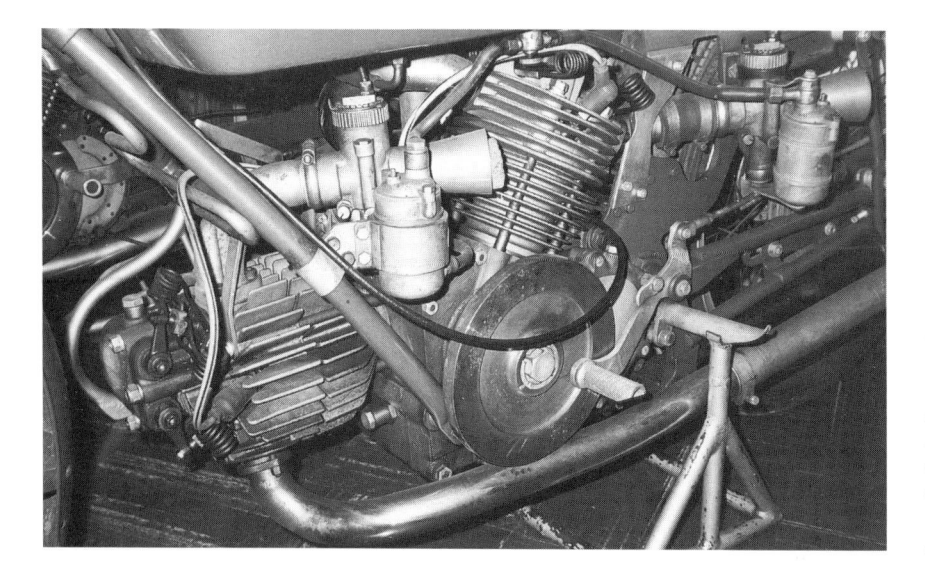

Post-war 120 degree Guzzi V-twin power unit, showing the alloy heads and barrels, Dell'Orto SSI carburettors, remote float chambers and the traditional Guzzi 'bacon slicer' outside flywheel.

In-Line V-Twin Development

The original rigid frame 500 V-twin at Monza, 1 September 1933. Carlo Guzzi is third from the left next to rider Amilcare Moretti seated on the bike.

Terzo Bandini leaves the checkpoint at Rome during the 1934 Milano–Napoli on his works Guzzi 500 V-twin.

Bosch-made magneto, mounted between the cylinders.

Dry sump lubrication was specified, the oil being carried in a wedge-shaped 4ltr (0.8gal) tank mounted above and to the rear of the 20ltr (4.4gal) fuel tank. The gear-type oil pump was external and driven from the timing gear on the offside (right) of the engine.

The traditional 'bacon slicer' outside flywheel – a feature of many Guzzis up to the early 1950s was on the nearside (left); this meant that a smaller area could be used for the vertically split, aluminium crankcases.

Bicilindrica 500 1935

Engine	Air-cooled, sohc, 120 degree V-twin with two valves per cylinder, iron heads and barrels, hairpin valve springs, inclined valves, vertically split crankcases
Bore	68mm
Stroke	68mm
Displacement	494.8cc
Compression ratio	8.5:1
Lubrication	Gear-type pump, dry sump
Ignition	Magneto
Carburation	2 × Dell'Orto 28.5mm
Gearbox	Four-speed, foot-change
Clutch	Multi-plate, wet
Final drive	Chain
Frame	Full cradle, tubular steel construction
Suspension	Front, girder forks; rear, rigid
Brakes	Drums front and rear
Tyres	Front 3.00 × 21; rear 3.25 × 20

General specification

Wheelbase	1390mm (55in)
Dry weight	151kg (333lb)
Fuel capacity	20ltr (4.4gal)
Maximum power output	44bhp at 7,000rpm
Top speed	112mph (180km/h)

43

The 1935 Senior TT-winning 500 V-twin, as ridden by Stanley Woods, now with rear suspension.

The drive for the rev counter was taken from the overhead camshaft (ohc) of the front cylinder.

At first, the power output was 44bhp at 7,000rpm. The prototype used a rigid frame, with a Brampton-type girder front fork. Details of this first version include cast-iron cylinder heads and barrels; a wheelbase of 1390mm (54.7in); a four-speed gearbox; a wet, multi-plate clutch; 3.00 × 21 front and 3.25 × 20 rear tyres. Straight-through exhaust pipes were used instead of megaphones. The frame design featured widely splayed twin front downtubes that pressed either side of the front cylinder.

By the beginning of 1935, the 190 degree single overhead camshaft (sohc) V-twin was putting out an additional 1bhp (making 45bhp in all), but the biggest news was the adaptation of a spring frame, based on that already in use on the 250cc racing model. This was of the cantilever type, with horizontal springs passing under the engine in box-like containers.

Heads and cylinders were now in cast iron or light alloy – depending upon whether the fuel used was alcohol (as was permitted during the 1930s) or petrol (gasoline). The horsepower figures are those for petrol.

Stanley Woods

During February 1935 came the first hints that the great Irish rider Stanley Woods was considering the V-twin Guzzi for the Senior TT (a 250 from Moto Guzzi had already been agreed).

By May it was revealed that not only would he be riding a Guzzi in both the Senior and Lightweight TTs, but he would be backed up by the Italian Omobono Tenni and fellow Irishman Gordon Burney.

The first appearance of the Guzzi squad came during the practice session of Friday 7 June, when, according to *Motor Cycle*: 'Tenni and Burney riding Lightweights and Stanley

In-Line V-Twin Development

Woods a Senior model. Tenni shaped [up] particularly well, being one of the 3-lappers, Stanley jogged along in his own inimitable style, but did not trouble about speed'. *Motor Cycle* also reported that: 'the spring frame on the Senior mount model seems good, for Woods' performance is a model of steadiness'.

The practice report for Monday 10 June commented:

> The 'foreign menace' is becoming stronger every day – those twin Guzzis are terrifically fast – and both Stanley Woods and O Tenni are riding them splendidly. They – the machines – seem to have a good degree of reliability too, and if they stay the course – well, we shall see.

In their issue of 13 June 1935 *Motor Cycle* published an article entitled 'Man of the Moment'. This set out to bring readers: 'some interesting facts about the riders entered for next week's three great races':

> Race number 2 Stanley Woods (Senior & Lightweight)
> Needs no introduction. Two years after competing in his first motor cycle event – a reliability trial – he finished fifth in the 1922 Junior TT. Has won numerous Continental races and pulled off 'doubles' in the Junior and Senior TTs of 1932 and 1933. Represents, perhaps, the most serious of the continental challenges.

> Number 14 O. Tenni (Senior & Lightweight)
> An Italian rider of no mean ability. Finished second to J.H. Simpson in the Swiss Grand Prix last year. Should prove an admirable team-mate for Stanley Woods.

> Number 25 J.G. Burney (Lightweight)
> Stanley Woods' brother-in-law. A well-known Irish speedman who is coming back to the TT after several years' absence. Finished sixth in the Lightweight in 1926 and tenth in the same race in 1928.

Who Will Win the Senior?

In the issue of 20 June 1935 *Motor Cycle* stated: 'The 1935 Senior comes nearer justifying its proper title of "International" than any of its predecessors. Four teams of foreign

Stanley Woods being congratulated after his victorious 1935 Senior TT-winning ride on the Guzzi V-twin.

In-Line V-Twin Development

machines, largely ridden by foreign riders, contest the issue with the cream of the stars from the British Isles'.

The continental challenge consisted of three German NSUs, three Czech Jawas, a German DKW – plus the Guzzi pair of Woods and Tenni.

The same issue also contained a report entitled 'Final Days of Practice', in which the main issue was that Woods had broken the lap record. *Motor Cycle* describing it thus: 'We have been having a taste of Guzzi speed at odd moments since practising started, but this morning Stanley Woods took out his actual race machine with astonishing results. The official time given out for lap 2 was the amazing one of 26 minutes 50 seconds, which is easily a record and equals 84.3mph (135.5km/h)'.

The 1939 version of Guzzi's 120-degree V-twin engine, with exposed hairpin valve springs and a 'bacon slicer' flywheel.

Woods Wins the Senior TT

Woods rode a tactical race. In a seven lap, 264.1 mile (425km) event, Jimmy Guthrie led for all but the last part of the final lap. In fact after the Norton star had crossed the finishing line he was declared the winner! But Woods, starting $14\frac{1}{2}$ minutes after Guthrie, rode an absolute blinder of a final lap, set a new lap record and in the process won the race. The top six finishers were as follows:

1st   S. Woods (Guzzi)
2nd   J. Guthrie (Norton)
3rd   W.F. Rusk (Norton)
4th   J. Duncan (Norton)
5th   O. Steinbach (NSU)
6th   E.A. Mellor (NSU)

At the end, Woods' victory margin was a mere four seconds. What a race, what a performance from man and machine! Team-mate Tenni, after lying second for several laps in the Light-

In-Line V-Twin Development

The Guzzi V-twin circa 1945–46.

weight race, had crashed and so had been unable to ride the V-twin in the Senior TT.

The 'Foreign Menace'

The lead story in the 27 June 1935 issue of *Motor Cycle* was headlined: 'A Sensational TT Week', with the sub-heading 'Spring-frame, Unit-construction – Foreigner's Double Success. Multi-cylinder Victory in the Senior – The Effect of This Year's Races on Future Design'. Part of this editorial is reproduced below:

> TT week deserves that much misused word sensational, for the first time since 1911 the so-called 'foreign menace' has proved more than a menace on paper. Two of the three races have been won by foreign machines, handled by that famous Irish rider, Stanley Woods. Important as this is, there is something of even greater importance: both these foreign machines had spring frames and unit construction of their engines and gearboxes, while the Senior TT winner had a multi-cylinder engine.

Equipment

The winning Guzzi V-twin used the following equipment:

- Amal carburettors (in place of the usual Dell'Ortos)
- Andre steering damper
- Bosch magneto
- Bowdemex control cables
- Brampton forks
- Dunlop tyres
- Ferodo brake and clutch linings
- Lodge spark plugs
- Moseley air cushions
- Pirelli tubing
- Renolds chain
- Shell fuel
- Tecalemit greasing
- Terry saddle
- Vacuum oil
- Wellworthy piston rings

LEFT: Works Guzzi star Omobono Tenni with one of the 120 degree V-twins at Genoa in the summer of 1945; one of the first meetings staged in Italy after the end of hostilities.

BELOW LEFT: Omobono Tenni's 1945–46 V-twin on display in the Guzzi museum at Mandello del Lario during the 1980s.

BELOW: Fergus Anderson pushes the latest version of the Guzzi V-twin into action at Nice in 1948; the first year of the telescopic fork model.

48

In-Line V-Twin Development

ABOVE: *Official Guzzi factory photograph of the 1948 machine, showing the front and rear suspension and the revised tank design (shared with the 250 parallel twin of the same year).*

RIGHT: *Bob Foster outside his showroom in Poole, Dorset with his factory 500cc Guzzi V-twin prior to leaving for the Isle of Man TT in 1950. Foster acted as Guzzi's UK distributor during the early post-war years.*

In-Line V-Twin Development

The 1949 V-twin, now with leading-link front forks and new full-width brakes. Note the streamlined tank and front number plate.

LEFT: *A works Guzzi V-twin at the TT, June 1950.*

BELOW: *The V-twin in its definitive form, 1951.*

In-Line V-Twin Development

Staying Competitive

The manoeuvrability and reliability of the 500 V-twin were major reasons why, like the Norton single, it remained competitive long after other more powerful bikes had come on to the scene.

The 1951 V-twin produced 48bhp at 8,000rpm, but it was the running gear that had really received the changes including:

- High-level exhaust
- Larger diameter brakes
- Megaphone exhaust
- Partial streamlining
- Revised bodywork
- Revised riding position
- Telescopic front forks (later replaced with leading-link type)

Of course, many of these mirrored the development put into the 250cc single that went on to win the World Championship that year in the hands of Bruno Ruffo.

Exploded view of the various major components of the 500 V-twin, circa 1951.

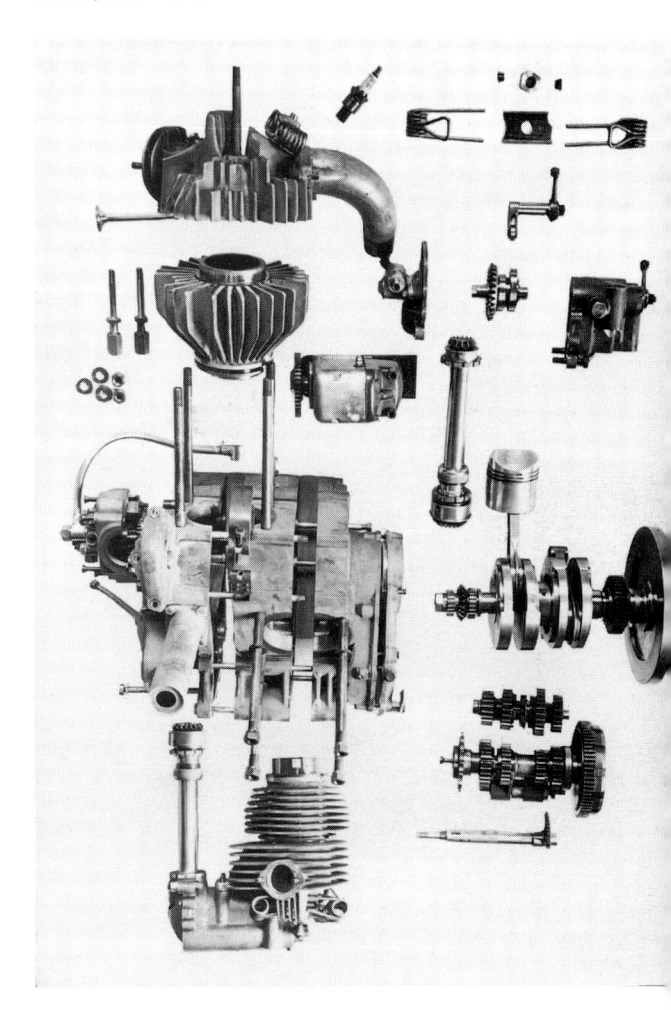

Bicilindrica 500 1951	
Engine	Air-cooled, sohc, 120 degree with two valves per cylinder, alloy heads and barrels, hairpin valve springs, inclined valves, vertically split crankcases
Bore	68mm
Stroke	68mm
Displacement	494.8mm
Compression ratio	9.0:1
Lubrication	Gear-type pump, dry sump
Ignition	Magneto
Carburation	2 × Dell'Orto 30mm
Gearbox	Four-speed, foot-change
Clutch	Multi-plate, wet
Final drive	Chain
Frame	Full cradle, steel construction
Suspension	Front, leading-link forks; rear, sprung
Brakes	Front, double-sided drum; rear, drum
Tyres	19in front and rear
General specification	
Wheelbase	1390mm (54.7in)
Dry weight	155kg (342lb)
Fuel capacity	22ltr (4.8gal)
Maximum power output	48bhp at 8,000rpm
Top speed	118mph (190km/h)

In-Line V-Twin Development

ABOVE: *Fergus Anderson on his way to victory during the Swiss Grand Prix at the end of April 1951; it was the design's last major success.*

LEFT: *One of the official Guzzi team entries for the French Grand Prix at Albi in May 1951.*

In-Line V-Twin Development

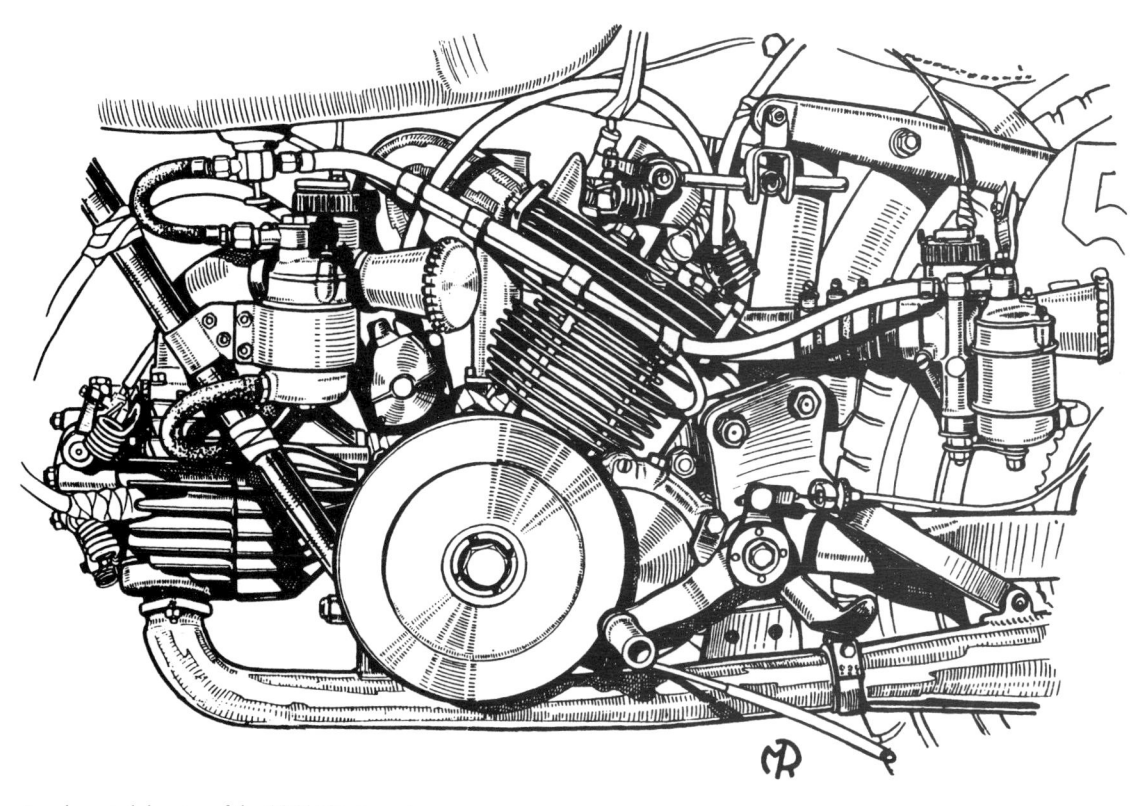

Lovely period drawing of the 1951 V-twin engine.

Anderson Wins the Swiss Grand Prix

The final victory came during the second round of the 1951 Grand Prix season, when Fergus Anderson took the machine to a famous win in the Swiss Grand Prix at Berne. Despite the heavy rain, the V-twin and its rider outlasted many more fancied runners such as the massed ranks of four-cylinder Gilera and MV Agusta models, to say nothing of the British AJS Porcupine and single-cylinder Nortons.

This twenty-eight lap, 127-mile (204km) marathon was all about lasting the course. *Motor Cycle* concluded its report of the race by saying: 'Anderson continued to lap in impeccable style and came home an easy and very popular winner. Mechanics smothered his face with kisses as both British and Italian flags were hoisted'.

The 500 V-twin was finally retired at the end of 1951.

5 Three Cylinders

The most famous use of three cylinders in motorcycle design has been by Triumph, Laverda (across-the-frame), and DKW and Honda (V-formation). But all these came many years after Moto Guzzi had built triples in both production roadster and Grand Prix racer forms.

The Tipo Tre Cilindri

Carlo Guzzi was no stranger to multi-cylinder engine design, having already built and extensively tested a four-cylinder racing bike in 1930/31 (*see* Chapter 1). Like the ill-starred four-cylinder, the original three-cylinder featured an across-the-frame layout with a horizontal cylinder. However, unlike the four, the newcomer was just about as far removed from the race circuit as was possible, because its role was that of a luxury street bike – a dream bike that few could afford.

The first Guzzi across-the-frame three-cylinder design was a luxury street bike, sold in limited numbers during 1932–33, preceding the later supercharged racer by several years.

Three Cylinders

Designed by Carlo Guzzi in 1939, the Tre Cilindri (three-cylinder) was only raced once, at Genoa in May 1940.

Guzzi believed, in common with other manufacturers of similar high-cost exotic models, that the world economic depression of the early 1930s did not provide the right conditions for launching such machinery.

In fact, Guzzi did go ahead with the launch of the Tre Cilindri, a superb model of particularly advanced design. It confounded observers by offering the power of a multi with the riding characteristics of a single. The Tipo Sport 15, which had a virtually identical engine capacity produced 13.2bhp at 3,800rpm from its ioe single-cylinder engine, against 25bhp at 5,500rpm for the triple.

However, it was not a commercial success and ultimately its performance, glamour and practical dimensions could not ensure the design's continuation.

The Engine
The engine displaced 494.8cc, with long-stroke dimensions of 56mm × 67mm. The valves were placed in parallel and operated by pushrods; the valve gear being exposed. Both the heads and barrel were in cast iron, with a single bolt-in aluminium casting for the single Amal carburettor that was mounted above the cylinders on the nearside (left) of the engine – later transferred to the offside (right).

The Gearbox
On the left on the engine's crankcase were the primary drive gears and clutch (both running in oil); whilst on the right were the ignition distributor and oil pump. Behind the crankcases was the gearbox, which was in a unit with the engine. This featured a three-speed cluster

Three Cylinders

The engine was an air-cooled, supercharged, dohc, across-the-frame triple with steeply inclined cylinders. A particularly advanced design.

and was hand operated via a lever on the offside of the 11.5ltr (2.53gal) chrome-plated fuel tank.

The Lubrication System
The gear-type oil pump worked in co-operation with the wet sump lubrication system – the latter having a capacity of 3ltr (0.66gal), and being unit construction, supplied the engine, gearbox, clutch and primary gears. Although a neat layout, full unit construction of this type – which included the clutch – meant that the oil became contaminated more quickly than would otherwise have been the case.

The Header Pipes
A trio of exhaust header pipes joined up in a single-cylindrical collector box was situated at the very front of the engine beneath the cylinders. The collector box exited on the offside (right) end into a single chrome-plated silencer. The noise emitted was totally at odds with Guzzi's other production roadsters, which were all single-cylinder machines at that time. Instead of the plonk, plonk every lamp post of the single, there came the high-pitched yowling noise of the triple – wonderful by early 1930s standards!

The Brakes
With the same drum brakes as the Tipo Sport 15 single – 177mm (6.9in) front and 200mm (7.8in) rear – readers might assume that the Tre Cilindri would perhaps be deficient in this area of its performance. However, they would be incorrect, as the difference in weight between the two contrasting designs was not as great as might have been expected, just 10kg (22lb). The Tipo Sport 15 weighed in at 150kg (331lb) against 16kg (35lb) for the Tre Cilindri.

The Wheelbase
Another area where surprises were in order was the wheelbase, which had been kept relatively short at 1440mm (56.6in). This had been achieved by positioning the cylinder heads between the twin front frame downtubes – a ploy Carlo Guzzi was also to exploit in his 1933 design of the 120 degree V-twin racer (*see* Chapter 4).

Ing. Fabio Taglioni was to follow with his 90 degree V-twin range that débuted in 1970. But Guzzi were there four decades earlier!

The Suspension
A high degree of comfort was assured in giving the triple both front and rear suspension – very rare in those days. The front came courtesy of girder forks featuring a massive single central spring, whilst at the rear was an early form of cantilever suspension pioneered in the 1928 GT single-cylinder road bike. This operated on the basis of horizontal springs located

underneath the engine and gearbox unit. These springs were contained within a box-like device.

The Wheels

Another way of obtaining a relatively compact motorcycle had been by using 19in wheel rims and tyres; this in an age when larger sizes were often specified.

As with his other designs, Guzzi used a horizontal cylinder layout, which kept the centre of gravity as low as possible, increasing manoeuvrability.

1940 Tre Cilindri Corsa

Even though the original production roadster failed to make the grade, this didn't mean that the engine type was not viable; a point made by Carlo Guzzi when he designed an entirely new three-cylinder motorcycle at the end of the 1930s. Although it was an air-cooled across-the-frame three-cylinder like its older roadster brother that was where any resemblance ended.

The racing-only design featured inclined rather than horizontal cylinders. The 491.8cc (59 × 60mm) engine featured double overhead camshafts (dohc), whilst both the heads and barrels were cast in aluminium, rather than iron. Official Guzzi figures give the power output at 65bhp at 8,000rpm.

Placed above the crankcase and behind the inclined cylinders, the Cozette supercharger was one of the reasons for the impressive power output and top speed of 143mph (230km/h). Although the engine could not be described as beautiful, the layout gave the engine unit a particularly impressive look.

Not only did the supercharged 500 triple have foot-operated gear change, but there were no less than five ratios – this in an era when many bikes still had three, and four was considered a luxury. In traditional Guzzi fashion, the clutch was a multi-plate device running in oil, with straight-cut primary gears and chain final drive.

The triangulated open frame was very much akin to the type used by Honda during the early 1960s – but with the Guzzi cantilever rear suspension system. The girder front forks were of the Brampton type. There were large drum brakes; each in excess of 200mm, with liberally finned hubs and ventilated brake plates. Components such as wheel rims, the fuel tank and engine casing were either in aluminium or electron. Even so, the 1939–40 Tre Cilindri weighed in at 175kg (386lb) dry.

Tre Cilindri 500 1940	
Engine	Air-cooled, supercharged, dohc, across-the-frame three-cylinder with inclined cylinders
Bore	59mm
Stroke	60mm
Displacement	491.8cc
Compression ratio	8:1
Lubrication	Gear-type oil pump
Ignition	Marelli magneto
Carburation	Cozette supercharger
Gearbox	Five-speed, foot-change
Clutch	Multi-plate
Final drive	Chain
Frame	Open type, with engine as stressed member
Suspension	Front, sprung girder forks; rear, cantilever with horizontal shock absorbers
Brakes	Drum, front and rear
Tyres	Front 2.75 × 21; rear 3.00 × 21
General specification	
Wheelbase	1470mm (57.8in)
Dry weight	175kg (386lb)
Fuel capacity	22ltr (4.8gal)
Maximum power output	65bhp at 8,000rpm
Top speed	141mph (230km/h)

Three Cylinders

ABOVE: Nearside view of the 1940 supercharged 3-cylinder, with the supercharger unit to the rear of the cylinders, above the crankcase.

LEFT: This view shows off the massive structure of components such as the Cozette supercharger, frame and timing case of the 1940 three-cylinder racing model. Sadly, the FIM post-war ban on superchargers was to sound its death knell.

With its weight and power, the bike would probably have been something of a handful around some circuits – but on those with fast straights and smooth tarmac it would most definitely have been a serious challenger at Grand Prix level had not the war intervened to stop play. When the conflict ended, FIM (the governing body for motorcycle sport) banned superchargers and so the triple, outlawed from competition, was abandoned. The only time the bike was ever raced was at the Circuito de Lido, Genoa (ridden by Guglielmo Sandri), in May 1940.

6 The Albatros

On both the street and the race circuit, Guzzi's 250cc horizontal singles played just as important a role as the larger 500cc family from the 1920s right through to the 1950s. In fact, as an over-the-counter customer racer, the 250 single was the more successful engine size for the Italian marque.

The Albatros

Following in the footsteps of its larger-engined brothers, the production racing Albatros made its début in 1939. It was conceived very much with the 'Gentleman racer' category (*see* Chapter 3) in mind. Although it could be purchased by the private rider, the design was right at the forefront of contemporary technology – in fact, virtually one of the latest supercharged works machines with the blower removed!

Going on sale in Italy for 12,500 lira, the international situation in the summer of 1939 hampered its progress – a situation that only changed once peace finally returned some six years later.

When production resumed at the Mandello del Lario plant after the war, the Albatros was offered for sale in full racing guise with an open pipe, the road-going accessories having been axed. This new edition met with immediate approval and was the preferred choice for many of the top privateers at this time.

After the war until the end of the 1948 season, Guzzi factory team riders were equipped with what were essentially specially

The original Albatros sports model as it appeared in 1938 was intended for both long-distance road events and conversion into a short circuit racer.

The Albatros

By 1939, the Albatros had become a full-blown racing motorcycle.

tuned and assembled versions of the Albatros production racer (*see* Chapter 6). These generated around 23bhp and could top 100mph (161km/h). In many ways they were similar to the pre-war supercharged machine, but without the blower and modified to run on low-grade fuel. With these machines, Guzzi were able largely to dominate racing in the 250cc class at Grand Prix level with only the lone Benelli of Dario Ambrosini posing a real challenge.

Manliff Barrington rode to victory on an Albatros in the Lightweight race of the first post-war Isle of Man TT in June 1947. Maurice Cann made it another Isle of Man TT win in 1948 (*see* Chapter 2). Throughout Europe, and indeed the whole world, the Albatros was soon clocking up hundreds of victories.

Due to the failure of the Grand Prix twin-cylinder model (*see* Chapter 8), the factory used the Albatros for its 'works' from 1946

Albatros 1939

Engine	Air-cooled, sohc, single with two valves, horizontal cylinder alloy head and barrel, hairpin valve springs, inclined valves, drive to camshaft by shaft and bevel gears, vertically split crankcases	Final drive	Chain
		Frame	Cradle type, steel construction
		Suspension	Front, girder forks; rear, sprung
		Brakes	Drums front and rear
		Tyres	Front 2.75 × 21; rear 3.00 × 21
Bore	68mm		
Stroke	68mm		
Displacement	246.8cc	**General specification**	
Compression ratio	8.5:1	Wheelbase	1430mm (56.2in)
Lubrication	Gear pump, dry sump	Dry weight	135kg (298lb)
Ignition	Magneto	Fuel capacity	20ltr (4.4gal)
Carburation	Dell'Orto SS30M	Maximum power output	20bhp at 7,000rpm
Gearbox	Four-speed, foot-change		
Clutch	Multi-plate, wet	Top speed	87mph (140km/h)

The Albatros

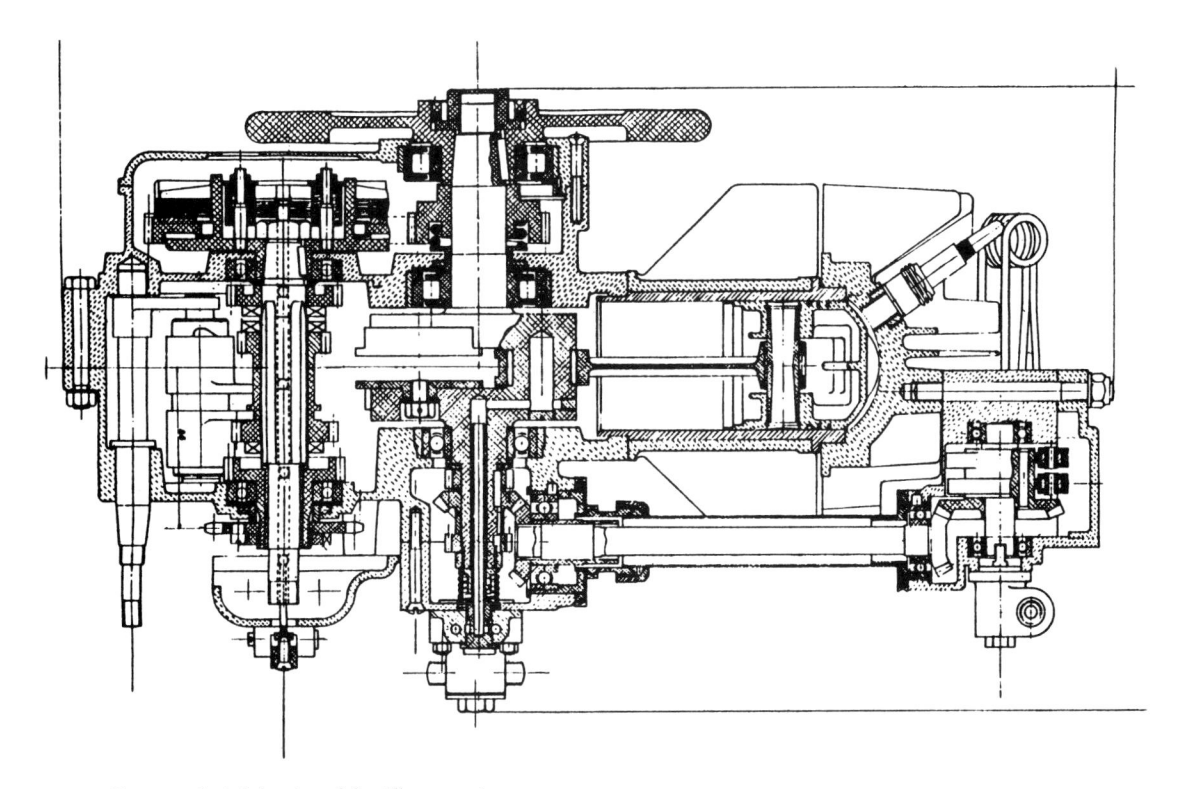

ABOVE: *Factory technical drawing of the Albatros engine.*

BELOW: *Official 1948 photograph of the Albatros as it appeared during the immediate post-war years.*

ABOVE: Les Diener of South Australia with his recently imported Albatros production racer, winner of the 1947 Victorian TT 250cc class.

LEFT: Unknown Albatros rider competing at Brough airfield, East Yorkshire, summer 1954.

BELOW: Isle of Man, early 1950s. The Albatros was the favoured 250cc mount for privateers – or at least those lucky enough to be able to afford one.

until 1948; after which it was replaced by the more highly developed Gambalunghino (*see* Chapter 7).

The Design

The Albatros turned out 20bhp at 7,000rpm and reached a speed of 87.5mph (141km/h). Like the 500 Condor it was supplied with a full set of road-legal equipment (lighting equipment, horn, silencer and the like). The single overhead camshaft (sohc) 246.8cc (68 × 68mm) horizontal single-cylinder engine featured a forged three-ring piston with a compression ratio of 8.5:1, and breathed through a Dell'Orto SS30M carburettor. The gearbox was a foot-operated, four-speed, close ratio unit.

To a large extent the Albatros reflected existing Guzzi thought, with girder front forks and the factory's own rear springing courtesy of the spring-in-a-box under the engine together with an adjustable friction system on either side next to the rear wheel. Other features included 21in alloy wheel rims fitted with 2.75 front and 3.0 rear tyres, 20ltr (4.4gal) fuel and 5ltr (1gal) oil tanks. It is interesting to note that both the tanks were larger than those on the Condor at that time.

Fergus Anderson

As far as British Commonwealth riders went, it was the Scot, Fergus Anderson, who stole the show in Continental Europe on the Albatros. Anderson went on to become double World Champion on Guzzis in 1953 and 1954, then in 1955 he became the racing team manager for the Italian marque. But before all of that, during the late 1940s he notched up a vast array of victories and leader board places as a privateer throughout Europe.

Anderson was a true member of that select band who shared the experiences and adventures of their racing careers in Europe before

Fergus Anderson after winning the Grand Prix of Prague on his privately entered Albatros model, 15 June 1947.

the era of motorways and air travel, which changed the pattern. These riders were both friends and rivals in a sport largely untainted by big money and corporate sponsorship. Anderson was one of a close band of competitors who were real men rather than today's hyped-up superstars. Sport then still meant sport – where the unwinding tarmac was their bread and the fumes of Castrol R their nectar.

Maurice Cann

1948 TT winner Maurice Cann was another hero of the time. Although he never competed on the Continent, he nonetheless helped put the Albatros on the map by making a surprising number of outstanding performances within the British Isles. Like Anderson, Cann was a loyal devotee of the Guzzi marque, and

The Albatros

who knows what success he might have garnered if he had been able to allow more time to go racing? As it was, his business interests restricted his efforts to the home circuits – the Isle of Man and that most famous of his stamping grounds, the Ulster Grand Prix. For several seasons in the late 1940s and early 1950s, this venue became almost his exclusive preserve where he annihilated reigning World Champions on full factory bikes. On the Clady circuit, Cann was 'King of the 250s' as one journalist of the era described the Leicester-based rider.

Cann was also an engine tuner of considerable ability. For the 1951 Isle of Man TT, he produced his own home-brewed double overhead camshaft (dohc) Guzzi. As he was unable to ride because of a practice injury, the bike was handed over to Australian Harry Hinton, who also crashed in practice and so failed to ride it in the race. Even so, one of Hinton's practice laps on Cann's dohc Albatros was faster than any laps recorded by the official Guzzi team riders! This so shook them that Cann was asked if he would allow his bike to be taken back to the Mandello works for inspection – to which he most sportingly agreed.

Just how much of Cann's design was subsequently incorporated into the later works bikes has never officially been revealed. But what is certain is that Guzzi engineers, headed by Carcano, did embrace the concept of twin overhead camshafts (ohcs).

An extract from *Motor Cycle*, dated 14 July 1955 serves as a fitting tribute to one of the most unsung members of the Guzzi team. This piece also presents the reader with an insight into a typical Cann/Guzzi performance:

> The flag falls, the riders start pushing, a dozen-or-two engines roar into life, but not Maurice Cann's. His engine gives only an apologetic cough and not until he has pushed the length of a cricket pitch does it burst into song. He then proceeds to race like a celluloid cat evacuating the hot regions, gobbling up riders who have made a rapid start; towards the end, usually, he engages in a duel with the leader.

Lorenzetti Turns Privateer

At the end of 1954, long-serving Guzzi works rider Enrico Lorenzetti left the official team, mainly because he was approaching his fortieth birthday and he wanted to ride a 250 rather than the 350s and 500s that Guzzi

Maurice Cann, Albatros production racer, circa 1949.

Scarborough, 1949: the first-ever meeting at the Oliver's Mount circuit, with Guzzi Albatros-mounted Dickie Dale at Mere hairpin.

E.A. Barrett with his Moto Guzzi Albatros during the 250cc race at Boreham Airfield, Essex, summer 1952.

were concentrating on by now. He therefore chose to ride a 250cc Guzzi as a privateer, although it is a fact that he was provided with considerable assistance by the factory. Lorenzetti's personal mount was an ex-factory Gambalunghino engine in his own special frame, which was to prove so successful that the design was later taken up by Guzzi.

During some three seasons as a privateer, Lorenzetti concentrated mainly on the Italian National Championship series and the Italian Grand Prix but he also competed in selected foreign Grand Prix events. His best year was 1956, when he finished third in the 250cc World Championship series (with a third in Holland and runner-up at Monza). His swan-song was a superb third behind Tarquinio Provini (FB Mondial) and Remo Venturi (MV Agusta). Appropriately enough, the end of Lorenzetti's long career came at the same time

65

LEFT: *The vast array of awards garnered by leading Guzzi privateer Arthur Wheeler up to the end of the 1955 season. Note the aluminium 'dustbin' fairing, very much like the factory bikes of the day.*

BELOW LEFT: *Arthur Wheeler (21) and an NSU Rennmax rider (20) at the Surtees Day, Brands Hatch, 1981.*

BELOW RIGHT: *Arthur Wheeler with his 250cc Guzzi at the Surtees Day, Brands Hatch, 1981.*

as Moto Guzzi withdrew from racing (*see* Chapter 7). His career spanned more than fifteen years and saw him survive an incredible number of accidents, some of them serious.

Arthur Wheeler

Another privateer who is very much part of the Moto Guzzi racing story is Englishman, Arthur Wheeler. A dealer from Epsom in Surrey, he first became a Guzzi convert back in 1951 when, to quote the man himself, despite finishing fifth in the Lightweight TT and third in the Ulster Grand Prix for Velocette, the Birmingham company 'never even said thank you'. At that point he decided to make the switch to Guzzi, influenced by the fact that not only had the Italians won the 1951 World Championship, but they had dominated the class at every Grand Prix since the fatal crash of Benelli's lone star Dario Ambrosini in the French round at Albi earlier that year.

Wheeler's first Guzzi was a three-year-old Albatros purchased from Belgian rider Leon Martin. The winter closed season saw the bike return to its birthplace at Mandello del Lario to be refurbished, and it was duly collected from the Italian works by its new owner in early 1952.

After taking in meetings at Pau and San Remo, Wheeler returned to Britain for a full season including the TT and Irish meetings, the latter including the North West 200 and the Ulster Grand Prix. His first victory with the Albatros came in the Leicester 200. In the Isle of Man his KTT Velocette 350 stopped with a bang, and then the Guzzi did the same thing in the Lightweight TT. But on the Italian bike this didn't happen until near the end of the final lap, and he was able to push it from Brandish to snatch ninth position. He also finished fourth at the Dutch TT (behind the works Guzzi trio of Lorenzetti, Ruffo and Anderson) and sixth at Solitude, scene of the German Grand Prix.

What followed was a brilliant career aboard Guzzi bikes. During one of his many conversations with the author, he said that: 'the Isle of Man TT is the best race in the world'. And in a decade of Guzzi TT rides he finished fourth three times, sixth once, seventh once, eighth once, ninth once, eighteenth once and twenty-third twice.

He was equally impressive in the World Championship series, highlights being fourth position in 1954 and third in 1962 (his final season).

1954 saw Wheeler finish fourth in the Ulster Grand Prix, sixth in the Dutch TT, fourth in the German Grand Prix and, the highlight of his career up to then, a magnificent victory in the Italian Grand Prix at Monza. This result so pleased Moto Guzzi that they provided him with a 350cc model for the 1956 and 1957 seasons.

Another feature of Wheeler's Guzzi career was the special frames he had made to house the Italian engine. The first of these, constructed by Birmingham-based Reynolds Ltd in 531 tubing, was built by Ken Sprayson to Wheeler's own design in 1959. From then onwards all his Guzzi singles (both 250 and 350cc) employed these frames.

The essence of this design was a massive top frame rail that incorporated the steering head and ran backwards to the rear tank/front seat area. There were much smaller diameter twin front downtubes and massive flat aluminium

Arthur Wheeler commissioned Reynolds to construct a special frame for his 250 and 350cc Guzzis; this is as it appeared in early 1962.

The Albatros

plates supporting the rear of the engine. The Guzzi-type leading-link front fork was retained, with conventional twin shock absorbers at the rear. The fuel tank was manufactured in aluminium. Other features included 18in rims and tyres and a well tucked-in megaphone exiting on the nearside (left) of the machine.

John Kidson

John Kidson built various home-brewed Guzzi specials. His first involvement with Guzzi machinery came in 1960, when he acquired a sohc Guzzi (68 × 68mm) Albatros engine, which had been brought into Britain some years earlier by Anderson. This was built into a Norton Featherbed chassis, and given the name 'Nor-guz'.

The bike's TT début came in 1961, when it was raced in the Lightweight event. Following a crash in the practices, it was rebuilt and finished the race in fifteenth position.

In 1962, with the help of Eric Lee, a frame-maker at the cotton works in his home town of Gloucester, Kidson constructed his own spine-type frame, with an oil reservoir in the large diameter top tube. This meant a name change to 'Cotton-Guzzi'. However, the TT that year saw a retirement due to big-end failure.

The following year, the bike was renamed

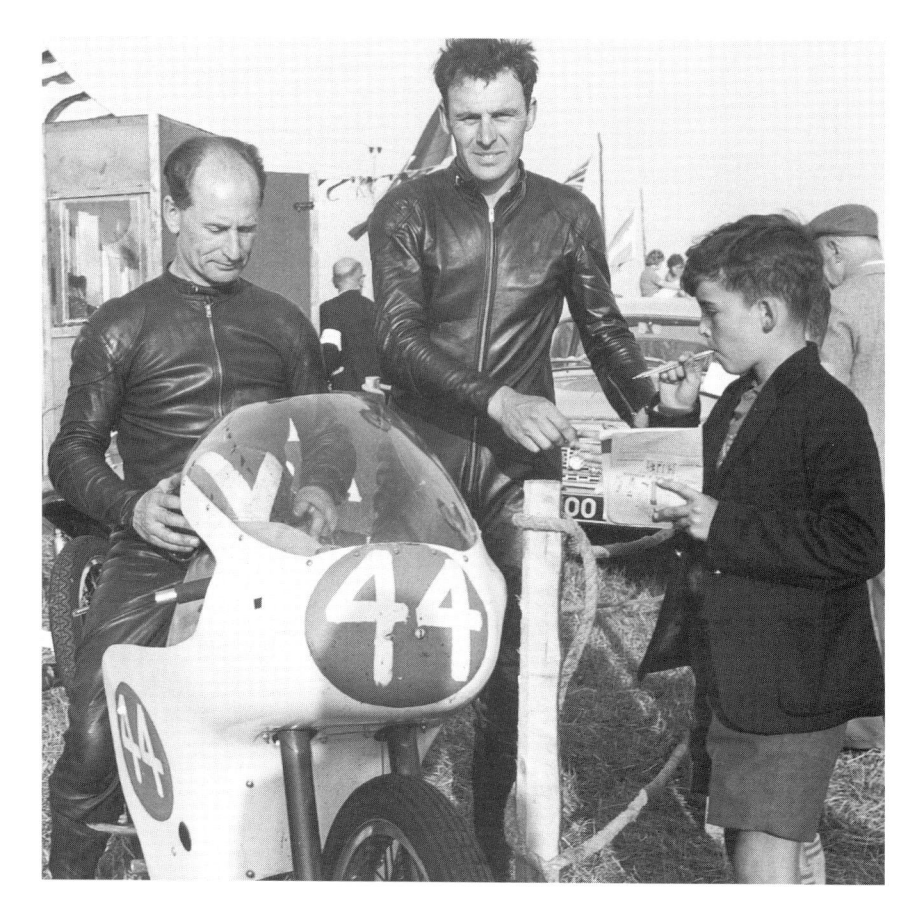

Arthur Wheeler (left) seated on bike, after winning the Southern 100 with his 250 Guzzi special, Isle of Man, July 1962.

yet again, this time as simply 'Guzzi'. The most notable technical invention was what Kidson described as a 'plenuim chamber'; a 2.5in tube from the front of the fairing to a chamber that was constructed in the front third of the fuel tank.

After a tremendous slide on melting tar Kidson took sixth place in the 1963 Lightweight TT, averaging 82.74mph (133km/h). Tommy Robb finished fifth on a factory Honda, beating Kidson into sixth place by a mere two-fifths of a second, which shows just how good a ride this was.

A Cotton Telstar joined the Kidson ranks in 1965, but it was back to the faithful Guzzi for the 1966 TT, where Kidson used Cann's double-knocker cam box, but the bike retired in the second lap due to severe misfiring. Then came three consecutive TT finishes: 1967, twentieth position averaging 77.75mph (125km/h); 1968, twenty-second position averaging 83.70mph (134.6km/h); and finally 1969, sixteenth position averaging 81.15mph (130.5 km/h).

Kidson acquired the majority of the Maurice Cann (now deceased) Guzzi racing équipe, including his home-engineered dohc cam box. Kidson discovered that it had been designed primarily to allow additional engine revolutions and also to prevent valve spring breakage, which was by far the biggest weakness on the sohc Albatros series of engines. So Cann had solved two problems by using dohc: more power and increased reliability.

The ex-Cann machine was stolen from the Silverstone paddock in 1964 during the annual Hutchinson 100 meeting. All that was eventually recovered was the bare engine and main frame loop. This led to a frantic rebuild effort by Kidson so it could be raced in the TT. The deadline was met, and Kidson was in fifth position on the first lap, but crashed at Laurel Bank on the second circuit and his race was over for another year.

During his time with Moto Guzzi, Kidson

A photograph taken by the author of his great friend Arthur Wheeler in 1984 at Snetterton with one of his Guzzis.

The same machine with the fairing removed. Sadly, after continuing to ride all over the world in historic races, Arthur died during the late 1990s from blood poisoning.

built a few short-stroke engines. In place of the 'square' 68 × 68mm standard bore and stroke dimensions of the Albatros series, he used 71 × 61mm, employing either Aermacchi or BSA Gold Star pistons. In the early sixties it was found that this gave the engine a new lease of life, particularly on the short British circuits. However, as the decade advanced the growing number of new Aermacchis and the latest

'Nor-Guz'; Ted Fenwick shows off his Norton-framed, Albatros-engined special at Brough, 3 April 1955.

breed of two-strokes were outclassing the Guzzi. Eventually, only the TT remained where reliability, handling and braking scored over the faster but less robust two-strokes. Then at the end of the 1960s, Kidson purchased the ex-Geoff Duke/Glen Henderson NSU Rennmax twin and the Guzzi singles were put into retirement.

Trevor Barnes

Trevor Barnes had arrived in the Guzzi fold after purchasing an early Gambalunghino from Wheeler in 1959. He told the author that it was: 'fairly original except the Guzzi front wheel was mounted on a pair of BSA forks'.

Much of his early racing with the Guzzi was spent suffering braking problems. That was until he discovered that the Guzzi brake had been designed for the Guzzi-made leading-link front forks and certainly not BSA telescopics! To effect a cure without too much cost, he acquired a set of Norton Roadholder forks and a full width hub. This was fitted together with 19in alloy rims and the latest racing tyres and he was in business.

1962 was his first year of racing and the remainder of the season was very successful, with wins and places at both club and national level throughout southern England, notably Crystal Palace and Brands Hatch. Barnes sums up his original Guzzi, once the braking problems had been resolved as: 'a lovely bike to start racing with'.

When Wheeler retired it was perhaps the natural thing that the young Barnes should buy the great man's 250 for the following season. However, as Trevor recalled recently, the bike had: 'too many minor mechanical problems to get the best from riding it. One wanted to be a full-time mechanic and rider, with tuning experience'.

The 1964 season saw a complete turnaround, and Barnes was quite often the first privateer home in the Grand Prix events he contested – quite an achievement. But it was the non-Grand Prix continental European races, where he had a chance to prepare and set-up the bike fully between races.

A 350cc engine, front forks and wheel, together with an Oldani rear wheel, were purchased, again from Wheeler, and a complete bike was then assembled in the same style as the existing 250. Like the smaller mount, the 350 was to prove competitive.

But two machines were an even bigger

An Insider's View

Trevor Barnes raced Guzzi singles for most of the 1960s – here are his views of the motorcycles and their technical features.

Certainly people don't realize just how advanced Moto Guzzi singles were. Their early frames had, of course, cantilever suspension with springs underneath the engine. However, what most don't know – and I only realized long after I had retired from racing – is that they also had an anti-dive braking system. The front brake of their machines equipped with leading-link front forks was clamped to the link itself. The torque reaction was to lift the front of the machine – or at least stop it diving. This was the reason why my large Guzzi-made front brake, fitted to the BSA forks on my first machine [*see* page 70], didn't function properly. It had not been designed for this type of fork. The first season on the ex-Arthur Wheeler Reynolds-framed 250, the wheel spindle was clamped this way.

The following year I decided to alter the front brake by making it fully floating, the brake torque arm being the same length as the leading link. This caused problems that year (it was always bad but manifested itself then), when under braking due to insufficient baffles in the oil tanks, oil shot past these and out via the breather, hence on to the rear tyre!

When I purchased the 250 engine and accessories (this included the front forks and twin front brake), amongst the parts were the original torque arms – which were shorter than the leading links. Not knowing why, I then proceeded to construct others the same length as the links – so the handling of the 250 and 350 would be equal.

Only during the early 1980s when I was fortunate enough to ride an ex-Bill Lomas factory 350 did I realize the difference. With a shorter torque arm it counteracts the dive under braking, but the adverse effect is pattering of the front wheel when under 45mph [72km/h] for slower corners. I think I had the right idea, but Guzzi probably had the world's first anti-dive system.

I found on riding my 250 that it had absolutely no handling vices – at least recalling things years afterwards. But it was more at home on long circuits, although the roadholding was such that short, twisty circuits also suited it. It also ran very well in hot weather – in fact the hotter the better. The only black spot was when Dunlop triangular tyres were fitted. These caused problems on very long sweeping corners such as those found at the Belgian Grand Prix.

I would also say that at the time many riders admired the Guzzi, but I would not say that it was the easiest bike to get the best out of. One had to work with it and being a low revver it didn't seem fast. Without doubt its biggest 'failing' was that the valves, guides and springs were in a very exposed position and meant that you had to keep an eagle eye on them. Changing valve springs for a race and keeping the old ones for practice!

On looking through my old records, it seems that there were always problems one way and another, but in fairness this reflected racing machinery which was both relatively old and spares hard to come by, rather than a reflection on machine or rider. Truthfully, at the time, I simply wasn't an experienced enough mechanic/tuner, racing almost ex-works bikes on a shoestring, with no backing.

However, still having got my Guzzis now, almost 40 years on, I have succeeded in keeping them serviceable for classic racing events.

Even Arthur [Wheeler] admitted that if he had continued to race he would have had to look for an alternative mount and in my own experience by 1966, the Grand Prix scene was getting out of the Guzzi single's depth.

drain on Barnes' time and mechanical skill (which was swiftly growing through experience). A major problem was spare parts, which were already thin on the ground and getting more difficult to find. To race machinery every weekend you would need a full-time mechanic, machine shop facilities and unlimited supplies of components. In Barnes' case, these were all in short supply.

Also, this was a time of increasing competition from bikes such as the new water-cooled 250 Bultaco, the works Aermacchis, not to mention the latest technical juggernauts from Japan, in the form of Hondas, Suzukis and Yamahas. Even so, the combination of Barnes' riding skills and the Guzzi horizontal single-cylinder machines would occasionally pull off a major surprise.

Just such a thing occurred in the summer of 1964, with victory at the Dutch Tubbergen circuit, where Barnes not only set the fastest lap, but also beat the German rider Gunter Beer on a works-supported Honda twin. Then at Assen during the Dutch TT that year he again came out on top in a battle with Beer and would also have beaten Alberto Pagani riding a Paton twin had he not: 'mucked up my braking off the back straight near the end'.

There were several good results from the 250 in 1965, but the larger bike proved something of a headache. As Barnes said to the author: 'Heartbreaking. I knew what it was capable of, but trying to keep it together, because it wasn't 100 per cent to start with, was to say the least, difficult'.

Tubbergen saw Barnes achieve a fourth place after crashing, and he also set up the fastest lap. At the Austrian Grand Prix, Barnes was the fastest in practice of all the privateers, including all the Nortons and AJSs, and behind a trio of works Jawa twins. However, when the race started the Guzzi would not start cleanly and an entire lap went by before the engine would clear; even so, he gained seventh position by the end. After finishing fifth in the North West 200, the year ended with a broken collarbone at the Ulster Grand Prix.

Easter 1966 – victory at Crystal Palace and the fastest lap of the day respective of displacement, gave Barnes the title 'King of the Palace'. Another excellent showing came in September 1966 at the annual Scarborough Gold Cup international meeting, held around the ultra-demanding Oliver's Mount circuit. On his smaller-engined model, Barnes finished runner-up in his heat to Australian Kevin Cass (on one of the latest water-cooled Bultacos) and third in the final after the Guzzi slowed towards the end of the race. After leading for most of the way, Barnes was overtaken just before the flag. And as he rode into the pits, the engine clanked to a halt with a loose valve seat. Unable to take part in the final, the 350cc heat was the last race of his career.

In the author's opinion, Barnes and Kidson were the last of the line of riders who campaigned Guzzi singles without the luxury of sponsorship, often having to carry out their own mechanical work into the bargain. As such, these hard-riding privateers followed in the tracks of men such as Anderson (in his earlier non-works career), Cann and Wheeler. For these riders, the sport of motorcycle racing was just that – sport first. A fact lost on many of today's so-called superstars.

And in the Albatros and its brothers they raced a motorcycle that was so advanced that it was still racing at the top level almost three decades after it had made its début back in 1939. Very few designs can boast such a record – a fitting tribute to the engineers back at Mandello del'Lario.

7 The 250 Parallel Twin

The quarter-litre Bicilindrica Bialbero (twin-cylinder, double-camshaft) project was the responsibility of Ing. Antonio Micucci, who joined Moto Guzzi in the winter of 1942, becoming managing designer in 1945. In September of that year, Carlo Guzzi laid out the basic specification for a new machine, which Micucci subsequently proceeded to bring to life. Progress was rapid, and by early 1946, construction of the prototype had begun. Less than a year later, the machine was ready to undergo initial testing.

The Design

The original design had been for a supercharged machine, so the cylinder heads of the 247.2cc (54 × 54mm), double overhead camshaft (dohc) twin had been laid out with its valves inclined at 60 degrees. The change to a normally aspirated engine necessitated by the ban on superchargers entailed major modifications (a similar fate to the British AJS Porcupine twin). The most important of these was a new design of head with the valve guides at

The 250 parallel twin project was headed by managing designer, Ing. Antonio Micucci. Carlo Guzzi laid out the basic design in September 1945, which Micucci subsequently completed. The first version, shown here, appeared in 1947.

The 250 Parallel Twin

80 degrees to accommodate larger diameter valves (29mm inlet, 23mm exhaust).

At a very early stage in the engine's development, the power was superior to that being achieved by the existing single-cylinder racer. These tests were not only carried out on the bench, but also on the autostrada, where the new twin proved itself capable of speeds close to 100mph (160km/h) first time out. This equated to a shade over 20bhp at 9,100rpm – all this on low-grade 'pool' petrol! Ultimately, the power output was increased to 25bhp, with the engine revolutions trimmed back to 9,000rpm. Correspondingly, maximum speed went up to around 105mph (170km/h).

Widespread use of aluminium and electron meant that the machine had a dry weight of 116kg (266lb).

The Engine

The double overhead parallel twin engine had its cylinders facing forward at an angle of 30 degrees to the horizontal. Hiduminium was employed for both the cylinder barrels and heads. The former were cast as one, but featured a hair-line cut between the cylinder bases. Bronze hemispheres, cast-in, formed the combustion chambers.

The crankcase and gearbox housing were manufactured in electron. The crankshaft was supported by a trio of main bearings and had bolted-on bobweights on its two middle cheeks; the central bearing being of the needle roller type. On the timing side of the crankshaft there was a ball-bearing, which was located on the shaft; on the drive side there was a roller bearing, which accommodated lateral movement caused by expansion of the crankcase. Both the timing and drive shafts were 30mm (1.1in) in diameter; the crank pins 23mm (0.9in). On the drive side shaft there was an outside flywheel with a diameter of 190mm (7.4in) and a thickness of 16mm (0.6in). Drive to the twin camshafts was by a series of gears.

The Oil Pump

A double gear-type oil pump was located within the camshaft drive cover, whilst the return pump with gauze filter was below the crankshaft. Lubricant was fed from the 4.5ltr (1gal) oil tank, which was mounted in rubber beneath the saddle. The big ends were supplied at a rate of just over 180ltr (40gal) per hour, and the camshafts at 126ltr (28gal) per hour.

The Valves

The valves featured shim-set adjustment and had head diameters of exhaust: 23mm (0.9in) and inlet: 29mm (1.1in). The bronze valve guides were of an unusual design, featuring abnormally large external dimensions and being tapered on the outside to mate with similar tapers in the cylinder heads. On the outer portion there was a circular groove, which formed a bearing surface for the balls that carried and centralized the valve spring assembly. This was of the coil type, there being two per valve (inner and outer), whereas the 250 horizontal single of the period employed hairpin springs.

Manliff Barrington rode the Guzzi twin in the 1948 Lightweight TT but subsequently retired.

The 250 Parallel Twin

1947 250 parallel twin showing steeply inclined cylinders (not quite horizontal), dohc (with the rev counter drive taken from the exhaust cam) and the traditional Guzzi outside flywheel.

Definitive 1948 version of the 247.2cc (54 × 54mm) dohc parallel twin; heavily revised from the previous year.

Other Technical Details

Also specified in the design were a pair of 26mm Dell'Orto carburettors with a single, remotely mounted float chamber; a German Bosch magneto; geared primary drive; a four-speed, close ratio gearbox (one of the first where the gears could be removed without stripping the engine); a six-spring, fourteen-plate clutch; 21in wheel rims; and tyres having 2.75 front and 3.00 rear sections.

The Frame Design

Due to the steeply inclined nature of the cylinders (30 degrees from the vertical), the cylinder heads were used as mounting points from the steering head; there being no continuous frame rail round the engine. In the original 1947 model, a pair of aluminium plates connected the steering head and the top of the engine. However, on the definitive version built for the 1948 season, these plates were dispensed with and in their place came a single circular steel downtube from the steering head downwards. Halfway down this was a welded-in tube that then ran backwards to connect with the frame's top tube towards the rear of the fuel tank – thus forming a triangular brace (*see* photographs).

75

The 250 Parallel Twin

> **Parallel Twin 1947–48**
>
> | | |
> |---|---|
> | Engine | Air-cooled, dohc, parallel twin, with cylinders inclined 30 degrees from vertical, alloy heads and barrels, electron crankcase, three main bearings, drive to camshafts by gears |
> | Bore | 54mm |
> | Stroke | 54mm |
> | Displacement | 247.2cc |
> | Compression ratio | 10:1 |
> | Lubrication | Double gear pump, dry sump |
> | Ignition | Bosch magneto |
> | Carburation | 2 × Dell'Orto 26mm |
> | Gearbox | Four-speed, foot-change |
> | Clutch | Multi-plate, wet |
> | Final drive | Chain |
> | Frame | Engine used as a stressed member, mixture of steel and aluminium construction* |
> | Suspension | Front, telescopic forks; rear, sprung |
> | Brakes | Drums front and rear |
> | Tyres | Front 2.75 × 21; rear 3.00 × 21 |
>
> **General specification**
>
> | | |
> |---|---|
> | Wheelbase | 1420mm (55.9in) |
> | Dry weight | 125kg (275lb) |
> | Fuel capacity | 21ltr (4.62gal) |
> | Maximum power output | 25bhp at 9,000rpm |
> | Top speed | 105mph (170km/h) |
>
> *1948 version all-steel frame

In the 1947 design the frame was effectively bolted-up aluminium sheeting, but in 1948 this changed to a more conventional round tubular construction.

Telescopic Front Forks

Another feature of the design concerned the front forks. On the 250 parallel twin these were telescopic with a leading axle. Normal Guzzi racing practice was to use either girders or, on later designs, leading-link types. Except for the 1948 version of the long-running in-line V-twin, no other works Guzzi racer used telescopic forks.

Cantilever Type Rear Suspension

Even if the Mandello del Lario engineering team had gone for innovation at the front end, the rear suspension was the familiar cantilever type with springs running horizontally underneath the engine unit. Guzzi was one of the first to provide rear suspension – as early as 1928 it had been fitted to the GT 500 roadster.

The Brakes

These were massive, single-sided single leading shoe on both wheels. As an integral part of the construction, all versions of the 250 twin were equipped with a rear mudguard/seat pad support, which was large enough to carry the aluminium racing number plates. The fuel and oil tanks were also in aluminium.

A Test Session

So what was the 250 twin like to ride? Arthur Bourne, editor of *Motor Cycle*, was lucky enough to have already ridden the 250 twin (the 1947 prototype) in Italy during March 1948. Here is what he reported in the journal's 1 April issue:

> In the afternoon [during his March 1948 visit to the Guzzi factory in Mandello del Lario] I was told we would set off to a point about a mile from the works; the racing side would warm up the engines of the 250cc twin and Anderson's Gambalunga and meet us there. Picture a narrow stretch of road beside Lake Como – smooth, but with only a short straight, followed by a blind swinging-right bend flanked by a stone wall: and this with lorries and all manner of other traffic using the highway. Think, too, of the fact that the

two-fifty was their one-and-only, costing, if everything were charged against it, goodness knows what. My comment was that I would be going gently – just a flip or two up and down the road to get the feel of the machines. Ye gods, I could have spent the whole day on that glorious two-fifty, out and about on my own. Open her up with the clutch out – work her up to something over 5,000rpm; in comes the droning, zestful power. In with the clutch, keeping the revs right up. Round flies the needle of the rev indicator. At first I got the feel in bottom (1st gear): 7,000, 8,000, 9,000 plus. Then into second. Up the scale in second and third. Top. No, none of your peak revs here. To get the feel of the machine – the general handling, the braking, engine characteristics, that was the idea. Gear change, braking, engine smoothness: in each direction, superlatives, but what struck me as much as anything was the way the machine clings to the road and the effortlessness with which it heels over for a fast bend. While I was on the machine, two uniformed men arrived with a sidecar outfit, betrayed extreme interest and parked themselves on the far side of the blind right-hand bend. Were they policeman? I took pains to turn round before I reached them. Later I asked whether they were policemen and was told, 'Oh, yes, but they are policemen for bandits, not traffic police'.

Good though the single-cylinder racing two-fifty is, I put this new 250cc twin almost in a class apart. That Guzzis have a winner in more senses than one seems a mere glimpse of the obvious.

1948 Lightweight TT

At the end of May 1948 company president, Giorgio Parodi, together with Ing. Micucci, Omobono Tenni, Ing. Moretto (an engine specialist), two mechanics and a total of ten Guzzi motorcycles, arrived in the Isle of Man for the forthcoming TT. Included were two 250cc twins. Both machines were earmarked for Stanley Woods' protégé, Manliff Barrington's use.

The Guzzi party arrived at Ronaldsway airfield just before 6pm on the evening of Wednesday 26 May. The 3 June 1948 issue of *Motor Cycle* reported: 'Guzzis had a big reception at Northolt (London) when their special British European Airways aircraft (a Douglas Dakota) put down on its way from Milan to the Isle of Man'.

After completing a relatively trouble-free practice period, Barrington's twin was then fettled for the Lightweight race.

The *Motor Cycle* race report in their issue of 17 June 1948 reads: 'M. Barrington, as

Arthur Bourne, editor of Motor Cycle, *testing the Guzzi works parallel twin at the factory in March 1948.*

The Guzzi workshop at the 1948 TT. Mechanics work on the Barrington two-fifty parallel twin; it was destined to retire after leading the race.

expected, quickly assumed the lead, and his twin was about one-third of a second per mile too fast for Cann's single'. It continued: 'The pattern of the race was thus already clear – ie, small hope of a British win so long as the Guzzis kept moving'. And everything continued on this plain, with Barrington leading the race, having averaged 74.94mph (120.5km/h) on lap 1 and 75.64mph (121.7km/h) for lap 2.

However, this was all to change. As *Motor Cycle* put it: 'Lap 3 brought more retirements, two at least being of major importance. Barrington's twin Guzzi gave up the ghost beyond Kirkmichael – it is too new for immediate triumph, but will be hard to lick in 1949'. And as described in Chapter 6, Maurice Cann went on to a clear victory.

The Great Mystery

The 250 twin was not further developed after 1948. Instead, Guzzi chose to update its venerable horizontal single instead. This would prove to a short-sighted move, as the appearance of the twin-cylinder NSU Rennmax in 1952 halted Moto Guzzi's previous dominance of the 250cc class. If Guzzi had continued with Micucci's twin, it would have been in a much more favourable position to meet the German challenge when it came.

However, the mystery remains, just why was the 250 twin axed? No official explanation has ever been given. It must have either been due to a major design fault that only showed up when the model was raced in the TT, a financial one, or simply a change of policy. But the fact remains that Guzzi should have continued its development as it was a quantum leap ahead of the old-fashioned quarter-litre single that could trace its ancestry back to the mid-1920s.

It is also possible that Guzzi lost the will to continue with the development after the death of Ombono Tenni, a hero to all associated with the Moto Guzzi marque. Winner of countless races at home and abroad, Italian national champion on several occasions, Tenni was also the first Italian to win an Isle of Man TT (1937 Lightweight).

Having completed the 1948 TT, Tenni went with the Guzzi team to the European Grand Prix – held that year at the Bremgarten circuit on the outskirts of Berne. His practice session on the 250 parallel twin was held in heavy rain; when he did not return from this practice session Guzzi mechanics were sent to look for him. They found his body at the side of the circuit with his machine on the other side in the trees. And so died one of Italy's, and Guzzi's, greatest riders.

Also that day, the great Achille Varzi crashed his Alfa Romeo Grand Prix car and was also killed. A dreadful day for all concerned.

8 The 500 In-Line Four

Giorgio Parodi, co-founder of Moto Guzzi, instigated a series of events that were to lead to one of the marque's most unusual designs, the 492.2cc (56 × 50mm) double overhead camshaft (dohc) in-line four. In 1950 Parodi had seen his factory's existing 500 V-twin effectively outclassed by the new Featherbed-framed dohc Norton single and also by the emerging four-cylinder machines from both Gilera and MV Agusta.

So, in 1951, he commissioned the Rome-based engineer, Ing. Carlo Gianni, to design a rival four-cylinder engine. Together with Pietro Remor (and later Piero Taruffi), Gianni had been largely responsible for the forerunner of the Gilera, the supercharged, four-cylinder OPRA and Rondine models.

Both Parodi and Gianni felt that an across-the-frame four was a non-starter for two reasons. One was that they would be accused of simply copying existing designs, the other was that the in-line layout would provide the same frontal area as Guzzi's existing singles and V-twins, but with the advantage of more power.

In many ways, Gianni's design followed aeronautical rather than motorcycle engineering practice, looking very similar to designs such as the Daimler Benz DB601 and Rolls-Royce Merlin (which powered the Messerschmitt Bf 109 and Supermarine Spitfire aircraft respectively).

However, there were two serious problems with the design – torque reaction from the final drive shaft put the bike at a severe disadvantage on twisting circuits, while the engine-speed clutch made it virtually impossible to guarantee making clean gear changes at racing speed.

It is also probably true to say that if fairings had been in popular use, the Gianni engine would not have been contemplated; the full

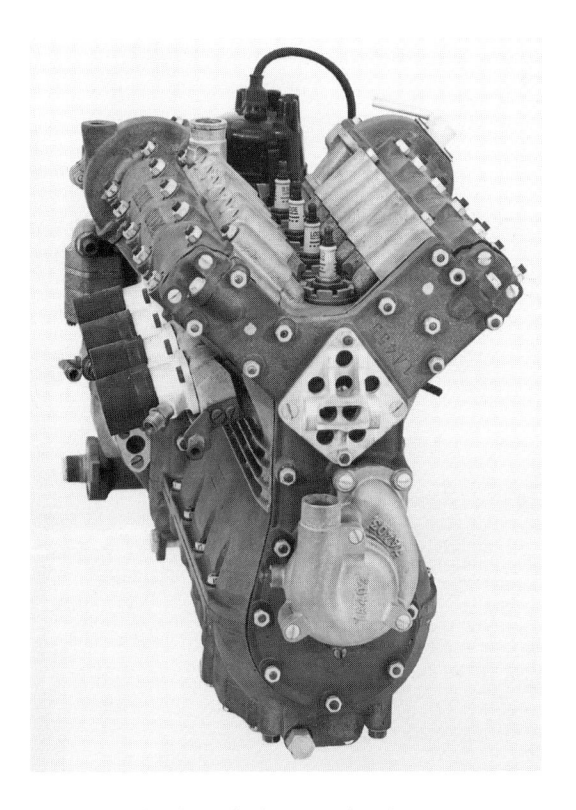

The 500 in-line four-cylinder engine that Guzzi commissioned from the Rome-based engineer, Ing. Carlo Gianni.

The 500 In-Line Four

ABOVE: 1953 in-line four, with a 492.6cc (56 × 50mm) liquid-cooled, fuel-injected dohc engine. It could reach 140mph (225km/h), but handling and road holding left much to be desired on shorter, twisting circuits.

LEFT: Enrico Lorenzetti at the Ospedaletti circuit during the initial testing of the new 500 in-line four-cylinder model; February 1953.

'dustbin' streamlining, which had become an almost standard feature of Italian racing bikes by the mid-1950s, ensured that the across-the-frame fours were not penalized so much for the increased frontal area.

The Design

The in-line four featured two valves per cylinder, spur gear drive for the double overhead camshaft (dohc), water-cooling, magneto ignition, a gearbox in the engine unit, and shaft final drive.

A feature of the engine was the use of a built-up crankshaft with one-piece connecting-rods and Hirth couplings. The crankshaft was supported by a total of five bearings: a ball race at the rear, a double-row roller in the middle, and a trio of single-row roller bearings. The connecting-rods were steel forgings with phosphor-bronze small-ends and single row, roller-bearing big ends.

Each high-dome forged piston featured a pair of compression rings, whilst below the gudgeon-pin boss was a slotted oil-scraper ring. The compression ratio was high, measuring 11:1.

A one-piece aluminium-alloy casting formed the upper half of the crankcase (it being horizontally split), the cylinder block and the cylinder head. Cast-iron wet liners were screwed into position. The lower half of the crankcase was retained by a series of nuts on long studs extending down into the main casting. Oil was contained within an integral sump at the base of the lower crankcase, there being 4.5ltr (1gal) of lubricant, which was distributed around the engine assembly by a gear-type pump.

The valves had head diameters of 30mm (1.1in) exhaust and 32mm (1.2in) inlet, and each valve had the unusual feature of having three springs. The outermost of the springs kept the cap in contact with its cam lobe (so the valve clearance was obtained between the underside of the cap and the top of the valve stem where shims were fitted as necessary).

The included angle of the valves was 96 degrees. To make it possible to withdraw the valves, the phosphor bronze guides were a push-fit into the head casting. The guides were retained by flanged collars held in place by the valve springs; the dismantling procedure was to take off the valve springs, the collar and the guide. Clearance between the guide boss in the cylinder head and the valve stem allowed the respective valve to be canted and removed down the cylinder bore.

Another unusual feature of the design was that the valves were seated directly in the light alloy cylinder head. In other words, there were no conventional inserts (a feature also employed on the 1960s Bianchi dohc twins).

Each camshaft was supported by crowded needle roller bearings at either end and a split bronze bearing in the centre. The cams operated directly on the tappets, which were, as already described, caps embracing the coil valve springs. The caps reciprocated in the

In-Line Four 1952–54

Engine	Liquid-cooled, dohc, two valves per cylinder, in-line four, alloy cylinder block/head, built-up crankshaft with one-piece connecting-rods and Hirth couplings supported by five bearings, one-piece crankcase, and coil valve springs
Bore	56mm
Stroke	50mm
Displacement	492.2cc
Compression ratio	11:1
Lubrication	Gear pump
Ignition	Magneto
Carburation	Fuel injection
Gearbox	Four-speed, foot-change
Clutch	Engine speed, dry
Final drive	Shaft
Frame	Trellis, open type, tubular steel construction
Suspension	Front, leading-link forks; rear, swinging arm with twin hydraulically damped shock absorbers
Brakes	Drums front and rear
Tyres	Front 3.00 × 19; rear 3.25 × 18

General specification

Wheelbase	1400mm (55.1in)
Dry weight	145kg (320lb)
Fuel capacity	28ltr (16gal)
Maximum power output	54bhp at 9,000rpm
Top speed	143mph (230km/h)

The 500 In-Line Four

electron cam box and took the side thrust imposed by the cams.

Perhaps the most unusual feature of all was the induction system, and this stemmed from the Moto Guzzi obsession with keeping down the width of their racing bikes. This meant that the prospect of four large Dell'Orto carburettors adorning one side of the engine and thus increasing width was a non-starter. Additionally, Guzzi had been attempting to devise a system to provide superior atomization of the fuel than was possible with conventional carburettors, and as early as 1950 the company had filed a patent covering a forced atomization mechanical carburettor.

A Roofs-type blower

Various changes were made to the 1950 prototype device, but except in one instance, the principle of forcing air to the fuel jets remained substantially unchanged throughout. Air supply was courtesy of a Roots-type blower housed within the gearbox shell to the quartet of atomizer assemblies, one in each induction tract. Operated by additional cams on the inlet camshaft were plunger-type valves timed to remain open for approximately the period of inlet-valve opening; hence at the required time for each cylinder, the air from the blower was released across the jet to atomize the fuel.

By way of six tangential grooves in the nozzle, some of the air released by the valve was provided with a swirl effect as it was drawn, with the fuel, into the combustion chamber by air passing through the induction tract. The tract was open to the atmosphere and was controlled in the conventional way by a butterfly throttle. The amount of air used for atomizing the fuel was relatively small and did not influence the degree of cylinder filling – hence induction was quite different to supercharging (which of course was banned).

Fuel was forced from a gear-type pump coupled to the inlet camshaft to syringe – like jets – one for each atomizer unit. The supply

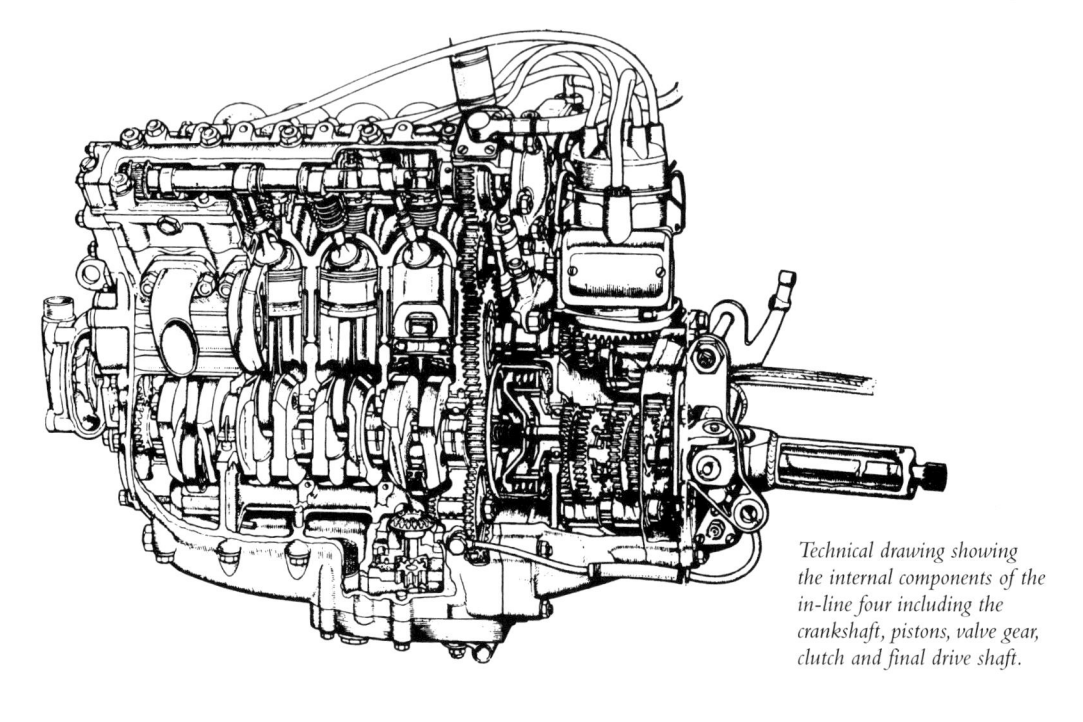

Technical drawing showing the internal components of the in-line four including the crankshaft, pistons, valve gear, clutch and final drive shaft.

The 500 In-Line Four

Fergus Anderson inspects the in-line four-cylinder model. He set the fastest lap at Hockenheim in May 1953, with Lorenzetti winning on a sister bike.

was continuous but was used only when the air valve was open. Excess fuel was returned by gravity to the pannier tanks (yet another unusual feature in the overall design of the in-line four), which had a total capacity of 28ltr (16gal).

The variant mentioned previously, took the form of injectors forcing fuel into the induction tract without the timed air supply. This system was by no means a new field for Guzzi who had employed the principle on supercharged record breakers during the inter-war years (*see* Chapter 11).

Changes to the Prototype

Lubricating oil from the sump was forced round the engine by a gear pump driven through bevels, a spur gear mating with the crankshaft pinion. Drillings in the crankcase casting led oil to the main bearings from where it escaped to lubricate the cylinders and the small ends and to cool the pistons. Flanges on the crank webs each side of the second and fourth main bearings trapped oil and passed it through drillings in the webs to the big-end bearings, since the Hirth couplings precluded the more usual arrangement of a main oil feed via the centre of the crankshaft.

For valve-gear lubrication, oil was forced up to the split bronze bearing at the centre of each camshaft then passed along the shaft in both directions before emerging at the lifting face of each cam and through the needle roller bearings at either end.

Water was circulated round the engine and radiator by an impeller bolted on the front of the cylinder block and driven by spur gears from the crankshaft.

A single-spring clutch of a type more usually seen on cars had four bonded friction plates separated by steel plates. A positive oil supply from the pump lubricated the clutch thrust mechanism. Positive circulatory lubrication from the engine system was a feature of the four-speed gearbox; which was mounted to the rear of the clutch and engine, in which all shafts ran on ball-bearings.

Within the gearbox shell was the bevel drive to the vertically mounted magneto. Later, Guzzi sources were to say that in light of experience a coil ignition would have been preferred, but in the early 1950s the magneto ruled supreme.

ABOVE: Fergus Anderson during the Belgian 500cc Grand Prix at Spa, 5 July 1953.

LEFT: 1954 version of the 500 Grand Prix in-line four with 'dustbin' streamlined shell.

140mph Potential

With a dry weight of 145kg (320lb) and a power output of 54bhp at 9,000rpm, the 500cc in-line four was capable of over 140mph (225km/h). And even though it suffered a mechanical failure during its racing début at Siracusa in April 1953, the design seemed vindicated when, in the following month, Lorenzetti won the 500cc race at the super-fast Hockenheim circuit in Germany. At the same event, Anderson set the fastest lap of the race at 113mph (182km/h) on a sister machine.

In September 1953, Anderson rode a revised version at the Italian Grand Prix. Besides more comprehensive streamlining, several modifications had been incorporated in an attempt to improve poor roadholding and handling characteristics. However, not only did the modified bike retire from the race, but its reliability glitches were never fully overcome, nor the problems caused by torque reaction and poor handling over short, twistier circuits.

In 1954, after a winning start to the season at Mettet in Belgium, the in-line four failed to live up to expectations. Thus this interesting design was replaced, first by a new single and ultimately by the big daddy of all racing Moto Guzzis, the incredible V8.

9 The Golden Era

This chapter charts Guzzi's racing developments and successes during this period in the history of the sport, largely concentrating on the technical evolution of the works racing singles (the multi-cylinder bikes being covered in Chapters 4, 8 and 10).

World Championship Series

Prior to 1949, there was no such thing as a road racing World Championship series – only individual Grand Prix events including the Isle of Man and Dutch Tourist Trophy races (TTs) and the Championship of Europe.

During that year, however, the FIM introduced the first World Championship for 125cc, 250cc, 350cc, 500cc and sidecar classes. Points were awarded on a sliding scale at a series of venues throughout Europe. This was a clear message that FIM wanted more manufacturers to take part – thus encouraging exotic works machines and star riders from the major factories.

From the very first event – the Isle of Man TT in June 1949 – Moto Guzzi was a keen and loyal supporter of the series. During the early and mid-1950s, the factory lived up to their enviable reputation of being amongst the

Fergus Anderson winning the 250cc race at Ferrena, Italy in May 1949. He was a tower of strength in the Moto Guzzi line-up and contributed twelve out of the factory's forty-six Grand Prix victories.

85

The Golden Era

leading contenders for honours – a position they were to hold until the marque's withdrawal from the sport at the end of 1957.

The Gambalunghino

In 1949, Guzzi produced a new 250 for the recently established World Championship races. The Gambalunghino was developed from the long-established Albatros (see Chapter 6). It shared the older machine's 246.8cc (68 × 68mm) horizontal single-cylinder power plant featuring a bevel-driven single overhead camshaft (sohc) and a four-speed close ratio gearbox, plus the same basic frame with twin front downtubes and cantilever rear suspension dating from pre-war days.

However, a number of important improvements were made to both the engine and cycle parts. First, power output was increased to 25bhp at 8,000rpm by using bigger diameter valves, a hotter cam profile and a larger (35mm) Dell'Orto SS carburettor. The compression ratio of 8.5:1 remained unchanged, as did the use of exposed hairpin valve springs.

New, more streamlined tanks (manufactured in lightweight aluminium) holding 21ltr (4.6gal) of fuel and 4ltr (0.8gal) of oil, plus a faired assembly comprising rear number plate background and mudguard, all gave a more modern appearance; as did the brand-new leading-link front forks and the larger and more powerful 200mm (7.87in) drum front brake. These and other changes added up to a much improved motorcycle that not only went faster, but stopped more quickly and held the road better.

The result was that the Gambalunghino was capable of producing a genuine 100mph (160km/h) performance with reliability, which is what the long races counting towards the World Championship demanded. These could be over 250 miles (402km) in length and take almost $3\frac{1}{2}$ hours to complete.

There is no doubt that the Guzzi development team was fortunate in being able to adapt an existing proven design so readily – and thus did not suffer the usual period of racetrack development during which sorting out bugs often meant a spate of retirements.

Following his victory at Ferrena, Anderson is shown here riding his works 250cc Guzzi single through part of the circuit, flanked by members of the local police on Gilera Saturno machines. This photograph vividly recalls the atmosphere of road racing in Italy during the immediate post-war years.

Gambalunga 1949

Engine	Air-cooled, sohc, single with two valves, horizontal cylinder, alloy head and barrel, hairpin valve springs, inclined valves, drive to camshaft by shaft and bevel gears, vertically split crankcases	Final drive	Chain
		Frame	Cradle type, steel construction
		Suspension	Front, leading-link forks; rear, sprung
		Brakes	Drums front and rear
		Tyres	Front 2.75 × 21; rear 3.00 × 21
Bore	68mm		
Stroke	68mm		
Displacement	246.8cc	**General specification**	
Compression ratio	8.5:1	Wheelbase	1420mm (55.9in)
Lubrication	Gear pump, dry sump	Dry weight	122kg (269lb)
Ignition	Magneto	Fuel capacity	21ltr (4.6gal)
Carburation	Dell'Orto SS35	Maximum power output	25bhp at 8,000rpm
Gearbox	Four-speed, foot-change		
Clutch	Multi-plate, wet	Top speed	112mph (180km/h)

A TT Victory

The first race to be eligible for World Championship points in the 250cc class was the Isle of Man TT in June 1949. Guzzi got off in great style courtesy of Manliff Barrington, protégé of the famous pre-war Guzzi star and fellow Dubliner, Stanley Woods. His Gambalunghino was followed over the line by the similar machine of Tommy Wood, whilst another Guzzi ridden by Ernie Thomas was sixth.

Swiss Grand Prix

Next came the Swiss Grand Prix, held at the 4.5-mile (7.2km) Bremgarten circuit just outside Berne. As was usual on the Continent at the time, the 250cc entry list was made up entirely of Italian machinery: eleven Guzzis, a trio of Parillas and two Benellis. One of these models was ridden by Dario Ambrosini (who was destined to become the 250 Champion in 1950). Two of the Guzzis were official factory entries ridden by Ferdinando Balzarotti and Bruno Ruffo; whilst two British riders, Fergus Anderson and Wood, were mounted on production bikes.

Off the line, it was Ambrosini who led, but soon Balzarotti forged ahead followed by team-mate Ruffo. These three rapidly opened up a lead of some quarter-mile over the remainder of the field, headed by Anderson. As the race wore on, Balzarotti overdid things and eventually crashed. Anderson tried hard to make an impression on Ambrosini, and set the fastest lap of the race – a just reward for his efforts. The race finished with Ruffo in first place, Ambrosini second and Anderson third.

The 350cc race was far less rewarding for the Moto Guzzi team, whose sole 350 V-twin (see Chapter 4) was ridden by Bertacchini. This motorcycle was a smaller version of the long-running 120 degree V-twin 500. It finally finished seventh, the best position it was ever to achieve, as it was axed at the end of that year, never to appear again.

Ulster Grand Prix

During these early post-war years, a skilled privateer could still cause a stir by occasionally beating the works boys. For example, in the third round of the 1949 World Championship, the Ulster Grand Prix; Maurice Cann beat

ABOVE: Maurice Cann on his way to victory in the 1949 Ulster Grand Prix.

RIGHT: Maurice Cann was the master of the famous Clady circuit in Northern Ireland, where he won the 250cc Ulster Grand Prix in 1948, 1949 and 1950 – all on Guzzi machines.

World Champion elect Ruffo into second spot by dint of some fantastic riding on his production Albatros-based machine. Even more incredible is Cann's record in the Ulster Grand Prix – three consecutive wins in 1948, 1949 and 1950. Then, in 1952, Cann won yet again on his home-tuned Guzzi, beating the official works team of Anderson, Enrico Lorenzetti and Wood.

The 1949 title was staged over only four rounds, the final one being at Monza in September. Although Ruffo could only manage fourth place, it was good enough to secure the first-ever 250cc World Championship.

A New 350

The Moto Guzzi racing engineering team, now led by Ing. Giulio Cesare Carcano, spent most of the 1949–50 closed season working on a new design for the 350cc class to replace the unsuccessful V-twin used the preceding season.

By March 1950, they were bench testing a 349cc (78 × 73mm) short-stroke horizontal single featuring a double overhead camshaft (dohcs), driven by shaft and bevel gears from the crankshaft and thence to the pair of cams by spur gears. An unusual feature was the use of no less than four hairpin springs radially disposed around each valve. With a five-speed gearbox, the newcomer did not match the V-twin for power, but it was considerably lighter and able to take advantage of the more manoeuvrable handling of the 250cc rolling chassis.

Thus, instead of using a smaller version of the 500cc V-twin, Carcano and his team had created a 250cc motorcycle with a larger engine. This was an innovative move, giving a much superior power-to-weight ratio at a time when most of Guzzi's rivals in the 350cc class were using scaled-down 500s. Several variations of the engine were built and tested, including experiments with twin plug ignition, forged slipper and full-skirt pistons, even water-cooling of the exhaust valve. However, the eventual definitive design was to feature a single plug and a sodium-filled valve.

Début and Demise of the 350

By the time the lightweight 350cc model made its race début at Mettet in Belgium during late April 1950, the engine was producing a respectable 31bhp at 7,000rpm. With a weight of only 116kg (256lb), here seemed a bike with considerable potential. And in the race, Lorenzetti was able to mix it with the eventual victor, works AJS star Les Graham (who had won the 1949 500cc World Championship for the British marque on a Porcupine twin), until the Guzzi's engine seized.

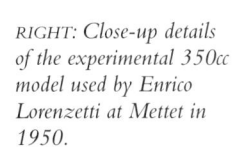

RIGHT: *Close-up details of the experimental 350cc model used by Enrico Lorenzetti at Mettet in 1950.*

BELOW: *Enrico Lorenzetti riding the prototype 350cc Guzzi at Mettet in 1950.*

The Golden Era

The short-stroke 350cc model was then taken to the Isle of Man for the TT, but without Lorenzetti, who had put himself out of action following a crash in a non-championship meeting in Switzerland, fracturing an elbow in the process.

British Moto Guzzi importer, Bob Foster, then brought the 350 over to the Isle of Man for Cann to ride; and as a back-up, Cann had the services of a works-supplied Gambalunghino bored out to 310cc (72 × 78mm). After Cann had practised on both bikes, he said that he had: 'a preference for the smaller-engined one'.

The 349cc short-stroke machine went back to Mandello del Lario, never to be seen at a race circuit again, whilst the overbored 250 failed to challenge the leaders in the Junior TT and retired on lap 3 after a valve dropped in. This too went back to the factory and was to languish under a thickening layer of dust in a corner of the race shop.

So why had the short-stroke 350 been axed? On paper it seemed to have a lot going for it. But in reality there were problems with severe vibration and a narrow power band, which made it difficult and tiring to ride in long Grand Prix type events. Added to that were mechanical problems highlighted by Lorenzetti's seizure at Mettet. All in all, not the success story that everyone at Guzzi had expected.

Strange Goings-On

The withdrawal of direct factory support meant, in practice, that no work was carried out on any of the racing machines for the rest of the 1950 season. This was exceedingly strange, considering that Moto Guzzi had signed Anderson and a number of Italian riders to contest the 1950 series. These very same riders, now 'unofficial', continued to contest the remaining rounds of the World Championship series and in fact finished the 1950 season second, third and fourth (Cann, Ruffo and Anderson, respectively) in the final championship table!

Any mention of the 1950 250cc championship must include Cann's Ulster Grand Prix

A works 250 bored out to 310cc and ridden by Maurice Cann in the 1950 Junior TT.

The Golden Era

victory. Cann, who rode either as a private or a 'semi-works' entry aboard Moto Guzzi machines was the undoubted master of Ireland's Clady course. In the 1950 race he was to win by over eight minutes from Ambrosini in the 198-mile (318.5km) race and in the process set up a new class record of 84.18mph (135.4km/h).

However, the failure of the short-stroke 350 was not Guzzi's only problem in 1950. Things were faring little better for the 250cc's defence of the title it had won in 1949. This was because Benelli's star rider, Ambrosini, was soundly beating the entire Guzzi team and would eventually take the title. However, Guzzi felt they at least saved some face by announcing that they were: 'withdrawing from official works entries', so that: 'more time could be spent developing new series production machines'. And Carlo Guzzi was on record with his 'disappointment' at how the 350 project had progressed.

A New Effort

For 1951, Guzzi went back to running an official team in the World Championship series. This consisted of Anderson, Lorenzetti, Ruffo and newcomers Gianni Leoni and Sante Geminiani. This team was something of a mixed bag – Anderson was well over 6ft tall, whilst in contrast Ruffo and Leoni were so short that the official factory team photograph taken at the beginning of the year depicted Anderson using his team-mates' heads as arm rests – with all three standing upright! It was always a source of amazement just how Anderson was able to tuck himself away on the diminutive Guzzi singles to such good effect.

A Wind Tunnel

A landmark for the Moto Guzzi factory in 1951 was the commissioning of a wind tunnel. This building was not only to become a land-

Bruno Ruffo became the first 250cc World Champion on a Guzzi in 1949. In 1950 he took a second title (125cc – FB Mondial), before becoming a champion for the third and last time in 1951 on a Guzzi 250.

mark on the site, but more importantly it provided vital information and testing facilities that helped Guzzi to stay ahead of its rivals in matters of aerodynamics and streamlining. Initially, this tunnel was powered by a government surplus aero-engine, and one of its first tasks was putting into practice a theory that Anderson had been known to exploit in the past with considerable success: riding with his feet up alongside his Guzzi's faired seat/tail section on the faster straights of the long Grand Prix-type circuits. He had always claimed that this gained an additional amount of speed; and the wind tunnel tests proved him right.

91

The 1951 Moto Guzzi works team left to right: Bruno Ruffo, Fergus Anderson, Enrico Lorenzetti and Gianni Leoni.

1951 Isle of Man TT Races

The first notable event in the 1951 World Championship was the Isle of Man TT. Anderson seemed set for a popular victory after lifting the class lap record to 83.7mph (135km/h). However, it was not to be, a broken con-rod forcing him to retire at Ballig. In a very close finish, Tommy Wood on another Guzzi held off Ambrosini's Benelli to win by 8.4 seconds after almost 120 miles (193km) of racing.

After the win, *Motor Cycle*'s George Wilson was able to sample Wood's victorious machine. The journalist discovered that, like an earlier Guzzi 250 he had tested the: 'engine began working properly at around 6,000rpm and only delivered the dynamite necessary for winning races when it was revving between 6,400 and the maximum revs of 8,000, with peak torque some 400–500 revs below so that upward gear changes were conducted at 7,500'. Wilson went on to say: 'Of all the racing machines it has been my good fortune to try, I regard the Guzzi as my particular baby. I love it'.

When one considers that Wilson had just tested Geoff Duke's Junior TT-winning factory Norton with the famous Featherbed frame, this was high praise indeed.

It was also informative to read that Wilson was towed to a suitable point on the course for this test by race-winner Wood, it is impossible to imagine one of today's stars doing the same – as it would be towing a factory Grand Prix bike by way of a piece of rope!

Pre-Heating the Oil

Prior to starting the engine, a ritual had to be carried out – a familiar one known to many factory teams (and also some privateers) that of pre-heating the lubricating oil. The procedure was as follows: the oil (usually vegetable-based, such as Castrol R), was poured into the oil tank after it had been pre-heated over a gas stove. Guzzi themselves were strict about this – saying that the oil had to be thoroughly warm before their racers could be revved hard.

More Experimentation

A little-known fact was that Anderson had practised for the 1951 Junior TT using an

ABOVE: Bruno Ruffo, the 1951 250cc World Champion, descending Bray Hill in the Isle of Man TT that year.

BELOW: An experimental 260cc 4-valve Guzzi used by Fergus Anderson during TT practice in 1951.

The Golden Era

overbored (260cc) Gambalunghino with dohc, four valves and twin carburettors, but did not use the experimental machine in the race. Even then it was quite obvious that the notion of using a 250cc chassis with a 350cc class engine was still alive – Anderson must have realized its potential; his nickname of 'The Old Fox' was not for nothing!

Victory in France and Ulster

After the TT came the French Grand Prix. Tragically, Ambrosini crashed and was fatally injured in practice, and took with him the heart and soul of the Benelli team.

With the main threat removed, Ruffo won the World Championship for the second time, following victories in France and Ulster (where Cann had something of an off-day and could only finish runner-up). Wood was fourth. Splitting the squad was future Guzzi star Arthur Wheeler, riding a Velocette.

Sadly, the 1951 Ulster Grand Prix will also be remembered for another reason. During a highly unofficial practice session on open roads, Guzzi works newcomers Gianni Leoni and Sante Geminiani collided and were both fatally injured.

In those days there was no safety regime as there is today, in fact the author remembers crashing during practice for the Manx Grand Prix, being taken to hospital and simply released with no check on machine or riding gear at all, so lax were the 'rules'.

Meanwhile, Anderson had suffered a crash in Italy on one of the V-twins (*see* Chapter 4) and was sidelined until the end of October.

A Disastrous Year

Although Guzzi took the first six places at the Italian Grand Prix at Monza in September, 1951 had been a disastrous year. No less than seven of their best riders had been killed. In addition to Ambrosini and the two Ulster fatalities, Leoni (another Guzzi factory rider) and Raffaele Alberti had been killed at Ferrana, Claudio Mastellari at Schotten in Germany, and finally Renato Magi met his death attempting to break the 125cc world speed record on an MV Agusta streamliner.

Back to the Drawing Board

Making a clean start for the 1952 season, the 500cc V-twins had finally been pensioned off

One of the factory 250s at Albi, the scene of the 1951 French Grand Prix. In the background is one of the 500cc V-twins.

The Golden Era

and the factory's race shop personnel concentrated their efforts on the 250cc class. This enabled them to focus on development work on the singles, including the design of a new frame that had been tested in prototype form by Anderson at Mettet, Belgium at the end of 1951.

In place of the traditional sprung frame with friction damping at the rear, there was now a modern swinging arm with a pair of vertically-mounted hydraulically-damped rear suspension units. The exhaust system had been switched to the offside (right), and there were a number of other modifications that were race tested at the early pre-Grand Prix races. These included a fully downdraught carburettor (complete with a horizontal mixing chamber and integral float chamber) and also a 4-valve engine with twin carburettors based on the concept first tried out by Anderson during practice for the 1951 Junior TT.

After all this experimentation, the definitive 1952 250cc works specification was a 2-valve head, single carb, and five-speed gearbox. But there were variations, for example Lorenzetti's bike sometimes had a twin cam, 4-valve head and only four speeds – strange but nonetheless true. Also, on this engine the valve gear was

Enrico Lorenzetti after winning the 250cc Italian Grand Prix at Monza on 9 September 1951.

Prototype dohc 250 single as tested in spring 1952. The machine employed four valves and twin carburettors.

95

ABOVE: Fergus Anderson testing the ultimate version of the Gambalunga at the Ospendaletti circuit, San Remo, February 1952.

LEFT: Official Guzzi photograph of the 1952 Gambalunga 250cc horizontal single.

Experimental dohc 350cc, 1952.

96

ABOVE: Débuting in 1933, the in-line 500 V-twin ran until 1951; this is the 1948 version – still very much as it was in pre-war days.

BELOW: 1948 Guzzi 250 parallel twin with dohc, front and rear suspension and large brakes. It should have been a world beater, but it was never fully developed.

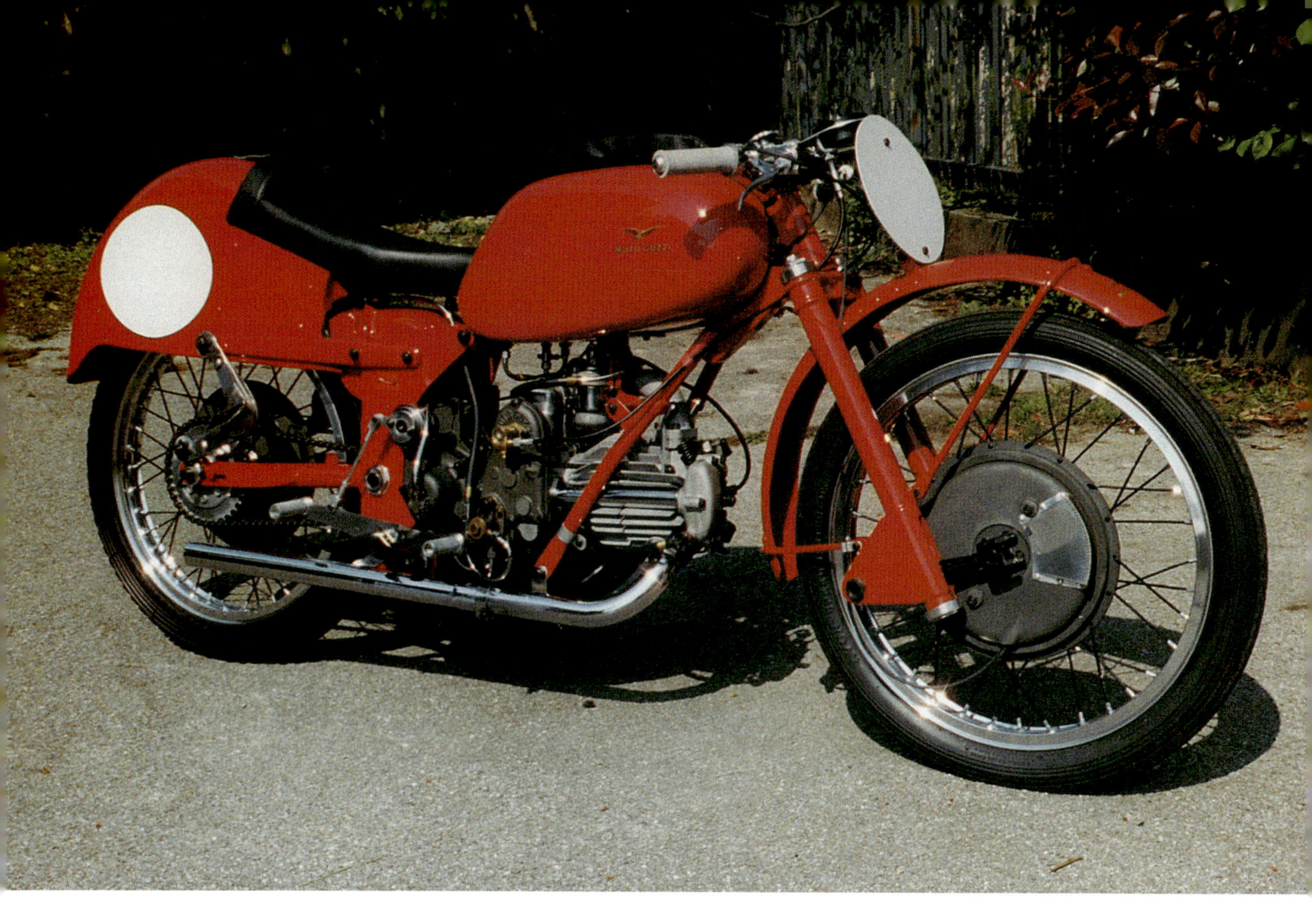

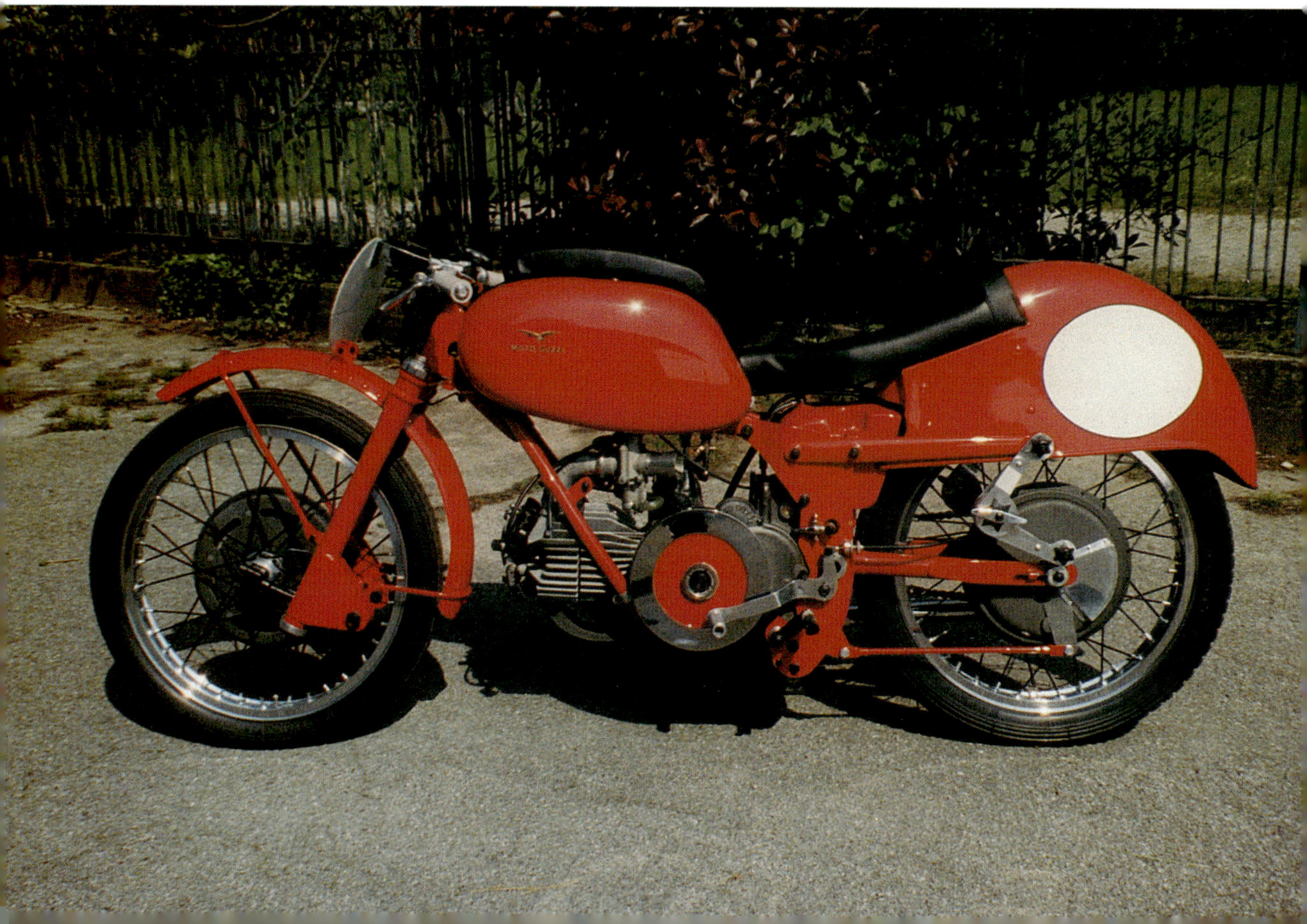

ABOVE: Late 1956 type Guzzi dohc works 350 single with trellis frame, leading-link front forks with additional dampers and swinging-arm rear suspension.

OPPOSITE, TOP: 1951 Gambalunga, a 500 horizontal single cylinder offered as a customer racer from 1946 until 1951.

OPPOSITE, BOTTOM: The Gambalunga was built in two versions, one with the marque's traditional 88 × 82mm bore and stroke, the other with long-stroke 84 × 90mm dimensions.

RIGHT: A late 1950s Moto Guzzi brochure for the Lodola 175cc showing Dickie Dale with the 350cc works single.

ABOVE: V8 with 'dustbin' streamlined fairing. Keith Campbell was timed at 178mph (286km/h) during the 1957 Belgian Grand Prix.

LEFT: V8 engine from the offside (right) and aluminium fuel tank.

BELOW: V8 engine from the nearside (left) showing many details including the twin contact breaker circular covers, carburettors, clutch and rev counter drive gearbox.

ABOVE: Lino Tonti transformed the staid-looking V7 tourer into the exciting V7 Sport; a 1972 bike is shown.

RIGHT: The V7 transverse 90 degree V-twin arrived during the mid-1960s and set Moto Guzzi on a totally new track – one that is still in vogue today.

The even more sporting Le Mans was the next stage in the Guzzi transverse V-twin racing story; this is a Mark 1 dating from 1976.

ABOVE: *A Le Mans III transformed into an endurance racer photographed at the Bol d'Or in 1982.*

BELOW: *This Guzzi V-twin kneeler sidecar racing outfit, seen at the Coupes D'Legends, Dijon, in May 2004, was originally constructed in the 1970s using a Le Mans 850 engine.*

ABOVE: Part of the Guzzi Museum in the Mandello del Lario works. In the foreground is a V8 and spare engine.

BELOW: Another Guzzi Museum view, this time showing a trio of record breakers.

ABOVE: Three Cross/Raceco Daytona-based racer, circa 1996.

LEFT: Moto Guzzi's sports/racing engine of the 1990s, the four valves per cylinder Daytona with belt-driven ohc.

BELOW: Jim Blomley's very special Guzzi big V-twin racer after rider Greg Burkett had scored a victory in the Norman Hyde Championships at Mallory Park, circa 1989.

The Golden Era

ABOVE: Fergus Anderson with the new experimental dohc 250 single – clearly based on the Gambalunga sohc model, spring 1952.

BELOW: Nearside (left) view of a 2-valve, single carb bike.

ABOVE: Two views showing the experimental 4-valve, two-carb engine as tested in 1952.

fully enclosed, using parallel valves with coil springs in a pent-roof cylinder head in which each inlet port had its own carburettor.

1952 World Championship

By the final round of the World Championship contested by the Guzzi team, Lorenzetti was leading the table with twenty-six points, ahead of Anderson who only had twenty. Everyone expected a straight fight between the two Guzzi men, but a young unknown German rider, Werner Haas, on an NSU twin upset the applecart by matching race leader Lorenzetti for almost the entire distance. As the flag finally fell, the Italian took the victory and with it

97

The Golden Era

the 1952 250cc World Championship title. However, the warning signs were clearly there and everyone was to hear an awful lot more concerning Haas and NSU in the future.

Experimental 250cc Singles

When Anderson and Lorenzetti went testing in February 1953 at the Ospidaletti circuit in San Remo, they not only took the new four, but also several 250 singles. These included an experimental dohc machine and a pair of streamlined racers – one with a conventional 2-valve motor, the other a 4-valver. On the two streamlined bikes the fuel tanks were placed underneath the top frame tube con-taining the oil, and a fuel pump at the end of the magneto pumped fuel up to a header tube above the carburettor.

Both these motorcycles wore freshly created streamlining of hand-beaten aluminium sheet with deep arm and leg fairings and what can best be described as a 'bird beak' projection; which acted not only as a fairing but also as a front mudguard. This form of aerodynamics had been perfected, thanks to the newly opened wind tunnel facilities at the Mandello del Lario works, and would be a standard feature of the 1953-model works Guzzi single-cylinder racers.

Another innovative feature tested at Ospidaletti and later adopted on other machines was a new swinging arm in box-section tubing in place of the tubular design used in 1952. The new rear suspension also featured hand-adjustable pre-set hydraulic dampers.

The 1952 250cc German Grand Prix. Guzzi rider Enrico Lorenzetti (56) leads NSU Rennmax-mounted Bill Lomas (68).

The Golden Era

Prototype 249cc dohc with 2-valve head, February 1953.

Bialbero 250 1953

Engine	Air-cooled, dohc, single with two valves, horizontal cylinder, alloy head and barrel, coil valve springs, inclined valves, drive to camshafts by shaft and bevel gears, thence spur gears, vertically split crankcases	Suspension	Front, leading-link forks; rear, swinging arm with twin hydraulically damped shock absorbers
		Brakes	Drums, full-width, front and rear
		Tyres	Front 2.75 × 29; rear 3.00 × 19
Bore	68mm [1]	**General specification**	
Stroke	68.4mm [1]	Wheelbase	1420mm (55.9in)
Displacement	249cc	Dry weight	122kg (269lb)
Compression ratio	9.5:1	Fuel capacity	21ltr (4.6gal)
Lubrication	Gear pump, dry sump	Maximum power output	28bhp at 8,000rpm
Ignition	Magneto		
Carburation	Dell'Orto 40mm	Top speed	125mph (200km/h)
Gearbox	Four-speed, foot-change [2]		
Clutch	Multi-plate, wet		
Final drive	Chain	[1] later five-speed	
Frame	Cradle type, steel construction	[2] 1954 on 70 × 64.8mm	

The Golden Era

The definitive 1953 Bialbero (twin cam) 250cc Guzzi single, with 'bird beak' fairing. It won three of the World Championship rounds.

Early season dohc 250cc, 1953.

Late season dohc 250cc, 1953.

The Golden Era

345 GP 1953

Engine	Air-cooled, sohc, single with two valves, horizontal cylinder, alloy head and barrel, coil valve springs, inclined valves, drive to camshafts by shaft and bevel gears, exposed valve gear, vertically split crankcases
Bore	75mm
Stroke	78mm
Displacement	344.5cc
Compression ratio	9.8:1
Lubrication	Gear pump, dry sump
Ignition	Magneto
Carburation	Dell'Orto 35mm
Gearbox	Four-speed, foot-change
Clutch	Multi-plate, wet
Final drive	Chain
Frame	Cradle type, steel construction
Suspension	Front, leading-link forks; rear, swinging arm with twin hydraulically damped shock absorbers
Brakes	Drums, full-width, front and rear
Tyres	Front 2.75 × 19; rear 3.00 × 19

General specification

Wheelbase	1470mm (57.8in)
Dry weight	127kg (280lb)
Fuel capacity	21ltr (4.6gal)
Maximum power output	32bhp at 7,700rpm
Top speed	132mph (212km/h)

Early season 350cc single, 1953.

Late season 350cc single, 1953.

The Golden Era

Fergus Anderson with the 317cc (72 × 79mm) machine on which he finished third in the 1953 Junior TT, averaging 89.41mph (143.8km/h).

317 GP 1953

Engine	Air-cooled, dohc, single with two valves, horizontal cylinder, alloy head and barrel, coil valve springs, inclined valves, drive to camshafts by shaft and bevel gears, exposed valve gear, vertically split crankcases	Frame	Cradle type, steel construction
		Suspension	Front, leading-link forks; rear, swinging arm with twin hydraulically damped shock absorbers
		Brakes	Drums, full-width, front and rear
		Tyres	Front 2.75 × 19; rear 3.00 × 19
Bore	72mm		
Stroke	79mm		
Displacement	317cc	**General specification**	
Compression ratio	9.5:1	Wheelbase	1470mm (57.8in)
Lubrication	Gear pump, dry sump	Dry weight	127kg (220lb)
Ignition	Magneto	Fuel capacity	21ltr (4.6gal)
Carburation	Dell'Orto 35mm	Maximum power output	31bhp at 7,700rpm
Gearbox	Four-speed, foot-change		
Clutch	Multi-plate, wet	Top speed	131mph (210 km/h)
Final drive	Chain		

102

Disappointment at Floreffe

By now, Anderson had been appointed team leader of Guzzi's factory riders, who were all retained for the 1953 season.

He had the habit of taking in the early-season Belgian international meeting at Floreffe in April; and 1953 was no exception. In the 250cc race he had one of the latest 4-valve, twin carburettor Guzzi singles and soon piled up a substantial lead, breaking the existing class lap record several times into the bargain. However he was eventually forced to retire with a blown engine.

A Potential World Beater

If Floreffe was a disappointment, then Hockenheim on 10 May 1953 was a red-letter day in Moto Guzzi racing history. Not only did they win the 350cc class, but this race also set Guzzi on the road to unparalleled success and a string of 350cc world titles.

This breakthrough came courtesy of the 310cc engine that Cann had sent back to the Mandello del Lario works after the 1950 TT. It had been rebuilt using the latest technology, and it stunned factory personnel when bench tested.

Anderson had been largely responsible for the recommissioning of the engine, having realized that with the arrival of the new NSU Rennmax dohc twin, the 250cc class would prove difficult for Guzzi in 1953. He reasoned that they were more likely to be competitive in the 350cc class, due to Guzzi's superior power-to-weight ratio and effective streamlining.

Anderson mounted the rebuilt engine (not of course the unreliable short-stroke 349cc unit discussed earlier) in one of the latest 1953 rolling chassis. The result was so encouraging that he then convinced Dr Enrico Parodi that he should be allowed to proceed to Hockenheim.

Fergus Anderson shown here with one of the works 250s at the Ospendaletti circuit, San Remo in early 1953.

His faith was found to be totally justified, because the 310cc lapped faster in practice than all but three of the 500cc models! Although forced to start from the rear of the grid due having taken over someone else's ride, things looked promising. He soon sliced his way through the pack to take the lead by the end of the first lap – and went on to totally annihilate the opposition, which included the entire works DKW squad.

By now Guzzi realized the machine's world-beating potential, but with the first round of the World Championship – the Isle of Man TT – due to commence in only three weeks time, they had to act quickly.

There was also a major problem to

103

The Golden Era

overcome – Anderson had no 350cc (Junior) race entry. This was eventually solved after Les Graham, leader of the MV Agusta team, convinced his boss Count Domineco Agusta that the Guzzi rider could take over one of the MV entries in the programme. This sporting gesture by one of its main rivals could hardly be imagined today.

The next move was entirely an engineering one. The stroke of the existing 310cc was lengthened by the simple expedient of providing the cylinder barrel with a 1mm thick aluminium spacer to give a displacement of 317cc (72 × 79mm). This gave a maximum power output of 31bhp at 7,700rpm, but the bike's greatest asset proved to be its amazing power-to-weight ratio.

'Who will win the Junior?' asked *Motor Cycle* in its TT Preview issue, dated 4 June 1953. It went on to say: 'Fergus Anderson is quite capable of flogging his 320cc Guzzi to victory. But is such a rehashed antique worth his efforts? We shall see'.

1953 Isle of Man TT Races

On June 8, after seven laps and 264.11 miles (424.9km), Anderson's 317cc Guzzi finished in third place, averaging 89.41mph (143.8km/h), behind the works Norton pair of Ray Amm and Ken Kavanagh.

In the 250cc (Lightweight) TT, Guzzi suffered a major setback when Ruffo crashed during practice. Although his bike was not badly damaged, Ruffo was hospitalized with a fractured leg that effectively ended the racing career of the three-times World Champion (two 250cc titles with Guzzi in 1949 and 1951, plus the 125cc crown for FB Mondial in 1950).

For the second year running, Anderson won the Lightweight TT. During his victorious four-lap ride, he completed the 150.92 miles (257.5km) at a record average speed of 84.73mph (136.33km/h) and in the process broke the class lap record by setting a speed of 85.52mph (137.60km/h). Werner Haas, riding

Enrico Lorenzetti airborne at Ballagara during the 1953 Lightweight (250cc) TT.

in his first TT race finished runner-up on his factory NSU, with DKW rider Siegfried Wünche third.

End of the Road for the 250

The 1953 TT was the end of the road for Guzzi's long-running 250, because it could not compete with NSU (1953, 1954 and 1955) that dominated the class together with MV Agusta (1956) and FB Mondial (1957). In those years, the best Guzzi could achieve was third place in 1953 (Anderson), fourth place in 1954 (Wheeler), third place in 1955 (Cecil Sandford) and third place in 1956 (Lorenzetti).

In its final 1953 guise, the 246.8cc dohc single still retained the square 68 × 68mm bore and stroke dimensions. Power was up to 28bhp at 8,000rpm, fed by a massive 40mm Dell'Orto SS carburettor, which gave the bike a top speed of 110mph (177km/h). Even though an experimental short-stroke 249cc (70 × 64.8mm) engine was built in 1954, Guzzi was no longer aiming for the World Championship.

350cc Class to the Fore

From then on it was the 350cc class on which Guzzi's hopes of single-cylinder glory rested. The next step in the evolution of the concept came with the début of a new 344.5cc (75 × 78mm) engine at Assen for the 1953 Dutch TT. Unlike its predecessor, this featured only a single ohc, but offered 31bhp at 7,700rpm running on a 35mm Dell'Orti SS carburettor.

Other details of the engine's specification included an alloy cylinder head and barrel (still placed horizontally); a gear-type oil pump; dry sump lubrication; a wet, multi-plate clutch; a four-speed gearbox with straight-cut primary gears, and chain final drive. The '345' tipped the scales at 246lb (127kg) dry weight and could reach 131mph (210km/h).

There is no doubt that their rivals were

Bialbero 350 1954

Engine	Air-cooled, dohc, single with two valves, horizontal cylinder, alloy head and barrel, coil valve springs, inclined valves, drive to camshafts by shaft and bevel gears, thence spur gears, enclosed valve gear, vertically split crankcases
Bore	80mm
Stroke	69.5mm
Displacement	349.2cc
Compression ratio	9.4:1
Lubrication	Gear pump, dry sump
Ignition	Battery/coil
Carburation	Dell'Orto 35mm*
Gearbox	Five-speed, foot-change
Clutch	Multi-plate, wet
Final drive	Chain
Frame	Cradle type, steel construction
Suspension	Front, leading-link forks; rear, swinging arm with twin hydraulically damped shock absorbers
Brakes	Drums, full-width, front and rear
Tyres	Front 2.75 × 19; rear 3.00 × 19

General specification

Wheelbase	1470mm (57.8in)
Dry weight	127kg (280lb)
Fuel capacity	20ltr (4.4gal)
Maximum power output	33.5bhp at 7,500rpm
Top speed	136mph (218km/h)

*37mm or 40mm on some circuits

caught out by the speed with which the Guzzi race engineers had developed their new single. The fact was that only when personnel returned from the Isle of Man could work begin in earnest – and a mere seven days after the '345' had been fired up for the first time, Lorenzetti took it to victory at Assen. But

The Golden Era

although Lorenzetti gave the newcomer its maiden victory, it was Anderson who really put Moto Guzzi at the top of the 350cc class.

1953 350cc World Championship

There were seven rounds counting towards the 1953 350cc World Championship series: Isle of Man TT, Dutch TT; Belgian, French, Ulster, Swiss and Italian Grand Prix.

Anderson came out victorious in the title chase with wins at Spa Francorchamps and Rouen, plus runner-up to Lorenzetti at Monza, and third in the Isle of Man.

The top five in the 1953 350cc World Championship were:

1st   Fergus Anderson (Guzzi)
2nd   Enrico Lorenzetti (Guzzi)
3rd   Ray Amm (Norton)
4th   Ken Kavanagh (Norton)
5th   Jack Brett (Norton)

As can be seen, the British Norton team was Guzzi's main rival in the class that year.

End of Season in Spain

With no 350cc race in the Spanish Grand Prix, which was staged over the twists and turns of Montjuich Park in Barcelona during October 1953, Guzzi still took part, contesting the 250cc and 500cc classes. A newcomer to the Guzzi team was former Norton works man Ken Kavanagh.

With no NSUs entered, Guzzi dominated the 250cc race, with Lorenzetti taking the win. But it was the 500cc race around which most of the interest centred. Not only did the bigger event provide the best racing, but it also featured factory entries from AJS, DKW, Gilera and MV Agusta – plus a trio of 350cc Guzzi's ridden by Anderson, Kavanagh and Lorenzetti.

The race was run, like the 250cc event, in atrociously wet conditions and both Kavanagh and Lorenzetti retired. Anderson, however, scored one of his greatest victories, finishing ahead of several four-cylinder models including Carlo Bandirola's Gilera and Dickie Dale's MV Agusta.

Technical Problems

Despite the jubilation surrounding Anderson's Spanish victory, the two retirements provided proof of the teething troubles that had been encountered by the 350cc class Guzzi's that year but never reported in the press at the time. Essentially these problems affected both the engine and the cycle parts due to the larger engine displacement and the extra performance this generated. The development team responded to the weaknesses by carrying out a major rethink of both engine and cycle parts in time for the 1954 season.

A new Ultra-Short Stroke

This resulted in a new ultra short-stroke double overhead engine (dohc) displacing 349.2cc (80 × 69.5mm). The new engine featured fully enclosed valve gear, together with a five-speed close ratio gearbox. Not only this, but various measures had been taken to improve reliability. A thicker cylinder liner and new design of piston (9.4:1) were fitted in an attempt to curb the excessive oil consumption by eliminating distortion. Premature big-end failure had been tackled by reverting from a one-piece crankshaft with a split connecting-rod and a mass of uncaged rollers to a three-piece crank with a separate crank pin and a caged roller big-end bearing. There were also new valve sizes – 32mm (1.25in) exhaust and 37mm (1.45in) inlet, together with a 35mm carburettor (for some circuits 37mm or even 40mm instruments were fitted).

As a result of all these changes not only was reliability greatly improved, but the maximum

The Golden Era

1954, full streamlined 'dustbin' faired 350cc Guzzi as used by Fergus Anderson to win the World Championship that year.

power output figure was raised to 33.5bhp at 7,500rpm.

Dual Ignition

An unusual feature of the new short-stroke engine was the use of a dual ignition circuit; this being intended to provide both reliable performance and a higher top speed, plus improved acceleration. The system comprised two coils feeding two spark plugs, and two distributors housed within a single magneto casing. Separate switches mounted on the handlebars could bring one circuit into action independently of the other, giving a retarded setting for starting and a considerable degree of advance for use once under way.

Changes to the Chassis

Besides the engine development, there were two vitally important innovations concerning the chassis. The first of these was a brand-new trellis frame comprising a series of small diameter tubes, which in Carcano's opinion offered not only a substantial weight saving, but also gave improved handling. The other was a new swinging arm with the box-section tubing replaced by a circular-section tube flattened at the rear for over half its length. The twin rear shock absorbers had been moved to a slightly angled mounting, rather than the vertical fitment employed previously.

'Dustbin' Fairing

Of all the changes for the 1954 season, the most obvious was the use of a full 'dustbin' fairing. Manufactured in aluminium, this had been developed throughout the closed season as a replacement for the 1953 'bird beak' type. The full streamliner had been developed with the use of the wind tunnel testing facilities and would prove a decisive factor in Moto Guzzi's bid to stay at the top of Grand Prix racing.

A New 500cc Single

1954 also saw the début of a new 500cc Moto Guzzi single-cylinder racer. Still featuring the

The Golden Era

500 GP 1954	
Engine	Air-cooled, dohc, single with two valves, horizontal cylinder, alloy head and barrel, coil valve springs, inclined valves, drive to camshafts by shaft and bevel gears, thence spur gears, vertically split crankcases
Bore	88mm
Stroke	82mm
Displacement	499cc
Lubrication	Gear pump, dry sump
Ignition	Battery/coil
Carburation	Dell'Orto 42mm
Gearbox	Five-speed, foot-change
Clutch	Multi-plate, wet
Final drive	Chain
Frame	Cradle type, steel construction
Suspension	Front, leading-link forks; rear, swinging arm with twin hydraulically damped shock absorbers
Brakes	Drums, full-width, front and rear
Tyres	Front 2.75 × 19; rear 3.00 × 19

General specification

Wheelbase	1470mm (57.8in)
Dry weight	127kg (280lb)
Fuel capacity	20ltr (4.4gal)
Maximum power output	42bhp at 7,000rpm
Top speed	140mph (225km/h)

classic horizontal layout, this had a capacity of 496cc (88 × 82mm). In many respects the bike was a larger version of the new 350. It was introduced as an emergency stopgap in the line-up, caused by the failure of the liquid-cooled in-line four (see Chapter 8) until a suitable replacement could be designed and built. The 496cc single featured enclosed valve gear.

Official Opening of the Wind Tunnel

Back in Mandello del Lario, 12 April 1954 saw the official opening of Guzzi's extended wind tunnel facilities in a ceremony performed by Emilio Battista, Under-Secretary of the Italian Ministry of Industry and Commerce.

Incorporating part of the smaller, early gallery, the new tunnel was of the closed-circuit type. At the entrance to the tunnel, air was drawn in through a honeycomb filter by a three-bladed variable-pitch airscrew. In place of the original Piaggio aircraft engine, this was now driven by an electric motor rated at 310bhp (brake horsepower).

Coppa d'Oro Shell

Two weeks later, Guzzi reaped the benefit of another recent construction – the new 3.1-mile (4.9km) Dino Ferrari road circuit at Imola some 20 miles (32km) east of Bologna. On Sunday 26 April 1954, Moto Guzzi proceeded to clean up both the 250 and 350cc classes at the international Coppa d'Oro Shell (Shell Gold Cup) meeting. Alano Montanari won the 250cc race at 74.34mph (120km/h), whilst Lorenzetti took the 350cc at 83.04mph (133.6km/h) with team-mate Kavanagh as runner-up.

Mettet

On the very same day, Anderson was starting his season in Belgium. At Mettet he won the 500cc event on the new single and also led the 350cc race until forced to retire with a broken frame.

Kavanagh then joined Anderson the following weekend at Floreffe, where both competed over the 8.5-mile (13.6km) road circuit near Namur. In the 350cc race, Anderson hit engine problems while in the lead, and Kavanagh won on one of the

The Golden Era

1953 machines – from Norton-mounted Ray Amm.

In the 500cc class both Guzzi riders failed to finish: Kavanagh went out with engine troubles while leading; Anderson, riding a 1953 350 retired in protest against a number of spectators crossing the track while racing was in progress!

1954 Isle of Man TT Races

Moto Guzzi probably wished they had not bothered to attend the 1954 Isle of Man TT races. Anderson and Kavanagh both rode singles in all three classes (250, 350 and 500cc) – and the best result out of a total of six Guzzi starts was a fifth in the Lightweight TT by Anderson. All the rest had the big 'R' for retirement marked on their respective scoreboards opposite the grandstand on the start/finish line. As Kavanagh was to openly admit: 'There are bugs in this which we never knew existed'. And that of course was followed by countless hours of bench running and circuit testing out on the track.

Dial photographed by the author in the early 1980s.

Anderson Bows Out

Even though Anderson effectively missed the first three opportunities to score any points in the bid to retain his title, the Guzzi team leader was ultimately successful, gaining four wins and a runner-up berth in the six remaining

BELOW: *Commissioned in 1951, the Guzzi wind tunnel facilities at the Mandello del Lario factory were completed in 1952*

The Golden Era

rounds (Belgium, Holland, Germany, Switzerland, Italy and Spain).

But before the World Championship season got underway, Anderson could not resist the call of those early season Belgian meetings. He therefore transported himself and a 350cc single to Floreffe in April where he finished in third position behind winner Dale and runner-up Sandford, the latter having reached an agreement whereby the 1952 125cc World Champion (MV Agusta) would have the use of F1953 type 250 and 350cc Guzzis.

Reports at the time claiming that Anderson was a very reluctant champion turned out to be true. At the end of the 1954 season he announced his retirement, to become director of the Moto Guzzi racing department. The plan was for him to act as a non-riding team manager for 1955, with riders Kavanagh, Duilio Agostini (no relation to Giacomo) and new signing, Dickie Dale.

Anderson rounded off his Moto Guzzi riding career in superb style a few days later at Mettet, by scoring a double 350/500cc victory. This was his last outing for Guzzi, from then on he concentrated on running the team, rather than taking part as a rider.

Technical Changes for 1955

Several technical changes were incorporated over the closed season in preparation for the 1955 campaign. The iron cylinders on the 350 and 500cc singles were replaced by a process of hard chroming straight on to the aluminium cylinder barrel – with an etched effect to retain lubricating oil. Not only did this save weight, it also allowed closer tolerances. To provide improved breathing, the 350's carburettor was changed to 37mm and the valve head diameters increased to 30mm (1.1in) for the exhaust and 41mm (1.6in) for the inlet. Ignition was now by battery/coil with dual 10mm spark plugs firing simultaneously. The motorcycles were now clothed in an even more efficient streamlined shell, once again constructed from hand-beaten aluminium.

Three-fifty Guzzi (Anderson's bike) at the 1954 TT, showing frame, tanks, carburettor and other details.

1955 – A Vintage Year

1955 was to prove a real vintage year for Guzzi's racing efforts. In Lomas and Sandford, the factory had two riders who could cope on both road courses such as the Isle of Man or Ulster, and purpose-built circuits like Monza.

There were seven rounds counting towards the 1955 350cc World Championship – and Moto Guzzi won them all:

French Grand Prix – Duilio Agostini
Isle of Man TT – Bill Lomas
German Grand Prix – Bill Lomas
Belgian Grand Prix – Bill Lomas
Dutch TT – Ken Kavanagh
Ulster Grand Prix – Bill Lomas
Italian Grand Prix – Dickie Dale

The French Grand Prix was the first to stage a 350cc race. Here Guzzi were virtually unopposed: Agostini scoring his first and only classic victory from Dale, and Ricardo Columbo, riding a two-year-old Guzzi equipped with 'dustbin' streamlining. Also competing was teamster Kavanagh, who after holding runner-up spot had his engine stop with an ominous bang as he entered the main straight on the 5.18-mile (8.3km) French circuit.

Next came the Isle of Man TT and with it the inspired signing of Bill Lomas by Anderson. Lomas had previously ridden home-brewed Royal Enfield machinery and works Velocettes, Benelli, AJS, NSU and MV Agusta. But it was with Moto Guzzi that the Derbyshire rider really stamped his mark on motorcycle racing history, which he did straight away by winning his first ever race for the Italian marque – the Junior TT!

Lomas finished runner-up in the Dutch TT and Italian Grand Prix. He also won the 500cc class at the Ulster Grand Prix on one of the singles. A truly superb performance for what had been his Guzzi début year.

Duilio Agostini, Ken Kavanagh and Dickie Dale with one of the factory's streamlined 350cc singles and the wind tunnel as a backdrop, early 1955.

Moto Guzzi dominated the 350cc class of the 1955 Italian Grand Prix, taking five of the top six places. This is one of the team bikes in the Monza paddock.

After the season was over, Lomas, Dale and Anderson took part in a successful bid for world speed records at Montlhéry, France – setting no less than thirteen new records (*see* Chapter 11).

Lomas and Dale had spent the European closed season racing in Australia, taking some Guzzis along with them. They were impressed by several of the Australian circuits and the riders, whose high standards surprised them both. Interestingly, one of these riders was none other than Keith Campbell, later to feature in Guzzi's final Grand Prix season.

Anderson Quits

Under Anderson's guidance, Moto Guzzi had enjoyed what appeared to be an excellent season. But behind closed doors, things were rather different. As team manager, Anderson felt he should be allowed unlimited authority to do his job. However, this brought him into dispute with the man who previously had the job, Dr Enrico Parodi.

Anderson was not a man to accept this state of affairs, and at the end of 1955 he quit. At that time he had his own column in *Motor Cycle*, 'Continental Chatter', and he used this as a platform to explain why he had come to this decision:

> I believe that to be run efficiently a ship should be in the full operational control of the Captain. The ship in which I thought I was assuming command 12 months ago turned out to have a couple of captains besides me – as well as an admiral! When I wrote to Dr Parodi, in resigning, I told him that I was severing my connection with Moto Guzzi with great regret, because it brought to a close an association which had lasted during the ten happiest years of my life. The pity is that it was too good to last!

The comparison to a sea captain may have seemed unusual if apt, but Anderson was talking from personal experience, having been the skipper of a British Admiralty ferry during the Second World War. At forty-seven, he could have been expected to retire peacefully to pursue his other interests – apart from journalism he was a top-class golfer. But that was not his style. His driving passion was racing motorcycles, and after talks with several parties (including a test session with DKW), he found that BMW were only too happy to supply him with one of their latest Rennsport Boxer twins. Sadly, a crash at his beloved Floreffe circuit in early May 1956 was to cost him his life. It is not known why the fatal accident happened, but whatever the real reason, the motorcycling world lost one of its greatest names.

A New Frame for 1956

For 1956, the main change to the all-conquering works 350s was that after two season's use, the 'Bailey Bridge' trellis-type frame would be replaced by a design very reminiscent of the chassis employed by the team bikes in 1953. The basis of this was a very large (à la Vincent) diameter tube that acted as an oil tank and formed the backbone of the frame. The steering head was an integral part of this tube, which also provided support for the fuel reservoirs. The swinging arm was fully triangulated and was pivoted in a tunnel cast at the rear of the crankcases, while the front forks with their short leading links now featured external two-way damper units provided by British specialists Girling, who also supplied the twin rear shock absorbers.

1956 World Championship

The official factory riders chosen by Guzzi to contest the 1956 World Championship rounds were once again Lomas, Kavanagh and Dale.

Except for a fifth by Lomas in the Isle of Man TT, the 496cc single had a poor year, but once again the 350cc more than made up for this. Not only did Lomas retain his title, but he did it against much stronger opposition in the shape of extremely determined challenges from DKW, Gilera and MV Agusta.

Although Kavanagh won the Junior TT and Lomas the Dutch round, Guzzi suffered several retirements during the early part of the

The Golden Era

ABOVE: Chassis from one of the 1956 350cc Guzzi racers. Note the additional Girling damper units on the front forks and the open, trellis-type frame.

RIGHT: 350/500cc dohc single-cylinder engine, 1956.

113

The Golden Era

350 GP 1956

Engine	Air-cooled, dohc, single with two valves, horizontal cylinder, alloy head and barrel, coil valve springs, inclined valves, drive to camshafts by shaft and bevel gears, thence spur gears, vertically split crankcases	Final drive	Chain
		Frame	Cradle type, steel construction
		Suspension	Front, leading-link fork; rear, swinging arm with hydraulically damped shock absorbers
		Brakes	Drums, full-width, front and rear
		Tyres	Front 2.75 × 19; rear 3.00 × 19
Bore	80mm		
Stroke	69.5mm		
Displacement	349.3cc	**General specification**	
Compression ratio	10:1	Wheelbase	1470mm (57.8in)
Lubrication	Gear pump, dry sump	Dry weight	107kg (236lb)
Ignition	Battery/coil; twin spark plugs	Fuel capacity	20ltr (4.4gal)
Carburation	Dell'Orto 42mm	Maximum power output	38bhp at 8,000rpm
Gearbox	Five-speed, foot-change		
Clutch	Multi-plate, wet	Top speed	138.5mph (223km/h)

Bill Lomas gets a flyer off the starting line at the Junior race in the Australian TT, January 1956. Also in the picture are a collection of AJS, Norton, BSA and Velocette machines.

Bill Lomas winning the 500cc race at Bandiana, Australia in January 1956.

1956 season. Poor quality fuel was causing the valves to burn out, and in the case of Lomas, a valve actually broke.

However, the team had got things sorted by the German Grand Prix at Solitude. Here, Lomas and MV's number one John Surtees had a battle royal. Surtees made his usual flying start, then Lomas began to close in steadily before finally overtaking the MV star and going on to build up quite a lead. Surtees later crashed, fracturing his left arm. Lomas set the fastest lap (a new record) at 92.58mph (148.9km/h).

Lomas Seals a Second Championship Title

At Dundrod, the scene of the Ulster Grand Prix, another victory for Lomas ensured that he would retain the 350cc world title. How-

Australian works Guzzi rider Ken Kavanagh pushes off his dustbin-faired three-fifty single at the start of the 1956 Junior TT, which he won.

The Golden Era

1956 Italian Grand Prix, Dickie Dale's machine came in second place, averaging 108.26mph (174.1km/h) for the twenty-seven laps.

BILL LOMAS, WERELDKAMPIOEN 1956 OP 350 CC MOTO GUZZI

MOTO GUZZI "Zigolo"

ABOVE: *Dutch Moto Guzzi brochure (for the Zigolo model) showing Bill Lomas, 350cc World Champion 1956.*

LEFT: *Enrico Lorenzetti (left) and Stanley Woods at Monza with one of the latest 350cc singles in October 1956. The youngster is Lorenzetti's son.*

ever, the race was marred by the fatal accident of Manxman Derek Ennett, who had been making his début ride for the Guzzi works team.

The final Grand Prix of the six-round, 350cc championship took place at Monza, where Lomas was sidelined with a broken wrist and Gilera-mounted Libero Liberati came home first. Lomas soon recovered from his injuries, but his riding career was to suffer much more severely after he crashed heavily during the Coppa d'Ora Shell international races at Imola in April 1957 – before the new Grand Prix season had even got under way. His place in the Guzzi team was effectively filled by the Australian Keith Campbell (Geoff Duke's brother-in-law) who had joined the Mandello del Lario squad towards the end of the 1956 season.

The Definitive 350 Single

With both Gilera and MV Agusta now in the position of having fast and fully developed four-cylinder 350 and 500cc models, Carcano, Guzzi's racing design chief instituted another round of updating measures to his flat single models, and although he could not have known it at the time, the result was to be the final, definitive version of the breed – in fact the ultimate fully streamlined, lightweight, single-cylinder Grand Prix racing motorcycle.

Carcano felt that the additional speed of the 1955–56 models had been achieved at the expense of bottom-end torque. Comparison tests on the twisting Modena circuit established that the 1954 350cc machine was faster on initial acceleration and lap times than the later bikes. He decided that what was needed in the 1957 model was improved low-end punch and an even better power-to-weight ratio, to be achieved by paring off yet more weight.

The first objective was achieved by a return to the long-stroke format. With new bore and stroke dimensions of 75 × 79mm respectively, the capacity was 349cc. To improve low-down urge he employed smaller valves (33mm exhaust, 39mm inlet). A return was also made to magneto ignition with a single 10mm spark plug; this was because dual ignition required less advance and if one plug fouled, the engine then misfired and lost all power.

350cc Guzzi dohc engine with two valves and a single carburettor…

…neat lines of the 1957 engine; still with outside flywheel.

350 GP 1957

Engine	Air-cooled, dohc, single with two valves, horizontal cylinder, alloy head and barrel, coil valve springs, inclined valves, drive to camshaft by shaft and bevel gears, thence spur gears, vertically split crankcases
Bore	75mm
Stroke	79mm
Displacement	349cc
Compression ratio	11:1
Lubrication	Gear pump, dry sump
Ignition	Magneto; single spark plug
Carburation	Dell'Orto 45mm
Gearbox	Five-speed, foot-change
Clutch	Multi-plate, wet
Final drive	Chain
Frame	Open tubular
Suspension	Front, swinging link; rear, swinging arm with twin hydraulically damped shock absorbers
Brakes	Drums, full-width, front and rear; front, four leading shoe
Tyres	Front 2.75 × 19; rear 3.00 × 19

General specification

Wheelbase	1460mm (57.4in)
Dry weight	95.25kg (210lb)
Fuel capacity	22ltr (4.8gal)
Maximum power output	40bhp at 8,000rpm
Top speed	140mph (225km/h)

500 GP 1957

Engine	Air-cooled, dohc, single with two valves, horizontal cylinder, alloy head and barrel, coil valve springs, inclined valves, drive to camshafts by shaft and bevel gears, thence spur gears, vertically split crankcases
Bore	88mm
Stroke	82mm
Displacement	499cc
Lubrication	Gear pump, dry sump
Ignition	Magneto
Carburation	Dell'Orto 45mm
Gearbox	Five-speed, foot-change
Clutch	Multi-plate, dry
Final drive	Chain
Frame	Large diameter top tube supporting engine
Suspension	Front, link forks with dual Girling shock absorbers; rear, swinging arm with dual Girling shock absorbers
Brakes	Drums, full-width, front and rear
Tyres	Front 2.75 × 19; rear 3.00 × 19

General specification

Wheelbase	1470mm (57.8in)
Dry weight	106.5kg (235lb)
Fuel capacity	22ltr (4.8gal)
Maximum power output	42bhp at 7,000rpm
Top speed	145mph (233km/h)

The changes resulted in an increase of 2bhp (up to 40bhp) at 8,000rpm, with a safe limit of 8,400rpm. Another benefit was increased torque, which meant that the internal gear ratios could be standardized, where previously different ratios had been needed for each circuit, entailing a lot of additional work for the support crew.

However, the most impressive achievement in the development of the post-war singles was probably the weight reduction. For example, the 1949 Gambalunga weighed 122kg (269lb), whereas the 1957 350 works model came out at a mere 95.25kg (210lb) and 97kg (216lb) complete with streamlining.

Whilst the last 500cc flat single stood very much in the shadow of the new V8, this too was a triumph of power-to-weight efficiency.

Weighing some 106.5kg (235lb), it was good for around 145mph (233km/h) despite a modest 42bhp (rear wheel reading).

Rider Changes

In January 1957, a press conference was held to announce the team riders for the coming season. This was to consist of Lomas (although in practice he was to play no part in the Grand Prix season), Dale, Campbell and the Italian veteran Giuseppe Colnago – although the latter's task was very much confined to the Italian Senior Championship series.

Then in March it was revealed that the English privateer John Clark had been loaned one of the 1956 works 500cc singles, complete with aluminium streamlined fairing, for use at British short circuit events, plus the Isle of Man TT.

1957 – A Disappointing Year

The Guzzi team made a bad start. Lomas, their leading rider and double 350cc World Champion, suffered a pre-Grand Prix crash at Imola in April. The injuries he received were to take far longer to heal than anyone envisaged at the time – this was not only to keep him out of racing for the entire 1957 season, but influenced his decision to hang up his leathers the following year.

With such a major upset to their plans and the even stronger four-cylinder challenge from Gilera and MV Agusta, Guzzi could well have crumbled under the pressure. However, that would have reckoned without the contribution of Keith Campbell.

Although Campbell did not win his first World Championship race for the factory, his world-beating potential was displayed in his first Guzzi race at no less an event than the Diamond Jubilee Junior TT.

It was after the Isle of Man that Campbell really began to shine, winning three (Holland, Belgium and Ulster) of the remaining four races to take the title.

Isle of Man TT Races

This was one of the greatest ever TT races. Lined up on the starting grid was a vast array of factory machinery from Gilera, MV Agusta and, of course, Moto Guzzi, not to mention many excellent riders on British AJS and Norton bikes.

Bob McIntyre on a Gilera four was in the lead at the end of the first lap, then Dale took over for two laps before a broken windscreen forced him to pit on the third lap, where he lost $3\frac{1}{2}$ minutes and surrendered the lead. The incident had been caused by a large bird, the remains of which had to be removed from the motorcycle by his pit crew. However, this was not to be the end of Dale's problems that day, for at Quarry Bends a Norton-mounted backmarker had a con-rod break that sliced open the engine's crankcases. As oil spread across the track, the normally dry strip of tarmac was quickly transformed into something more akin to an ice-rink. First it brought down Norton works entry John Hartle, followed by the luckless Dale. Although he was not seriously hurt, his bike was too badly damaged to continue. Since Hartle and Dale had been in first and second positions, this let McIntyre back into the lead, a position he was never to surrender. Behind McIntyre came the hard-riding Guzzi newcomer, Campbell, followed by Bob Brown on another four-cylinder Gilera. John Surtees (MV) was fourth and John Clark came home eighth on the third works Guzzi (specially loaned to him for this race).

The same trio of Guzzi riders contested the Senior TT a couple of days later, but this time Dale was aboard one of the V8s, whilst Campbell and Clark rode singles. With no less than 298.96 miles (481km) to cover in eight laps, only the Guzzi singles had enough fuel to complete the race without stopping, but Clark

The Golden Era

was destined to retire, whilst Dale (whose V8 was running on only seven cylinders for most of the time), finished fourth ahead of Campbell who rode a well-judged race to come home fifth.

Monza

Monza 1957 was to be very much of an anti-climax. This was because all of Guzzi's big names were sidelined. Lomas, still believing he would race again, had been admitted once more to hospital in Bologna due to problems caused by the slow knitting together of the bones in his damaged shoulder. Dale was still hobbling around with his feet in plaster from an accident at the Dutch round; whilst Campbell, the newly crowned 350cc World Champion, was also in Bologna hospital receiving attention for an injury sustained in a non-championship meeting the previous month. And finally, the most recent of Guzzi's signings, Keith Bryen (another Australian) wasn't even offered a ride at Monza!

Even so, Giuseppe Colnago split the Gilera team to come second in the 350cc race, whilst Giuseppe Mandolini further upheld Guzzi pride by finishing fifth. Not bad for a 'reserve' team!

Moto Guzzi Pulls Out

Rumours were circulating concerning a planned mass withdrawal from racing by several Italian factories – including Moto Guzzi. As the Grand Prix season ended everyone held their breath, and waited for the truth to emerge.

The news was not long in coming. At the end of September the shattering announcement was made that Gilera, FB Mondial and Moto Guzzi would not be racing in 1958.

Dr Gerardo Bonelli, Director General of Moto Guzzi, made the official announcement at a press banquet (forever after known in Italy as 'The Last Supper') in the presence of representatives from Gilera and FB Mondial. In today's Moto Grand Prix this would be akin to Honda, Yamaha and Suzuki all quitting together – just think about it.

Various reasons were presented, including that all three companies had: 'demonstrated the undeniable technical excellence of their products and that recently there had been no foreign opposition'. Added to that had been the outbreak in Italy of an anti-racing lobby fuelled by the popular press and the restrictions introduced by the authorities following the Mille Miglia car tragedy (in which a car had run off the road killing several spectators). But the real reason, and one that could not be given at the time, was that motorcycling itself was in trouble. It was the beginning of an era in which customers would turn away from two wheels to small cars in ever-increasing numbers.

End of a Golden Era

So came to an end a truly golden era in the history of motorcycle sport, which has not been witnessed on quite the same scale before or since. The 1950s was a time when motorcycle ownership was at a peak and racing matched the sales boom, with crowds flocking in their thousands to watch the top riders and machines of the day all over Europe. During this period the Moto Guzzi legend had been irrevocably welded together and, besides the mere masterpieces of metal, had spawned human legends such as Anderson, Carcano, Lomas and their final champion, Campbell.

With no support forthcoming from Mandello del Lario in 1958, Campbell reverted to running a pair of privately funded Manx Nortons. It was on one of these that his

OPPOSITE: *Shell advertisement proclaiming the help Moto Guzzi had from the corporate giant in winning the 1957 title.*

The Golden Era

KEITH CAMPBELL'S INVISIBLE PARTNER

Keith Campbell, outright winner of the World Motorcycle 350 cc Championship for 1957 says

"A good deal of the credit is due to my partner." This remark from Keith Campbell seems unduly modest as no partner is anywhere to be seen. Nor has one been seen during the whole string of victories that won Keith the 350 cc World Motorcycle crown. But take another look and close at hand you will always see a drum of Shell Motor Oil. Like the rest of the Moto Guzzi team Keith Campbell has good reason for choosing Shell Motor Oil. Through the whole of last year's gruelling racing season the entire Moto Guzzi team relied on Shell Motor Oil. Their faith was rewarded. At the end of an extremely successful season all the machines were stripped down and found to be almost as good as new. Keith Campbell's tribute is typical of those paid to Shell Oils by many of to-day's greatest riders. Shell Motor Oils are especially popular, for they give motorcycle engines the most complete protection that science can devise. They cut to a minimum wear due to sludge, overheating and acid corrosion. They give an engine years more life. No wonder they're at home in the company of champions—they're the world's champion of oils.

"This last season has certainly proved to me the wisdom of using Shell Motor Oils. Another thing, whenever race regulations permit, Moto Guzzi team up this super oil with Super Shell with I.C.A., they like keeping things in the Shell family."

Keith Campbell of Australia, riding a 350 cc Moto Guzzi (No. 37), comes over Ballaugh Bridge, Isle of Man, during the International Tourist Trophy Race 1957.

SHELL

LEADERSHIP IN LUBRICATION

Guzzi's World Championship certificates awarded by the FIM from 1949 onwards.

Carlo Guzzi – the man behind the name, 1889–1964.

promising career was brought to a sad and premature end on 14 July 1958, when he crashed fatally on the first lap of an international meeting at Cadours, France.

And so the 'no racing' policy stood without retraction. Over the next few years there was a great deal of speculation as to whether Guzzi would return. All the fans were left with was Guzzi's record, which up to the end of 1957 totalled a magnificent 3,329 international racing victories, 47 Italian Championships, 55 National Championships (in other countries), 11 Isle of Man TT wins and 14 World Championships – a truly great achievement by any standards.

Although Moto Guzzi has been represented both at works and private level in racing all around the world in more recent years, none of these activities have been able to quite match the glorious record garnered by the marque in its Grand Prix era.

Lomas Has the Last Word

As double World Champion Lomas commented in an article written by the late journalist Charlie Rous for *Motorcycle Racing* magazine in the early 1980s:

> Japan has gained success with money and endless labour and colossal resources. Guzzi did it with the genius of just one man – Giulio Carcano [he was referring to 1955–57, his own time with the company] and his team of only eleven dedicated mechanics. I wonder what they could do today? I bet the old Guzzi team could still come up with something totally different from the rest, and they could still win.

Lomas spoke from the heart. He and thousands of others believed that this dedicated band of engineers had been responsible for building some of the world's greatest ever racing motorcycles during an extremely competitive era.

Replicas – the Ultimate Endorsement

With the rise of the classic racing scene since the beginning of the 1980s, many old racing bikes have been put back on the track. In Guzzi's case the original factory works bikes preserved in the Mandello del Lario works museum were occasionally given an outing (for example, by Lomas at Brands Hatch in 1981), but generally they were deemed too valuable to be risked in serious competition.

However, during the 1990s the first thought was given to producing replicas for sale to wealthy customers, which led to the Guzzi 350, the Grand Prix dohc singles and the V8 joining such exotica as the Benelli four and Honda six in the replica models market.

10 The V8

The most well-known and respected of all Moto Guzzi's racing designers was Ing. Giulio Cesare Carcano. It was he who largely created and honed the Guzzi singles that dominated the 350cc World Championship series between 1953 and 1957, and he also designed the world's only eight-cylinder Grand Prix racing motorcycle.

The fantastic V8 arrived in 1955; this is the first version, with hand-beaten aluminium 'dustbin' fairing. Note the air scoop shape.

This unique racing machine came about due to the failure of both the in-line four (see Chapter 8) and the single-cylinder model, which was simply not fast enough against the 500cc four-cylinder Gileras and MV Agustas. The defining moment for Carcano came at the Italian Grand Prix at Monza in September 1954. Sitting on the banking watching the practice, the designer suddenly realized that drastic action was needed if Guzzi were to be competitive in the Blue Riband class of Grand Prix racing. Nothing less than a brand-new bike would do.

123

The V8

V8 1955–57	
Engine	Liquid-cooled, dohc, 90 degree V8, two valves per cylinder with gear-driven camshafts, one-piece crankshaft, two-piece connecting-rods, coil valve springs, one-piece crankcase
Bore	44mm
Stroke	41mm
Displacement	498.5cc
Compression ratio	10:1
Lubrication	Gear pump
Ignition	Battery/coil
Carburation	8 × Dell'Orto 20mm (1957 21mm)
Gearbox	4-, 5- or six-speed, foot-change
Clutch	Multi-plate, dry
Final drive	Chain
Frame	Double cradle
Suspension	Front and rear, hydraulically damped shock absorbers; four in total
Brakes	Drums, full-width, front and rear; front, four leading shoe
Tyres	Front 2.75 × 19; rear 3.00 × 20

General specification

Wheelbase	1420mm (55.9in)
Dry weight	150kg (331lb)
Fuel capacity	34ltr (7.5gal)
Maximum power output	68bhp at 12,000rpm (1955), 76bhp at 14,000rpm (1957)
Top speed	170mph (273km/h)

The Design

At first Carcano considered a six-cylinder layout, but soon plumped for an eight. Although at the time this might have been viewed as being an extremely complex design, Carcano had good reasons why he selected a V8. The cylinders of a V8 were arranged in two blocks of four, at an angle of 90 degrees. The cubic capacity of each cylinder could be reduced to a minimum to provide very high engine revolutions and thus higher power output (something Honda was to exploit later). Also, the axis of the engine was laid across the frame to simplify the employment of chain final drive, which Carcano considered absolutely vital after his experience with the ill-fated in-line four.

There was also the attraction that the originality of the design gave great possibilities of development, while the overall dimensions, both longitudinal and transversal, could still be quite reasonable, enabling the engine unit to be housed in a conventional, double-cradle frame.

The project crystallized during the winter of 1954–55, in an atmosphere of total secrecy. However, Carcano was not only a brilliant designer, he also had a great sense of humour. Without adding any written explanation, Carcano sent his friends in the press, both at home and abroad (who were clamouring for information), a drawing of his latest project, seen only from the offside. He invited them to guess what it was, but not one journalist came up with the correct answer – one even going as far as suggesting that it was a turbine-powered machine!

Bore and Stroke Dimensions

With bore and stroke dimensions of 44 × 42mm giving each cylinder a swept volume of 62.31cc, the 498.58cc engine was very slightly oversquare, with a 0.932:1 bore to stroke ratio. During the early stages of its development, the power output of the V8 was in the region of 65bhp at 12,000rpm, but gradually this figure was increased. By the end of 1957, when unfortunately Moto Guzzi decided to withdraw from Grand Prix racing, it had been increased to almost 80bhp at 14,000rpm – almost 10bhp more than the rival Gilera and MV fours, and unsurpassed until the 1970s.

A point worth recording is that even at 14,000rpm, the linear speed of the tiny pistons

The V8

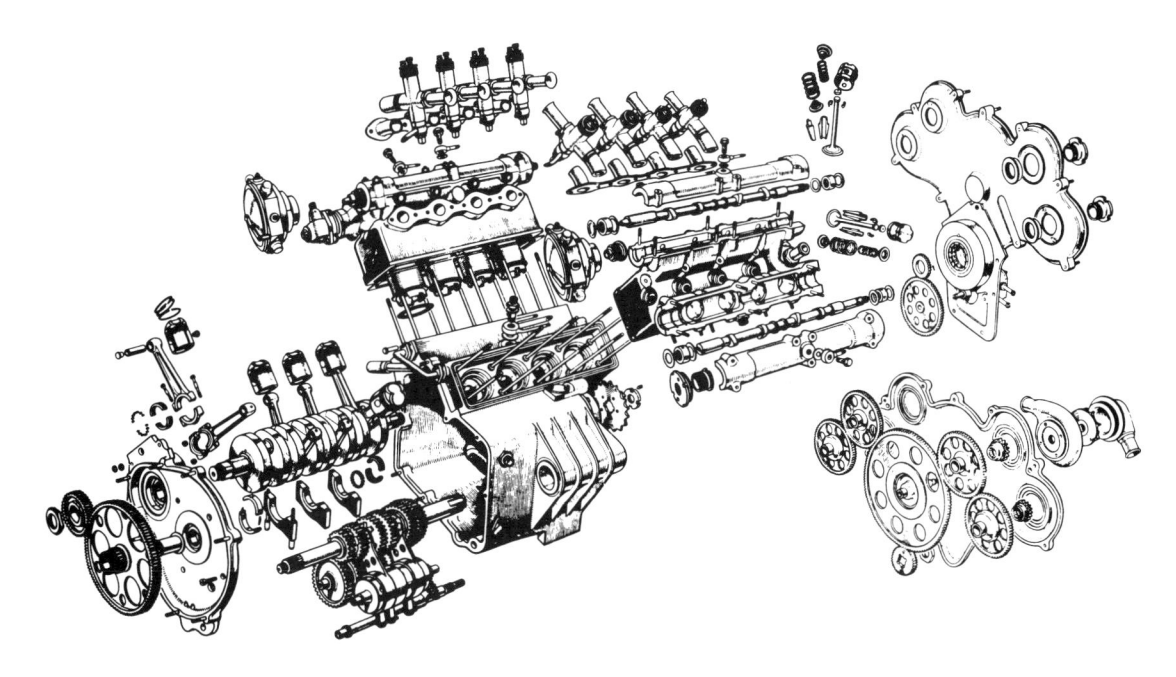

Exploded view of the V8 engine with a one-piece crankshaft and eight carburettors.

ABOVE: Side view of the 76bhp V8. Before it was retired, it powered the machine to almost 180mph (289.6km/h).

RIGHT: The compact nature of the unit is shown here.

The V8

was actually lower than that of a typical 500cc single-cylinder racing engine of the era, such as a Manx Norton or Gilera Saturno, turning over at 7,000rpm.

Water Cooling

Owing to its cylinder arrangement, the V8 engine needed water cooling, the radiator being situated ahead of the crankcase. The water pump was driven by one of a train of six timing gears (housed in an oil bath on the off-side of the engine), that operated the twin overhead camshafts (ohcs) for each bank of cylinders.

On the nearside of each inlet camshaft was a pair of distributors, each with four contact breakers. The coils, one for each cylinder, were mounted in two clusters of four on each side of the frame's front downtubes. Dual 6-volt batteries were housed on each side of the rear frame section, with the firing order being 1-8-3-6-4-5-2-7. To provide more space for two valves per cylinder in their hemispherical combustion chambers, 10mm spark plugs were specified.

The Crankshaft

A short, massive, one-piece, forged nickel-chrome crankshaft with circular flywheels, was supported by a total of five caged roller bearings, with split races between each throw. Split roller bearings were also employed for the big ends of the 90mm (3.5in) connecting-rods. The crankcase was a one-piece electron casting, whilst the cast-iron wet-liner cylinders were finned at the top, within the water jacket, for more efficient cooling.

The Valves

The valves, operating in split guides, were set at an angle of 58 degrees to each other, their diameter being 21mm exhaust and 23mm inlet. Each featured dual coil springs, over which large tappets came into direct contact with the cams. The highly domed forged pistons, deeply recessed for valve clearance and also to provide a squish effect, carried two compression rings and a single oil-scraper ring. Following conventional Guzzi racing practice, the lubrication system was of the dry sump variety, the oil pump being driven at half engine speed. The oil tank itself was in the large-diameter top frame tube and had a capacity of 5ltr (just over a gallon).

The Carburettors

Each of the tiny cylinders was fed by its own 20mm Dell'Orto carburettor, there being two float chambers on the nearside of the engine, each serving four instruments. A single cable from the quick-action twistgrip operated the eight throttle slides with an extremely efficient

Guzzi V8 engine complete with eight Dell'Orto carburettors.

The V8

1956 version of the V8. Note the revised air scoops on the fairing and stacked exhaust pipes.

X-ray view drawing of the fully faired Guzzi V8 500 Grand Prix bike.

The V8

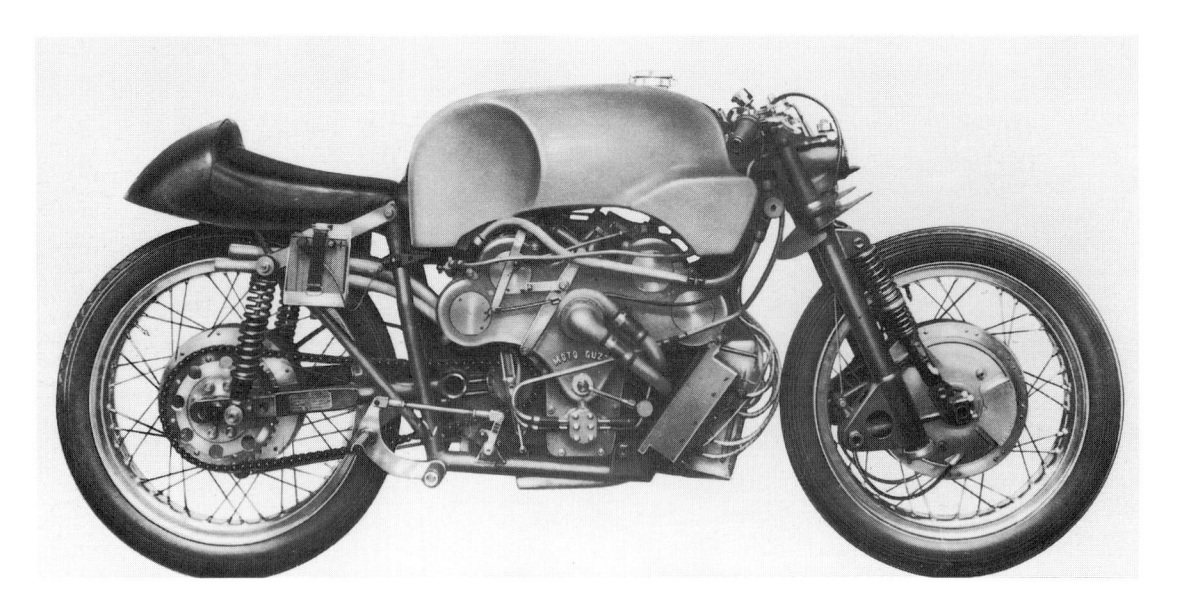

1956/57 V8 with the streamlining removed to show the engine, frame, brakes and suspension details.

linkage system, which reduced effort to a bare minimum.

The Transmission
Besides chain final drive, there was also a dry clutch, while the geared primary drive ran in an oil-bath casing and provided an engine-to-gearbox ratio of 2.75:1. Amazingly, there was a choice of four, five or even six-speed gear clusters available, depending upon the circuit or on individual rider's requirements. In practice, however, it was soon discovered that the massive torque generated by the V8 rendered the six-speed cluster redundant. Incidentally, this high torque figure at low engine revolutions meant the eight-cylinder engine was useful for both fast and slow going.

The Frame
Manufactured in chrome-moly tubing with a double-cradle frame, the pivot point for the round section swinging arm being incorporated in the crankcase casting to reduce the machine's overall wheelbase. As was the practice with the majority of post-war Guzzi racing bikes, the V8 was fitted with leading-link front forks.

The Shock Absorbers
Because of its immense power, certainly by the standards of the day, Carcano and his engineering team had seen fit to provide additional exposed shock absorbers to the front fork assembly. This was not only to be able to cope with the speed whilst in full flight, but to provide the rider with the stability to haul the bike down from these high speeds. Carcano provided the tools for the braking job in the form of a massive 240mm (9.4in) drum front brake; this featuring four leading-shoe operation. The rear brake was also large at 220mm (8.6in) diameter and of the single leading-shoe type.

The Fuel Tank
The fuel tank was made from hand-beaten aluminium, together with the streaming. At first, it was a fully-streamlined dustbin, but was

later axed in favour of a less-enveloping dolphin type. The change of fairing came about because the dolphin was found to improve the machine's handling, particularly in adverse conditions. Here, once again, Guzzi led the way, as from the beginning of the 1958 season FIM (the governing body for motorcycle sport) banned the use of the full enclosure type fairing on safety grounds.

The début

Carcano's masterpiece first appeared in public mid-way through 1955, at an Italian national meeting at Senigallia. For such a complex piece of machinery, the V8 was remarkably light, weighing in dry at 135kg (298lb), disproving the old argument that more cylinders meant more weight.

The newcomer caused a huge stir in racing circles throughout the world, even though it was not raced that day. The same thing occurred at its second appearance, during practice for the Italian Grand Prix at Monza later that year. Finally, its actual race début came at Imola on Easter Monday 1956, when Guzzi works rider Ken Kavanagh completed ten laps before retiring in the 500cc Gold Cup race.

Italian Senior Championship

Carcano, together with his two design assistants and a team of eight considered 1956 to be very much part of the V8's development period, and actual racing successes not to be important. In fact, the design's first success did not come until the following year at the

Stanley Woods celebrating his fiftieth birthday by riding the V8 at Monza in October 1956.

The V8

ABOVE: Dell'Orto carburettor company's display of the SSI 21 carbs as used on the 1957 V8.

LEFT: Stanley Woods with the V8 after his Monza ride in October 1956.

BELOW: 1957 V8 with dolphin fairing as used by Dickie Dale in the Isle of Man TT that year.

At the 1957 Senior TT Dickie Dale finished fourth on the works Guzzi V8, even though one of the cylinders was not functioning for most of the race!

Italian Senior Championship held in Sicily on 19 March 1957. During the first round of the series, over the 5.5 km (3.4-mile) course, veteran Giuseppe Colnago (nicknamed the 'Grandfather') won the 500cc race at an average speed of 93.15mph (149.8km/h).

World Standing-Start Record

Then, without resorting to any special tuning or fuels, the 1955 and 1956 350 cc World Champion, Bill Lomas, sprinted one of the V8s along the Terracina Straight to smash the world standing-start record of 10 km (6.2 miles) at an average speed of 151.5mph (243.7km/h), a record that still stood three decades later! Unfortunately, an injury sustained whilst racing was to keep Lomas out of action for most of that year.

Isle of Man TT

Because Lomas was sidelined, Dickie Dale rode the V8 in the 1957 Senior TT in the Isle of Man, in the process completing the last $6\frac{1}{2}$ laps on seven cylinders due to a burnt-out piston. He knew something was wrong, but as the entry had been made for test purposes only, he decided to carry on until it stopped, which it did not (in an eight lap, 302-mile race too!)

Belgian Grand Prix

During the Belgian Grand Prix a few weeks later, the V8 was timed at 178mph (286km/h), by far the fastest speed recorded by any racing machine during the 1950s. However, after setting the quickest lap at 118.06mph

131

ABOVE: Bill Lomas warms up the V8 in front of an admiring group of supporters, Brands Hatch, 1981.

LEFT: Bill Lomas piloting the V8 at the Surtees Day, Brands Hatch, summer 1981.

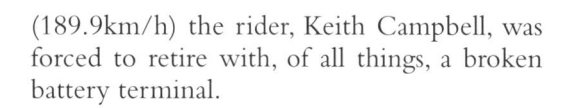

(189.9km/h) the rider, Keith Campbell, was forced to retire with, of all things, a broken battery terminal.

Italian Grand Prix

Racing accidents sidelined the top Guzzi stars for the final Grand Prix of 1957 at Monza in September that year. And so Guzzi's decision to withdraw from racing shortly afterwards (along with Gilera and FB Mondial), effectively meant that the V8 was never to show its full potential.

Future Development Potential

If the V8 had been continued, the early faults that dogged it – carburation, crankshaft and lubrication – would no doubt have been resolved.

Carcano and his team (which Lomas described as 'the best in the world') had spent a lot of effort ensuring the engine would respond at all throttle openings. They had also already beaten the lubrication problems by fitting two additional oil pumps, while Hirth had come up with a much improved crankshaft.

A smaller version displaced 348cc (36 × 41mm) and had already been bench tested and found to produce 52bhp. Another project was a 350 four (the front block of the V8), along with a similar 250. But of course all these projects were doomed once the fateful 'retirement' decision had been taken by Guzzi's management in 1957.

What Might Have Been?

It is the author's view, and one shared by Bill Lomas, that had Guzzi continued, the V8 would have ruled the racing world for many years. Certainly if this had been the case, MV Agusta would never have won the record-breaking number of Grand Prix and World Championships as it did from the late 1950s until the mid-1970s. And the riders who won these would probably have been Guzzi-mounted; men such as Surtees, Hocking, Hailwood and Agostini. (My book *John Surtees, Motorcycle Maestro* explains how he had discussions with Moto Guzzi.) All very interesting, but of course one is left only to speculate. The fact remains that Guzzi themselves killed off the V8.

11 Record Breaking

Besides its massive impact in road racing, Moto Guzzi were also extremely successful in another field of competition, that of record breaking. Over some two decades, which spanned the late 1930s until the late 1950s, the Mandello del Lario factory was to gain hundreds of world speed and endurance records, on two, three and even four wheels.

It was Omobono Tenni that set Guzzi on their record-breaking path. The first Italian to win the Lightweight TT, Tenni was generally seen as Guzzi's best rider at the time. Consequently, he was chosen to pilot a version of the factory's new supercharged 248cc model (*see* Chapter 2) that had arrived in spring 1938.

Although the supercharged bike was to prove less than successful in the Grand Prix-type races of the day, it was much more suitable for the shorter distances of the record-breaking requirements.

Record attempts were an important focus of attention for the Moto Guzzi marque. An early effort was this supercharged 250 single in 1938.

Record Breaking

Monza 1938

Tenni's Monza attempt came in November 1938. The records that fell to Tenni and the supercharged 250 were as follows:

5km (flying start)	116.714mph
10km	108.636mph
50km	112.8mph
10km	111.106mph
5 miles (flying start)	116.709mph
10 miles	110.902mph
50 miles	110.466mph
100 miles	111.794mph
1 hour	112.157mph

The records applied to Classes A (250cc) and B (350cc).

In 1939, Raffaele Alberti added more records on the 250 supercharged Guzzi.

A Third Wheel

Post-war a third wheel was added to the pre-war 250 supercharged machine, and with this Luigi Cavanna was to set more records, this time for the 250cc sidecar category. For the 1948 attempt Cavanna used the bike in naked form, even though the sidecar (essentially only a platform and wheel) was fully streamlined. In 1952, Cavanna was to improve on his 1948 performance with a fully streamlined motorcycle and sidecar device, which was still powered by essentially the same pre-war supercharged horizontal Guzzi power unit.

The Motoleggera

After the Second World War, Italy badly needed personal transport. Piaggio (Vespa) and Innocenti (Lambretta) took over the scooter market, and Guzzi did the same thing in the ultra-lightweight motorcycle field with an entirely new design powered by a 64cc (42 × 46mm) rotary-valve two-stroke engine. The result, at first known as the Guzzino (little Guzzi), was soon rebadged Motoleggera.

In February, Alberti took a specially prepared Motoleggera to Switzerland for an attempt at the 75cc world speed record. This

Raffaele Alberti, one of three riders to establish twenty-seven new world records in 1948, on a 65cc disc valve Guzzi 2-stroke.

Record Breaking

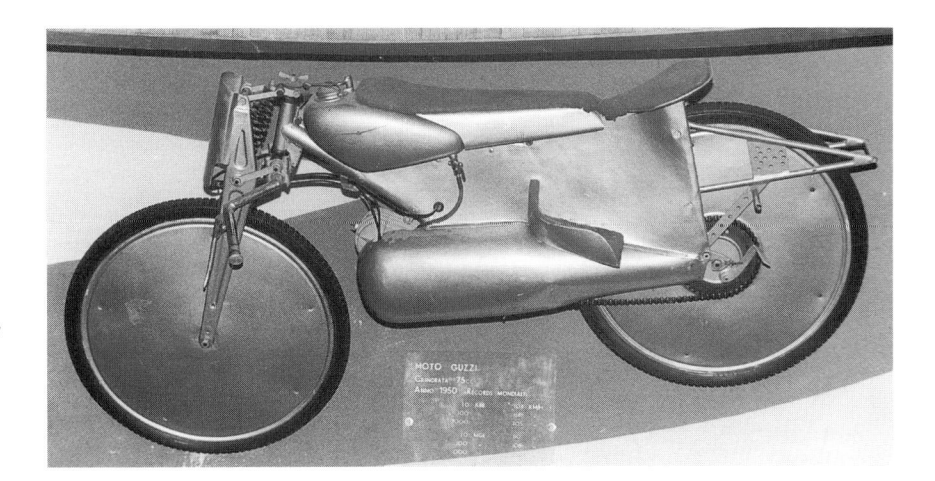

The 1948 machine was modified in 1950 to take a larger 73cc engine. But it was superseded by a new machine with a different chassis and full enclosure.

The streamlined 73cc model that established twenty-two more world records in the 75cc class at Montlhéry, France 14–17 September 1950.

he achieved over the Saxon-Charrat highway. Later that year, Alberti, Gianna Leoni and Bruno Ruffo established twenty-seven new records at Monza (again in the 75cc category) on the same machine.

Montlhéry 1950

With the engine displacement raised to 73cc (by increasing the bore size to 46mm), a fully streamlined version of the tiny two-stroke was taken to Montlhéry, just south of Paris, and between September 14–17 Alberti, Leoni and Ruffo established twenty-two more records in the 75cc class, several being at a higher speed than those for the 100cc category.

Official Guzzi performance figures for the 1950 73cc record breaker gave 3.6bhp at 6,300rpm, a compression ratio of 7:1 and a top speed of 80mph (128km/h).

Record Breaking

The new 73cc streamliner 'naked', showing the horizontal engine, fuel tank, wheels and 'kneeler' position for the rider.

Cavanna Again

On 26 August 1952, Cavanna once again hit the headlines – gaining yet more records and prestige for himself and the Moto Guzzi marque.

Taking advantage of a revision in the regulations governing the construction of sidecars for record breaking, and using what *Motor Cycling* described as a hinged 'wing-cum-wheel', it used one of the pre-war blown 248cc horizontal single-cylinder engines. Cavanna and the Guzzi outfit subsequently broke a number of records in Germany over the Munich-Ingolstadt autobahn.

The 'outfit' achieved a standing kilometre of 73mph and 84.5mph over the 1-mile distance; the flying kilometre and mile both at 137mph; 5 km at 128mph; 5 miles at 126mph; plus 10km at 117mph and 10 miles at 108.5mph. Not only did these speeds exceed those for the 250 and 350cc classes, but in many cases they also battered those in all the sidecar categories up to 1200cc.

Perhaps most amazingly of all, Cavanna had actually exceeded the speeds set by Tenni and Alberti on solo machines in 1938 and 1939 respectively. These latest achievements gave Moto Guzzi a total of 108 world records – unsurpassed at the time.

Besides the efforts with the 65 and 73cc 2-strokes, as this photograph shows, the factory also mounted a sidecar on the pre-war 250cc supercharged machine for yet more record attempts. The rider was Luigi Cavanna, circa 1948.

Record Breaking

ABOVE: Luigi Cavanna was back in the limelight in August 1954 when he set fourteen new world records with this 250cc Guzzi and 'sidecar' on the Munich–Ingoldstadt autobahn.

RIGHT: Guzzi had taken advantage of a revision of the FIM rules governing the construction of sidecars for record breaking, allowing this 'wing-cum-wheel' device for its 1954 attempts.

Using only a 250cc engine (one of the pre-war supercharged units) Cavanna broke all existing 10 mile and 10 kilometre sidecar records for engine sizes up to no less than 1200cc!

Record Breaking

A Return to Montlhéry

During almost ten hours at the Montlhéry speed bowl near Paris on Wednesday 23 March 1955, a 348cc Guzzi (essentially a 1953 sohc Grand Prix racer with a special dolphin fairing and revised gearing) gained twenty-two more world records.

The riders were Fergus Anderson, Dickie Dale, Ken Kavanagh and Duilio Agostini. Comprehensive streamlining was not employed because during long-distance record attempts, speedy access to the wheels for tyre changing was necessary. For the same reason, the less highly stressed single overhead cam (sohc) engine was preferred to the double camshaft layout.

Anderson got things under way at 7.30am during heavy rain and rode for the first hour, to be followed by Dale, Kavanagh and Agostini, each for hourly periods. After almost ten hours, with Agostini in the saddle the oil tank ran dry. The result was severe damage to the engine. However, a distance of 1,054.5 miles (1,696km) had been covered, sufficient to claim the eleven- and twelve-hour records. They had also set new eight and nine -hour records. The 1,000-mile (1,609km) distance

At Montlhéry on Wednesday 23 March 1955, a 348cc Guzzi broke twenty-two world records in less than ten hours. The riders were Fergus Anderson, Dickie Dale, Ken Kavanagh and Duilio Agostini.

Record Breaking

At Montlhéry on 1 November 1955, Guzzi gained another twenty-five world solo and sidecar records with a three-man team comprising Fergus Anderson, Dickie Dale and Bill Lomas.

was covered at an average speed of 107.92mph (173.6km/h). All these figures also applied to the 500, 750 and 1000cc classes.

The team also broke the existing twelve-hour record for the 350 and 500cc categories with an average speed of 87.88mph (141km/h) – even though they were two hours short!

A Fitting Tribute to Giorgio Parodi

On 28 August 1955, the death was announced of Giorgio Parodi, the man who together with Carlo Guzzi had founded the Moto Guzzi company. It was a fitting tribute to this great man's memory that his Mandello concern not only finished off the Grand Prix season in style

ABOVE: Dickie Dale with the 350cc Guzzi and 'sidecar' record-breaker at Montlhéry in November 1955.

LEFT: Factory photograph of the sidecar outfit used at Montlhéry in November 1955; it was powered by one of the 'old' 1953 sohc 350cc Grand Prix engines.

Record Breaking

by taking five of the top six places in the 350cc race at Monza, but also embarked on yet another (successful!) record-breaking spree.

This took place at Montlhéry, France on November 1 1955, with a team comprising the newly crowned 350cc World Champion Bill Lomas, Dickie Dale and team manager Fergus Anderson. The Guzzi trio attacked a number of records with Guzzi 350cc machines in both solo and sidecar guises, returning to Italy with another thirteen world records. This success enabled Moto Guzzi to proclaim themselves not only the holders of 135 world records, but also the 'The Record of Records' in subsequent advertising.

The sidecar machine featured the 'bird beak' streamlining similar to the 1953 works racers (*see* Chapter 9) whilst the solo, which bettered the 350cc Montlhéry lap record with a circuit of 133.18mph (214.2km/h), was a standard works racer save for a higher compression ratio. Both bikes ran on a 70/20/10 mixture of 80 octane petrol/benzole/alcohol fuel mixture.

Montichiari Airport 1956

At the end of October at Montichiari Airport new speeds were set by Enrico Lorenzetti and Dickie Dale.

Using both 350 and 500cc solos, Lorenzetti covered the standing kilometre at 92.06mph (148.12km/h) and the mile at 103.05mph (165.8km/h); whilst Dale on one of the V8s recorded 102.37mph (164.7km/h) and 115.53mph (185.8km/h).

The Last Record Attempt

In early 1957, yet more records fell to the marque. On 26 February, Dale and Lomas on the 350cc single and V8 respectively, attempted to break the 10km standing start for both engine sizes. Such was their success that new speeds were set for the 350, 500, 750 and 1000cc classes. Dale covered the distance on the 350cc model in 2 minutes 49.6 seconds – 131.89mph (212.2km/h), whilst Lomas on the V8 made a first run in 2 minutes, 35 seconds, then

Yet more records were broken in 1956 with this streamliner, powered by the multi-World Championship winning 350cc horizontal single-cylinder engine.

Record Breaking

Without special tuning or fuels, the V8 was used during February 1957 by Bill Lomas to smash the world standing start 10km record along the Terracina Straight at an average speed of 151.8mph (244.2km/h), a record that was to stand for over three decades.

improved upon this getting it down to 2 minutes, 27 seconds – 151.35mph (243.5km/h). The Lomas record was to stand for well over three decades.

Guzzi Withdraws from Racing

1957 had marked a dramatic end to Moto Guzzi's participation in both Grand Prix racing and record attempts, when along with fellow Italian marques Gilera and FB Mondial, they had withdrawn from the sport. At the time, it seemed as if the final curtain had fallen on what many would still argue was the golden age of the motorcycle industry. It was virtually inconceivable that Guzzi should abruptly give up something they had done so well, but it was a fact – and it took twelve years before they returned to serious participation in the sport.

The New 'Works' Guzzi

With much of Guzzi's reputation firmly established in both Grand Prix racing and setting new world records, it was hardly surprising that at the end of the 1960s, attention should once again turn to this latter area. Lino Tonti, recently appointed as chief designer to succeed Ing. Giulio Cesare Carcano, realized the importance of proving that Guzzi could still make successful high-speed motorcycles.

However, anyone studying the original V7 700cc model would have to be excused for failing to notice even a spark of competitive spirit in the make-up of the 90 degree transverse V-twin machine. But Lino Tonti had seen something beneath the skin of what most others viewed as simply an out-and-out tourer.

When the new 'works' Guzzi appeared in 1969, it was at first solely an attempt at getting the marque's name back in the record books, rather than a full-scale return to the racing circuits. However, Guzzi was not a factory to do things half-heartedly, and the V-twin machines that they turned out for the new record-breaking attempt were highly interesting in their own right.

With only the unlikely looking V7 as a basis, Tonti went to work. During the closed season of 1968–69, the competition department at the Mandello works began construction of a batch of specially-prepared V7s, stripped of everything that could possibly be removed, in a massive weight saving exercise.

This resulted in a motorcycle weighing only 158kg (348lb) in which the only stock components left were the basic engine and gearbox assemblies, the frame, swinging arm (and drive shaft), the wheels and front forks. To these were added a hand-beaten aluminium fuel tank of 29ltr (6.4gal), a single racing saddle, clip-ons, rear set foot controls, and a final drive box with modified ratios.

Each of the machines were carefully assembled, and their engines painstakingly blueprinted and tuned. The completed bikes were fitted with specially made three-piece aluminium dolphin fairings and (recalling the works racers of the 1950s) finished in a very pale green paint. This paint was applied to the fairing, tank and rear mudguard (there being no front 'guard). A large, 100mm (3.9in) white-faced Veglia rev counter kept the rider informed when he needed to change gear.

The V7 record attempt machines were made in two engine sizes. Although these were only of marginal difference, they allowed Guzzi entry into two distinct classes. The first engine, for the 750cc class, displaced 739.3cc (82 × 70mm). The second unit was for the 1000cc class and employed the dimensions of the newly released V7 Special, displacing at 757.486cc (83 × 70mm).

The result of these modifications was no less than 68bhp at the rear wheel; compared to 40bhp for the V7 700 and 45bhp for the larger-engined V7 Special. Maximum power was produced at 6,500rpm.

Selecting the Riders

With the bikes ready to go, the next stage was the task of selecting suitable riders. The eight who were finally chosen proved to be an excellent blend of experienced testers and road racers, including such well-known names as Vittorio Brambilla, Alberto Pagani and Remo Venturi, whilst the press was represented by racing journalist Roberto Patrignani. By June 1969, the team was ready to pay its first visit to Monza.

Monza 1969

It was immediately apparent that Guzzi had done their homework. What had formerly

1969 marked the return of Guzzi to the record-breaking trail with specially prepared V7 transverse V-twin models, using either 748 or 757cc engines.

Record Breaking

been very much a ponderous, essentially touring bike had been transformed into an entirely new creature with great athleticism and a fair turn of speed. Soon, team members were gunning the deep-sounding V-twin chargers around Monza's speed bowl with an enthusiasm that was clearly visible when team leader Brambilla set very respectable new 750cc class records in three categories: 1000km 125.6mph (201km/h), 100km 131.9mph (212.2km/h), 1-hour 132.9mph (213.8km/h).

LEFT: One of the 1969 V7 machines with its streamlining removed. Stripped down to the bare bones, the machine weighed in at only 158kg (348lb).

BELOW: Ex-Bianchi and MV star Remo Venturi at speed on the Monza banking during one of the June 1969 record attempts.

More Records Taken

Guzzi returned to Monza later that year to take more solo records and also went for honours in the sidecar class, something they hadn't done on their first visit.

In the solo section, the six-hour speed record fell at 125.76mph (202.3km/h), whilst the twelve-hour went at an average of 111.53mph (179.4km/h). The sidecars speeds were obviously less, but the one- and six-hour speeds were both successfully increased – with 115.64mph (186km/h) and 86.99mph (139.9km/h) respectively.

Besides the considerable amount of positive publicity these record attempts generated, Moto Guzzi's efforts at Monza in both June and October 1969 acted as a stepping stone towards the factory making a comeback into road racing. But this time, the emphasis would not be directed towards the highly specialized Grand Prix circuit but production-based racing, including 24-hour events such as the Bol d'Or and the Barcelona 24-hour race (see Chapters 12, 13 and 14).

Another set of record attempts was made in October 1969 with both solo and sidecar machines. Giuseppe Dal Toe is seen here helping establish new three records for one- and six-hour periods.

Alberti Pagani was another rider to take part in the October 1969 attempts, which resulted in fifteen new records being gained in two days.

145

Record Breaking

Four-Wheel Exploits

Besides its great success in the record-breaking sphere on both two and three wheels, Moto Guzzi were also to be found in the four-wheel sector when it came to speed and endurance record attempts.

The first four-wheel efforts came via Count Giovanni (Johnny) Lurani, who was already a well-known racing driver. Lurani approached Carlo Guzzi with a proposal that they should supply him with one of their 494.8cc (68 × 68mm) 120 degree V-twin racing engines. This was prepared in the Mandello del Lario factory to produce 50bhp (44bhp was standard at the time), running on alcohol. When one considers that the majority of 1000cc four-cylinder sports racing cars were hard pushed to reach 50bhp, that figure on half the displacement was most impressive.

Mounted in a streamlined car named Nibbio and helped in its preparation by Guzzi's son, Ulisse, Lurani set new speed records in the under 500cc category for the standing and flying kilometre and one-mile distances on the Firenze–Mare autostrada on 5 November 1935. In May 1939, Lurani took Nibbio to Berlin and set new records during which he topped 108mph (174km/h) on the Berlin–Munich autobahn.

Postwar, in 1948, the V-twin engine was used once again for a crack at breaking car records. But this time the driver was Piero Taruffi, a famous racer and record breaker on Gilera motorcycles in pre-war days. In his 'car', named Bisiluro (actually two cigars joined at the centre) Taruffi achieved speeds up to 129.6mph (208.72km/h) on the Bergano–Brescia highway. He had less power at his disposal – 45bhp at 7,400rpm. Why? Well, Taruffi didn't have the level of support that Lurani had enjoyed in pre-war days, and also his engine had to run on petrol rather than alcohol.

In 1955, Lurani returned to the scene and constructed an entirely new car named appropriately Nibbio II. This was powered by the very latest of the dohc 350cc Guzzi single-cylinder Grand Prix engines. With this car yet more records fell to the flying Count between 1956 and 1958. Not just in the 350cc class, but the 250cc also as Nibbio II was later fitted with a 250cc Guzzi engine. These record attempts were made on the banked high-speed section of Monza Autrodrome, near Milan.

Towards the end of the 1950s, Guzzi's chief designer, Ing. Giulio Cesare Carcano, teamed up with Gino Cavanna to construct a supremely streamlined tiny car powered by the pre-war Guzzi 250cc supercharged flat single engine that Cavanna had already used in 1948 and 1952 to set new sidecar world records (*see* page 134).

Cavanna had access to Aeronautica Macchi of Varese, and their engineer Ing. Barzocchi assisted in the design of the body shell for the car, named Cobra. Cavanna drove the car himself, although 'drove' is a somewhat misleading term as he lay flat on his stomach. This project resulted in yet more records, set at the Autostrada del Sole in May 1959, with speeds up to 145mph (233km/h); this being quite incredible for a car of only 250cc!

The final project, named Colibri (humming bird) came in 1963 when Italian racing car manufacturer Stanguellini, whose main business was Formula Junior teamed up with the Modena company Gransport to build a fully streamlined car to attack a series of medium-distance 250cc speed records. The engine used was one of the final Guzzi Grand Prix 250cc flat singles of the mid-1950s, with dohc and a five-speed gearbox. Driven by Campanello and Poggio, the team were successful setting new records for the 50–200 kilometres, the 50–100 miles, and 1-hour Class K international records.

So one can see that Guzzi have a pedigree second to none if one looks at their achievements across two, three and four wheels.

1935, the first Moto Guzzi car, the Nibbio, driven by Count Giovanni Lurani on the Firenze–Mare autostrada at speeds of up to 100.6mph (162km/h). Power came from the in-line 500 V-twin as used by Stanley Woods to win the Senior TT that year.

Record Breaking

ABOVE: 1948, Piero Taruffi, using one of the V-twin engines used by this car to reach speeds of up to 128mph (207km/h).

BELOW: 1955, the Ghia-bodied Nibbio II, powered by one of the Guzzi 350cc dohc Grand Prix single-cylinder engines.

Gino Cavanna's Cobra, powered by a supercharged 250cc Guzzi engine with aerodynamics in conjunction with Aeronautica Macchi. It reached speeds of up to 145mph (233km/h) in May 1959.

1963, the streamlined Colibri car – powered by a 250cc Guzzi engine it reached speeds of 103mph (165km/h) on only 29bhp – proof of the advantages of efficient aerodynamics.

147

12 Early Transverse V-Twin Development

Moto Guzzi quit Grand Prix racing towards the end of 1957. Many thought they would soon be back, whilst others believed that Guzzi had quit the sport for good.

As is often the case, the answer lay somewhere between these two extremes. To start with, the withdrawal created a vacuum within the factory itself. This was to some extent filled when in February 1958, the company announced that it was preparing a trials team for 1958 under the managership of Bruno Romano, once one of Italy's top trials aces and a member of the famous Sertum team. Subsequently, specially prepared Lodola and Stornello single-cylinder models were campaigned with considerable success, winning several gold medals in the International Six Days Trial (ISDT). Guzzi machines were also used to represent Italy in the ISDT, the highlight of this coming in 1963 when the entire Italian Silver Vase team all rode Guzzis. Then at the end of 1963, Guzzi withdrew from the world trials arena and although they continued at home for another year, finally retired altogether at the end of 1964.

The V-Twin

In 1964 the first prototype testing began of a motorcycle that was to revolutionize the Mandello del Lario company, the V7.

Although the original V7 was as far removed from a racing motorcycle as one could be, its development is important to the overall Guzzi racing history, as it was to sire an entire family of 90 degree transverse V-twins, many of which were to be raced with varying degrees of success over the following decades.

Inspiration for its power unit had come from the engine that powered the 3 × 3, a small military tractor built between 1960 and 1963 and used by the Italian army. In fact, the V7 project was created with military and police work very much in mind, rather than the civilian market.

Early the following year, the first pre-production bikes went for government inspection. But even before these official tests had taken place, the factory's management had realized that the machine was also suitable for sale to the general public, and soon a civilian prototype was built and tested. This machine was given its public début in December 1965 at the International Milan Show, where it proved to be the star exhibit. *Motor Cycle News* summed the newcomer up thus:

> There was the monumental Moto Guzzi 700cc V7, with a layout that was dictated by army and police designers rather than by the factory. It weighs in at a colossal 213.2kg (470lb), is a four-stroke pushrod ohv transverse V-twin, with a four speed 'box and a top speed in excess of 110mph (177 km/h).

Guzzi in Crisis

The V7 had been born into an industry that was struggling with declining sales and Japanese competition. Although Italy did eventual-

Early Transverse V-Twin Development

ly impose import restrictions, it was too late for several Italian factories where motorcycle production had already ceased, such as Rumi, MM, Sertum, Parilla and Bianchi. And many others, including Moto Guzzi were struggling badly. In fact bankruptcy was only avoided at the Mandello del Lario plant by expending the entire Parodi family fortune, and late in 1966 Moto Guzzi was forced into compulsory court administration (the Italian equivalent of receivership). On 1 February 1967, *Societa Esercizio Moto Meccaniche SpA* (SEIMM), a trusteeship company set up by the creditor banks and the state financing agency (IMI), effectively took over the financial control of the company to enable Guzzi to continue trading. The president of this controlling body was Prof. Arnaldo Marcartino.

Besides a falling market, there was another problem – the men at the top of the original management structure had by then left the scene, a process that had started during the Second World War, when Emanuele Parodi had died at almost the same time as his nephew, Angelo. His son Giorgio then died in 1955, and to complete the gloomy picture, Carlo Guzzi passed away in 1964 at the age of seventy-five, shortly after finally retiring from the company he had helped create some forty-five years earlier.

By 1966, the only remaining link was Giorgio Parodi's brother Enrico, who had joined

The first civilian production V7, powered by a 703.7cc (80 × 70mm) transverse 90 degree V-twin engine went on sale in 1966, after making its début at the Milan Show the previous November.

Early Transverse V-Twin Development

Moto Guzzi in 1942. Although in many ways a gifted man, he was not a prudent one, being responsible for a series of unfortunate speculations, many outside the motorcycle industry, which caused the entire Parodi empire to crumble just when Guzzi had to cope with its biggest crisis. This led not only to a large number of the workforce being made redundant, but a severe pruning of the model range which, except for the V7, was made up entirely of single-cylinder bikes of various engine sizes, both four- and two-stroke.

V7 Saves the Day

The one ray of hope lay in the V7 project. Thanks to its police and military heritage, the V7 had been created with priority given to

1969, the V7 Special had an unusually large 757.5cc engine size.

Otherwise it was largely unchanged from the original V7.

simplicity, ease of maintenance and reliability in service. In many ways, for a motorcycle it was surprisingly 'agricultural', especially when one compares it to the majority of its competitors in what was to emerge as the age of the Superbike, which began in the early 1970s and has matured into today's hyper-performance machines.

Engine Design

The V7 name was drawn from the engine's transverse 90 degree vee layout and its original displacement of 703.717cc (80 × 70mm). Running on a compression ratio of 9:1, the oversquare pushrod motor put out 50bhp at a relatively leisurely 6,000rpm.

The engine layout provided superb accessibility and its simplicity and relatively 'soft' state of tune made for a long, maintenance-free life.

Details of the design are listed below:

- One-piece steel crankshaft
- Steel connecting-rods with bolt-up big-end eyes running on this white-metal split end big-end shells
- Four-ring Borgo pistons (three compression, one oil scraper)
- 22mm (0.8in) gudgeon pin size
- Alloy cylinder heads with two valves per cylinder, coil valve springs
- Alloy cylinder barrels with chrome-plated bores
- Dell'Orto SS1 29 carburettors
- Screw and lock-nut tappets
- Detachable rocker box alloy covers
- Single camshaft located centrally between the cylinders
- Marelli car-type distributor
- 12-volt electrics
- Wet-sump lubrication, gear-type oil pump
- One-piece aluminium crankcase
- Separate timing chest at the front of the engine, with a helical gear drive to the camshaft and oil pump

V7* 1967

Engine	Air-cooled, ohv, transverse 90 degree V-twin, two valves per cylinder, one-piece crankshaft, one-piece crankcase
Bore	80mm
Stroke	70mm
Displacement	703.717cc
Compression ratio	9:1
Lubrication	Gear pump, wet sump
Ignition	Battery/coil, with Marelli distributor
Carburation	2 × Dell'Orto SS129D/DS
Gearbox	Four-speed, foot-change
Clutch	Twin driven plates, dry, car-type
Final drive	Shaft
Frame	Duplex cradle, tubular steel
Suspension	Front, telescopic forks; rear, swinging arm, twin hydraulically damped shock absorbers
Brakes	200mm drums front and rear; front 2LS operation
Tyres	4.00 × 18 front and rear

General specification

Wheelbase	1470mm (57.8in)
Dry weight	206kg (454lb)
Fuel capacity	20ltr (4.4gal)
Maximum power output	40bhp at 5,800rpm
Top speed	102mph (164km/h)

*1st series V-twin roadster

Soon, larger engine sizes were fitted into the heavy V7 cycle parts, 757.486cc (1969) and 844.057cc (1972).

The Frame

The greatest changes in transforming the Guzzi transverse V-twin into a sports/racing motorcycle were made to the cycle parts.

Transmission System

The V7's transmission system was closer to a car than a motorcycle. Securely bolted to the rear of the crankshaft was a large diameter flywheel that also formed the housing for the dry clutch. This consisted of two friction and two plain plates, and eight springs. The clutch assembly was retained inside the flywheel by the electric starter ring gear, but was held in place by eight screws and spring washers. Passing through the centre of the clutch shaft was a single long clutch pushrod, this in turn passed through the input shaft of the gearbox to finally exit behind the clutch operating lever on the right of the gearbox.

The gearbox housing was bolted on to the rear of the crankcase. It had four speeds and was of the constant mesh, front engagement type. The mainshaft was driven by the driving gear on the clutch shaft. All four gears were fixed to the mainshaft – in other words – a one-piece assembly.

The Layshaft

The layshaft was provided with four separate engagement gears, two sliding sleeves and also carried the speedo drive gear. The gears were selected directly by a traditional Italian heel-and-toe job on the outside. This pedal controlled the selector shaft which had a toothed sector in mesh with a gear on the selector drum. The drum carried a series of grooves in which the selector mechanism ran, so that its position, and the position of the gears that it selected on the layshaft, was governed by the rotation of the selector. In the drum were five holes, one for each gear, plus neutral; and a spring-loaded pawl ensured that it was positively located in each of the positions in turn as the gear lever was operated. This pawl was drilled and operated additionally as a gearbox breather.

Shaft Final Drive

Final drive was by Cardan shaft and bevel gears, another feature that displayed its military and police background. This took the drive from the rear of the gearbox via splines on the end of the gearbox layshaft that connected to a universal joint running in a $28 \times 58 \times 16$mm ball race housed in the end of the swinging arm. The exposed section between the swinging arm and the rear of the gearbox was protected by a rubber gaiter to accommodate the suspension movement. Inside the swinging arm, the universal joint mated up with the drive shaft which ran in a pair of $25 \times 52 \times 16.25$mm ball races, one at each end. At the rear, this was splined to the bevel drive pinion inside the rear drive box, an aluminium casting filled with EP90 oil to lubricate the drive. The crown wheel was meshed directly with the pinion, and mated up with the rear wheel through an internally-toothed sleeve in the rear hub. The rear wheel could be removed without the need to disturb the drive, simply by removing the wheel spindle and spacer which kept the wheel centred and in mesh.

Running Gear

The 1960s V7 chassis clearly displayed its government specification origins by way of a massive and extremely heavy duplex cradle steel tubular frame and equally robust swinging arm. One side of the swinging arm contained the drive shaft and carried a mounting for the rear bevel drive box. Because of the drive shaft, a conventional swinging-arm pin could not be used, so two separate, part-threaded stub spindles were employed on either side of the swinging-arm pivot. These ran on $17 \times 40 \times 12$mm taper roller bearings sealed from the outside by oil seals. Side play could easily be taken up by screwing the stub spindles in to tension the bearings.

Other components of the original V7 series included: Marzocchi fully enclosed telescopic front forks with 35mm (1.37in) stanchions and full-width 220mm (8.66in) drum brakes, with a 2LS front and SLS at the rear.

Early Transverse V-Twin Development

Last of the heavyweight V7 series, the GT850 was the first bike to have the 844cc engine size, later fitted to the Le Mans model.

Tonti's Project

The V7 Sport was the work of Ing. Lino Tonti, who had joined Moto Guzzi in 1970, effectively replacing Carcano who had retired. Tonti had previously worked for such companies as Aermacchi, Bianchi and Gilera. He had also played a major role in the birth of Paton and the Linto (the latter, a pair of Aermacchi cylinders in a common crankcase).

Tonti's first project for his new employers had been to enlarge the V7 engine from 703 to 757cc (and later to 844cc). As the creator of several pure Grand Prix-type racing motorcycles, his opinion was that pure increases in engine displacement were secondary to resolving the V7's biggest drawback – the sheer bulk and weight of its chassis.

He was less than enthusiastic about the existing, distinctly touring, heavyweight character of the V7, which was at odds with his view of just what a motorcycle should be like – both in terms of rider appeal and road behaviour. So Tonti turned his engineering skills to creating the Guzzi V-twin in his own mould – one that was lower, lighter, sleeker, faster and with better handling than its forebears.

The first problem Tonti encountered was the height of the engine between the vee of the cylinders. This was due to the position taken up by the belt-driven generator atop the crankcase, reflected by the exceedingly tall timing cover casting at the front of the engine.

This particular problem was solved by substituting the top-mounted generator with a Bosch G1 (R) 14V 13A 19 alternator, which was fitted directly at the front of the crankshaft. Changes to the design of the timing cover substantially reduced the overall height along the centre line of the engine, allowing the entire bike to be reconstructed in a lower, lighter and obviously much more sporting manner.

Created by Lino Tonti, it was the 1971 V7 Sport that really set Guzzi up in the sporting and racing side of things once again. Alan Walsh is seen here racing his V7 Sport at Brands Hatch, 6 August 1972.

The result was to be a true classic, one of the most beautifully efficient motorcycles constructed up to that time – at least for series production.

The newcomer was clearly stamped with Tonti's own commitment, not just to its design, but its testing too. This is clearly illustrated by the now classic tale of the man himself testing a prototype and crashing – breaking a leg in the process! How many designers today would actually get out there and ride, let alone carry out their own testing? The phrase blood, sweat and tears springs to mind in Tonti's case.

V7 Sport

The V7 Sport, probably the most important Guzzi series production bike of the post-war era made its public début at the Milan Show in November 1971. Essentially, this used a tuned version of the V7 engine which displaced just under 750cc and had the advantage of a five-speed gearbox.

Although never mass produced in the true sense of the word, the first V7 Sports for general sale began to leave the factory in early 1972. As well as the sports-minded road rider, the V7 Sport also found favour for long-distance racing, its strength being particularly appreciated both by works-supported and private riders alike.

There was little change throughout the model's production run. Although for the 1973 season the striking metallic lime green and Italian Racing Red gave way to a much more reserved finish of a red tank and panels with the remainder (including the frame) in black. The stock 'as supplied' mudguards remained in stainless steel.

Bikes for the American market were delivered with left-hand change and electric, instead of manually operated, fuel taps as standard equipment. Another difference between the European and American markets was that the V7 Sport was available in the USA throughout 1974, whereas in Europe it was superseded by a new machine.

Engine Design

As well as using an alternator in place of the dynamo, the other significant engine alteration was a change in displacement. The new capacity was 748.388cc, achieved by reducing the bore from 83mm on the 757cc engine down to 82.5mm, whilst the stroke remained unchanged at 70mm. The main reason for this move was to take advantage of the newly introduced FIM Formula 750 (Superbike) regulations, which limited all motorcycles taking part to a maximum of 750cc, irrespective of the number of cylinders. To achieve this level of performance a number of engine tuning measures were needed. These were as follows:

- Higher compression, four-ring pistons with a ratio of 9.8:1
- Fiercer cam profiles
- A pair of coil valve springs
- 30mm Dell'Orto square slide VHB carburettors

These changes resulted in power output rising to 52bhp at 6,300rpm (measured at the rear wheel). As with other V7 series motorcycles, the aluminium cylinder bores were chrome plated, and as before, this meant that pistons were offered in three matched sizes (relevant to cylinder bore measurement). For the V7 Sport, these were:

- Class 'A' 82.500 – 82.506mm
- Class 'B' 82.506 – 82.512mm
- Class 'C' 82.512 – 82.516mm

V7 Sport 1972

Engine	Air-cooled, ohv, transverse 90 degree V-twin, two valves per cylinder, one-piece crankshaft, one-piece crank-case, two-piece connecting-rods, plain bearing big ends
Bore	82.5mm
Stroke	70mm
Displacement	748.4cc
Compression ratio	9.8:1
Lubrication	Gear pump, wet sump
Ignition	Battery/coil, with Marelli distributor
Carburation	2 × Dell'Orto VHB 30CD/CS
Gearbox	Five-speed, foot-change
Clutch	Twin driven plates, dry, car-type
Final drive	Shaft
Frame	Duplex cradle, removable bottom members
Suspension	Front, telescopic forks; rear, swinging-arm twin hydraulically damped shock absorber
Brakes	Front, dual drum 220mm twin leading shoe operation; rear, drum 220mm 2LS
Tyres	Front 3.25 × 18; rear 3.50 × 18

General specification

Wheelbase	1470mm (57.8in)
Dry weight	206kg (453lb)
Fuel capacity	22.5ltr (4.9gal)
Maximum power output	53bhp at 6,300rpm
Top speed	119mph (191km/h) or 129mph (206km/h) with factory race kit

Endurance Racing

Monza, on the outskirts of Milan, was the venue for a 310-mile (500km) endurance race in June 1971. Guzzi supported a factory-backed team comprising Raimondo Riva and the Brambrilla brothers, Vittorio and Ernesto, plus newcomers Gino Carena and Luciano Gazzola. The motorcycles they used were specially prepared V7 Sport models. Not only did the team enjoy considerable success in this début event, but they went on to rack up a string of wins and places throughout Italy in the months that followed.

Like rivals Ducati and Laverda, Guzzi's arrival on the endurance scene enabled them to develop and test ideas that would otherwise have been much more difficult. Like the V7 Sport, endurance racing was to have a considerable impact upon the famous Le Mans model.

The Barcelona 24-hour race of May 1973 that heralded Ducati's prototype 860cc V-twin also saw Moto Guzzi make an equally important entry. This bike was based on the existing V7 Sport, but with the engine displacement increased to 844.957cc (83 × 78mm), as first employed on the GT850 Tourer which had débuted a few months earlier.

But unlike the GT, the newcomer was a pure-bred sportster. And unknown to observers at the time, the Barcelona prototype was the very first Le Mans. Raimondo Riva and Luciano Gazzola put up a good performance to complete the distance, coming home an impressive fifth in the overall rankings. Compared with the winning Ducati's record-setting 720 laps, the Guzzi completed 683 circuits of the tortuous Montjuich Park course.

After this successful début the factory continued to support endurance racing at international level until it quit at the end of 1975. By then the groundwork had already been laid for the entry into production of the Le Mans, so the need to race in such events had gone.

Production Racing

Right from the very first V7 Sport series, the Guzzi V-twin has been used in sports machine racing (more commonly known as production racing).

Both at home and elsewhere in Europe, the V7 Sport competed successfully in the early 1970s against bikes such as the BMW R75, Honda CB750, Kawasaki Mach 3 500, Norton Commando, Triumph Trident and BSA Rocket 3.

In 1974, rivals to the 750S included the Ducati 750 Sport/750SS, Laverda SFC, Kawasaki Z1 and BMW R90S.

In the 1975 Isle of Man TT, one of the newly released 750S3 models, ridden by the RAF Motor Sports Association pairing of John Goodall and Dave Featherstone came home a highly credible fifth against a huge entry including Honda, Kawasaki, Laverda, BMW, Benelli, Norton and Triumph machinery.

The production race at Daytona in the spring of 1976 saw more Guzzi success when Mike Baldwin aboard expatriate Reno Leoni's brand-new Le Mans scored an impressive fifth behind the Butler & Smith entered, factory-supported BMW R90S models of winner Reg Pridmore and runner-up Steve McLaughlin, Cook Neilson (Ducati 900SS) and Wes Cooley (Kawasaki Z900).

The same year also saw Guzzi make a brief return to the endurance scene, with a semi-works Le Mans, but with a 948.813cc (88 × 78mm) engine size, in the Barcelona 24-hour race. Ridden by Giuseppe Gazzola and Raimondo Riva, the bike came home ninth, with 701 laps completed. The winners, the British pairing of Stanley Woods and Charlie Williams (riding a works Honda) completed 741 laps.

In September, Gazzola together with a new partner, Alberto Rusconi, finished fifteenth in the French Bol d'Or, with Riva, now partnered by Davide Levieux, coming one place further down the field, in this, the most famous of all endurance races.

Like the previous year, 1977 began with Baldwin recording another fifth place on Leoni's Le Mans in the Daytona Production event (now referred to in the programme as 'Superbike Production'). Although the paper result remained unchanged from 1976, Baldwin's performance was of a higher level, coming through from the back of the field to catch the previous year's winner, Reg Pridmore (980cc BMW), and even though Pridmore eventually overtook the Guzzi rider, the verdict was by the narrowest of margins.

Early Transverse V-Twin Development

Tonti chose the best features of the various V7 series models to provide the best package. So, together with the recently announced 850, the V7 Sport benefited from a five-speed gearbox. In fact, this additional ratio had been created very much with the sportster in mind, rather than the other way around. As with the earlier versions of the V7, the gears themselves were helical cut, mainly, Guzzi claimed 'in the interests of quieter operation'.

The Frame

If the power unit formed an integral part of Tonti's design strategy, then it was the balance of the bike's specification that really set the V7 Sport apart from its touring brothers. This was due to the simply stunning lines – and why the newcomer was such a hit.

Lean, low, racy – it was a style that is as much loved today as it was when the original V7 Sport made its bow at the Milan Show in November 1971. It was not simply the flagship of the Moto Guzzi range, but also the pride of the entire Italian motorcycle industry. Almost thirty-five years later, its brilliance has not dimmed, such was its initial impact. Matching the stunning looks was an equally breathtaking paint job of metallic lime green for the handsomely sculpted 22.5ltr (4.95gal) fuel tank, and the equally eye-catching angular side panels. The V7 Sport's double-cradle frame was in an equally bright hue, this time in Italian Racing Red; the two colours contrasting perfectly.

The bike's length contributed to the low, sleek looks, but it was the exceptionally low seat height of a mere 750mm (29.5 in) that helped most. The frame and swinging arm

A works-prepared V7 Sport during the Dutch Zolder 24 Hours, 19–20 August 1972. Riders Raimondo Riva and Gino Carena lasted the distance. Note the non-standard twin disc front brake, later fitted as standard to the 750S/S3 and Le Mans.

Early Transverse V-Twin Development

consisted of near-straight steel tubing and the layout was masterful, resulting in a design that was to remain largely unchanged until the early 1990s and the arrival of the Daytona (see Chapter 14). Also new were the front forks, which were of Moto Guzzi's own design and manufacture and incorporated internal sealed damper assemblies – again a feature that was to endure over the years.

With such a low-slung frame, accessibility might have suffered, but this was not the case. The layout of the new frame included fully detachable bottom rails.

Drum Brakes Retained

Although the 220mm (8.6in) drum brakes were retained from the earlier models, the front was now double-sided, each having twin leading-shoe operation. This innovation, together with the machine's reduced weight (down from 234kg on the original V7 to 206kg) removed one of the major criticisms of the V7 series, poor braking performance.

Swan-Neck Clip-Ons

A feature of the V7 Sport to receive universal praise was the clip-on handlebars. These allowed a myriad of adjustments both fore and aft, up and down – one of the very few sports/racing machines to provide a stance to suit every size of rider.

The electrical equipment was a mixture of German Bosch (alternator, regulator, rectifier, starter motor) and local Marelli (distributor with twin contact breakers and condensers, dual ignition coils).

Jack Findlay riding one of three works 750cc Guzzis in the Imola 200-Miler on 23 April 1972. Prepared in just six weeks, the bikes finished eighth, tenth, and eleventh proving their reliability against the best bikes in the world.

750 Sport 1974	
Engine	Air-cooled, ohv, transverse 90 degree V-twin, two valves per cylinder, one-piece crankshaft, one-piece crank-case, two-piece connecting-rods, plain bearing big ends
Bore	82.5mm
Stroke	70mm
Displacement	748.4cc
Compression ratio	9.8:1
Lubrication	Gear pump, wet sump
Ignition	Battery/coil, with Marelli distributor
Carburation	2 × Dell'Orto VHB 30 CD/CS
Gearbox	Five-speed, foot-change
Clutch	Twin driven plates, dry, car-type
Final drive	Shaft
Frame	Duplex cradle, removable bottom members
Suspension	Front, telescopic front forks; rear, swinging-arm twin hydraulically damped shock absorbers
Brakes	Front, dual 300mm discs with two-piston Brembo calipers; rear, 220mm 2LS drum
Tyres	Front 3.25 H18; rear 3.50 H18
General specification	
Wheelbase	1470mm (57.8in)
Dry weight	206kg (454lb)
Fuel capacity	22.5ltr (4.9 gal)
Maximum power output	53bhp at 6,300rpm
Top speed	119mph (191km/h) or 129mph (206km/h) with factory race kit

750S

This 'new' machine was the 750S. And although clearly based on the original, there were nonetheless several important engineering and styling differences. The engine's big change was the replacement of the original timing gears by a chain and sprockets. The major reason for this was one of cost, and the 750S is important in the evolution of the Guzzi transverse V-twin series, because of this. The main change to the cycle parts was the replacement of the massive 220mm double-sided 2LS (actually a 4LS device) drum front brake by a pair of hydraulically operated 300mm (11.8in) cast-iron Brembo discs. Situated next to the front brake lever on the off-side of the handlebars was a master cylinder with a metal screw cap, which was connected by hydraulic hoses to the callipers carried at the front of each fork slider.

Another difference, at least for non-Americans, was that the gear lever was now on the left. The seat was exchanged for a new, more racy style featuring a bump-stop (this coming in place of the full dual seat as found on the V7 Sport). Matt black was now specified instead of bright chrome plate on the Lanfranconi-made silencers, although the H-section (balance pipe) under the engine and the exhaust header pipes remained in chrome.

For the first time, a hydraulic steering damper was fitted as standard equipment.

Factory Race Kit

The factory claimed a maximum speed of 130mph (209km/h), but neither the 750S nor its predecessor the V7 Sport were actually capable of this in 'as delivered' guise. The true figures were just over 10mph (16km/h) slower. However, if you needed more go for the street – or wished to go racing, a factory-supplied race kit was available. This kit,

Early Transverse V-Twin Development

1974 750S with twin discs at the front and a change from gears to a chain and sprockets at the front of the engine.

produced for Formula 750 events was made up as follows:

- Full race camshaft
- 36mm Dell'Orto PHF carburettors
- Straight cut close ratio gears
- Open, unrestricted exhaust system

To make full use of these components it was also necessary to have the cylinder heads ported and gas-flowed, the crankshaft dynamically balanced and the remainder of the engine components blueprinted. With a full fairing fitted, maximum speed then rose to between 132 and 134mph (212.4 and 215.6 km/h).

750S3

The final version of the 750 series of the 1970s was launched (together with the 850T3 touring bike) in spring 1975. The newcomer, known as the 750S3, looked much the same as the 750S and was even finished in the same colour scheme (black, with angled flashes on the tank and panels in either green, red or orange). In fact, there were several differences. Mechanically, the S3 owed more to the 850T3 than the 750S.

When *Motor Cycle* tester John Nutting put an S3 through its paces soon after its launch in 1975, he achieved a mean (two-way) figure of 114.2mph (183.7 km/h). But, as with the earlier sporting 750s, this performance could easily be bettered by fitting the factory's race kit.

There is no doubt that the launch of the 850 Le Mans a few months later effectively killed off the 750S3, but in many ways it was still an excellent sports and racing motorcycle that brought the benefits of the triple disc, linked brake system to the market first (together with

Early Transverse V-Twin Development

750S3 1975

Engine	Air-cooled ohv transverse 90 degree V-twin, two valves per cylinder, one-piece crankshaft, one-piece crank-case, two-piece connecting-rods, plain bearing big ends	Frame	Duplex cradle, removable bottom members
		Suspension	Front, telescopic forks; rear, swinging-arm twin hydraulically damped shock absorbers
Bore	82.5mm	Brakes	Front, dual 300mm discs; rear, single 242mm disc
Stroke	70mm	Tyres	Front, 3.25 H18; rear, 3.50 H18
Displacement	748.4cc		
Compression ratio	9.8:1	**General specification**	
Lubrication	Gear pump, wet sump	Wheelbase	1470mm (57.8in)
Ignition	Battery/coil, with Marelli distributor	Dry weight	208kg (458lb)
		Fuel capacity	22.5ltr (4.9gal)
Carburation	2 × Dell'Orto VHB 30CD/CS	Maximum power output	53bhp at 6,300rpm
Gearbox	Five-speed, foot-change		
Clutch	Twin driven plates, dry, car-type	Top speed	119mph (191km/h) or 129mph (206km/h) with factory race kit
Final drive	Shaft		

The first Guzzi 90 degree V-twin to appear on the British classic racing scene was this 750S3-based racer campaigned during the mid-1980s by Mark Wellings.

161

Mark Wellings in action on his 750S3-based racer at West Raynham, Norfolk on 27 September 1987.

the 850T3). This system was usually modified for racing purposes by converting it back to a conventional front brake twin disc and rear brake single disc function (the linked system operated largely by the rear brake pedal – to the rear disc and one of the front discs, whilst the front brake lever only operated a single disc at the front wheel).

Engine Design

In the engine room the only 'S' components were:

- Cylinder barrels
- Piston assemblies
- Carburettors/manifolds
- Crankshaft
- Clutch flywheel

The rest of the power drive chain was pure T3. The cylinder heads were T3 castings that retained the exhaust header pipes by means of bolt-up clamps rather than the threaded ring nuts of the earlier 750 vees, this meant new exhaust header pipes (shaped as per V7 Sport/750S) were required. This was a good move for potential owners, because the original retaining nuts had a nasty habit of working loose. Left unchecked this can lead to a damaged cylinder head casting.

Guzzi factory at Mandello del Lario as it was during the mid-1970s.

162

13 The Le Mans Series

Named after the legendary French race circuit, the Le Mans was the definitive Moto Guzzi sports/racing bike of the late 1970s and early 1980s. It was built over a longer period than any other Guzzi V-twin except the California tourer. However, when production really did get underway in spring 1975, they simply flew out of the dealers' doors.

With something of a laid-back, almost lazy, power delivery, the Le Mans often fooled even the most experienced of road testers into believing that it was somewhat lacking in performance. But as results were to prove, in production sports machine racing the Guzzi could beat the best there was out on the circuit.

Certainly, it ruled the roost from its introduction until the end of the 1970s, when newcomers such as the Suzuki GS1000 finally defeated it through sheer power. However, until this occurred, machines such as the Honda CB750 (in its various guises),

Roy Armstrong heels his Le Mans over around Snetterton's Coram Curve on his way to winning the final race and the 1977 Avon Production series Championship.

The Le Mans Series

Kawasaki 900 and 1000, Laverda Jota, Ducati 750 and 900 Super Sports were simply blown away by a well-prepared, well-ridden Le Mans.

The Guzzi also scored highly in long-distance endurance events, thanks to its combination of speed, reliability, low fuel consumption and good handling.

The Prototype

As described in Chapter 12, a prototype of the Le Mans was track-tested at no less an event than the Barcelona 24-hour race in July 1973. Riders Raimondo Riva and Giuseppe Gazzola finished fifth in a hotly contested test of endurance, performance, reliability and riding skill.

However, this exercise was very much part of an extended development and test period and the first series production model, the Le Mans 1, did not make its public bow for another two and a half years.

Le Mans Mark 1

When the production model arrived at the Milan Show in November 1975, it was known simply as the Le Mans and although clearly aimed at the sporting road rider, it also had a second role, that of a bike which could be successfully raced, thanks to a factory race kit. To many enthusiasts this original model was not only the best of the Le Mans breed, but also the finest Italian sporting motorcycle of its era. Of course, it could be argued that the Ducati 900 Super Sport was a rawer bike, or that the Laverda Jota was faster, but as an all-round machine the Le Mans was hard to beat, as its performance proved in subsequent production racing events including the prestigious and highly competitive British Avon Tyres series.

The Design

Technically, the sportster drew heavily on both the 750S3 and 850T3. In fact the 844cc (83 × 78mm) engine, together with the transmission were lifted from the T3, but given additional tuning.

To achieve the required additional power output, the Le Mans featured higher compression (10.2:1) pistons; larger valves (37mm exhaust, 44mm inlet); a more sporting

850 Le Mans 1 1976

Engine	Air-cooled, ohv, transverse, 90 degree V-twin, four-stroke, two valves per cylinder, ohv with pushrod operated valves, coil valve springs
Bore	83mm
Stroke	78mm
Displacement	844.057mm
Compression ratio	10.2:1
Lubrication	Gear-type pump
Ignition	Battery/coil with twin contact breaker points
Carburation	2 × Dell'Orto PHF 36
Gearbox	Five-speed, foot-change
Clutch	Double plate, dry
Final drive	Shaft
Frame	All-steel construction, tubular cradle
Suspension	Front, Moto Guzzi telescopic front fork with 38mm stanchions; rear, swinging arm, twin shock absorbers
Brakes	Front, dual disc 30mm; rear, single disc 242mm
Tyres	Front 3.50 H18; rear 4.00 H18

General specification

Wheelbase	1505mm (59.25in)
Dry weight	196kg (43lb)
Fuel capacity	22.5ltr (4.9gal)
Maximum power output	71bhp at 7,300rpm
Top speed	124mph (200km/h) or 134mph (215km/h) with factory race kit

The Le Mans Series

Avon Series

The Avon Production series – sponsored by the Avon Tyre Company of Melksham, Wiltshire was without question the premier British production-based sports machine racing event of the 1970s.

In 1976 the series was won by Pete 'PK' Davies riding for Laverda importer Roger Slater, backed up by Roger Winterburn on another Jota. But during 1977 the balance of success switched to Moto Guzzi.

Riding a 1976 Le Mans Mark 1, Manchester rider Roy Armstrong began the season with victory in the first round and went on to become the new champion.

Together with his younger brother Ian, both rode a pair of virtually stock Le Mans models throughout that year. Only towards the end of the year, when the competition grew hotter were special parts fitted, such as higher compression pistons, a B10 camshaft, racing valve springs, lightened and polished valve gear and a modified exhaust. The 1977 Avon series winning bike retained the stock 36mm Dell'Orto pumper carburettors. But, like several Le Mans machines used on the track, the linked brake system had been axed in place of conventional hydraulics.

Contrary to reports at the time, both the Armstrong bikes had been bought and paid for by the brothers, even though Roy worked as a mechanic for the Manchester-based Sports Motorcycles, headed by Steve Wynne. The director John Sear (a well-known

John Sear winning the Cadwell Park round of the 1977 Avon series on his Le Mans.

racer in his own right), also took part in the series riding a Le Mans. This bike, however, was very much more highly tuned; featuring as it did a 950 conversion from the V1000.

With the race kit, this machine was tested by *Motor Cycle* at 132.01mph (212.4 km/h), but the rider, John Nutting, had to sit up for half the length of the straight where the timing equipment was installed to prevent the engine over-revving in top gear. The standing start quarter-mile was achieved in 11.8 seconds with a terminal speed of 112.24mph (180.59km/h).

Other riders to campaign the Le Mans in the Avon series included Richard Gamble and Doug Lunn.

An interesting aside is that Sports Motorcycles claimed to have ordered a factory-prepared engine together with a consignment of racing parts, but the story goes that Luton-based importers Coburn & Hughes held this back for most of that year.

The following year, 1978, saw the rules for the Avon championship revised. One of the main features was to restrict the competition to competitors retaining their original cubic capacity (in Guzzis case, the Le Mans was therefore limited to 844cc). Compared with rivals such as the Laverda, Suzuki and Kawasaki, this meant having to give away some 150cc.

This rule change effectively put the Guzzi (and the 864cc Ducati) at an obvious disadvantage. And it was not just in Britain where things got tougher (*see* Coupe D'Endurance page 170).

Le Mans rider Richard Gamble racing in the Avon Production series at Croft in 1977. His machine used the 948cc engine size from the V1000 Convert model to provide more horsepower.

Le Mans-powered kneeler sidecar outfit.

camshaft profile and a pair of Dell'Orto PHF 36mm carburettors with accelerator pumps and large plastic bellmouths.

In terms of styling, the Le Mans (unofficially now referred to as a Mark 1) was a winner, and even today is regarded as being the best of the entire Le Mans series. With its clip-ons, rearset footrests, a race-style bump-stop saddle, bikini fairing, drilled brake discs, matt black frame and exhaust system, silver-finished cast-alloy wheels and a choice of colour schemes (bright red, ice blue metallic or white) the Le Mans was in the very best Italian sporting tradition. Red was by far the most popular choice – this being applied to the 22.5ltr (4.9gal) fuel tank, mudguards, sidepanels and fairing; the latter having its central section (around the headlamp) finished in a distinctive day-glo orange.

Performance

In standard ex-showroom guise, the power output was 71bhp at 7,300rpm, but with the factory race kit (including Lafranconi performance silencers) this rose to 81bhp at 7,600rpm. An open exhaust gave even more.

With the race kit fitted the maximum speed was 134mph (215.6 km/h); against 124mph (199.5 km/h) for the stock bike.

Even more performance was possible, by careful assembly (blueprinting) and also by increasing the engine size to 948.8cc (88 × 78mm) by using the cylinders from the V1000 Convert model. The stroke remained unchanged, which made the engine's dimension more short stroke than before.

Weaknesses

Generally, the Le Mans was a fast and robust bike that handled well.

However, there were a couple of notable glitches. One concerned the seat. This was a distinctive feature of the first Le Mans and should have been both a stylistic and ergonomic coup. Instead, the seat was to be one of the really poorly finished components on the entire bike. The interesting feature was the way in which it was moulded so that the nose extended over the rear of the tank, a curiously effective design that should have also enhanced rider comfort. The problem was that the whole contraption was moulded in one piece from dense foam rubber; but this was simply not robust enough for the task at hand, the result being that entire chunks could break away, particularly from the poorly supported nose section. A favourite and practical remedy was to fit a seat from the earlier 750S/S3 models.

Another component that was a source of nuisance to owners of these original Le Mans models was the battery – a puny 12-volt 20-amp hour device (compared to the 32-amp hour components on the other models).

Mark II

Even though the factory had never experienced problems selling all the Mark 1s they could build, it was still decided in early 1978 to revise the design, and so in September that year at the international biennial German Cologne Show the new model, the Mark II, was to make its début.

The most obvious change was the adoption of an SP1000-style three-piece fairing, which

The Le Mans Series

Le Mans II, which ran from 1978 through to the end of 1980.

Le Mans II 1979

Engine	Air-cooled, ohv, transverse 90 degree V-twin, two valves per cylinder, one-piece crankshaft, one-piece crank-case, two-piece connecting-rods, plain bearing big ends	Suspension	Front, telescopic forks; rear, swinging-arm twin hydraulically damped shock absorbers
		Brakes	Front, twin 300mm cast-iron Brembo discs with two-piston calipers; rear, single 242mm disc with two-piston Brembo caliper
Bore	83mm		
Stroke	78mm		
Displacement	844.057cc	Tyres	Front 3.50 H18; rear 4.10 H18
Compression ratio	10.2:1		
Lubrication	Gear pump, wet sump	**General specification**	
Ignition	Battery/coil, with Marelli distributor	Wheelbase	1470mm (57.8in)
Carburation	2 × Dell'Orto VHB 36 BS/BD	Dry weight	202kg (445lb)
Gearbox	Five-speed, foot-change	Fuel capacity	22.5ltr (4.9gal)
Clutch	Twin driven plates, dry, car-type	Maximum power output	71bhp (crankshaft) at 7,300rpm
Final drive	Shaft		
Frame	Duplex cradle, removable bottom members	Top speed	127mph (204km/h) or 136mph (219km/h) with factory race kit

167

Isle of Man TT

A little-known fact in the Guzzi racing story is that the factory officially entered the 1977 Isle of Man TT. This came about when a couple of works engines (of the Le Mans type) were shipped over with factory mechanic Bruno Scola. The engines were then fitted into the frames of Sears' and Armstrong's Le Mans production models and raced in the Formula 1 TT by Steve Tonkin and George Fogarty (father of Carl). Both riders did well during qualifying, with the engines proving both fast and reliable.

Unfortunately 1977 was a year when the Isle of Man weather was at its very worst during the TT race week, and both machines retired in truly awful weather conditions, due to sticking carburettor slides on their 40mm Dell'Orto carbs.

Both these engines sported all the factory race kit options, plus a '950' conversion, 47.5mm inlet and 39mm exhaust valves, and sintered metal clutch plates. Additionally, the bikes were equipped with higher ratio V1000 rear drive bevel gear sets (9/34 teeth) giving a ratio of 1:3.788 Because of this, it was also necessary to fit the V1000 universal joint with its extended rear section, and therefore the matching V1000 connecting tube to mate up with the rear drive bevel box assembly.

But if the Isle of Man had not been the success the factory had hoped for, they were secretly pleased with the result garnered that same year in the Avon Production series. Not only did Armstrong win on a Le Mans, but in addition Sears was third with Richard Gamble fourth.

---

endowed the Mark II with an altogether more angular stance. At the same time, it gained most of the fairing-mounted accessories from the SP model. These comprised the entire instrument layout and switchgear, including the quartz clock and voltmeter. The large, moulded rubber dashboard was suitably re-labelled with the 'Le Mans' logo.

The red paint job was as before, except that there was now more of it, whilst the frame continued to be finished in black. However, the metallic blue/grey and white options were dropped and replaced by a bright royal blue as an alternative to the ever-popular Italian racing red.

In their pre-launch publicity campaign, Guzzi claimed that the power output had been increased and the exhaust system modified. These comments later proved to be largely incorrect, as the changes were limited to cosmetic alterations, rather than anything more significant in technical terms. But even so there were a couple of worthwhile changes.

The first concerned the poorly finished single saddle. This had already received attention during 1977 for one which not only gave two-up abilities but also stayed in one piece, despite being manufactured from similar material.

Although the first batch of Mark IIs came with the original small-capacity battery, this was subsequently replaced by a more powerful 32-amp hour device from the second production batch onwards.

Other changes included the Brembo front brake callipers being relocated to the rear of the fork leg (something a lot of racers had already done with their Mark 1s).

Under test performances, figures for the fully faired Le Mans differed little from the original bikini-faired version. *Motorcycling* recorded an electronically timed 126.89mph (204.16km/h).

Modifications

During late 1980, a series of modifications were introduced for the Le Mans II. The chrome-plated cylinder bores (a feature of the V7 series and Le Mans were replaced by Nigusil (Guzzi's in-house coating process – very similar to Nikasil). However, it is worth noting that the V1000 948cc cylinder used steel liners (which several racers had fitted to their Le Mans models).

The internal fork dampers (manufactured by Lispa) were improved, and the forks converted to air-assisted operation (with valves on the fork top plugs). The rear shock absorbers were also changed, with the substitution of Paioli-made assemblies.

Special Editions for the UK and USA

At the same time, British importers Coburn & Hughes launched a UK-market only special. This was the Le Mans II in an overall black and gold livery, gold being used for the wheels, fork bottoms, and pinstriping on the black areas of the fairing, tank and side panels – altogether very much a Moto Guzzi take on the black and gold colour scheme which had proved so popular on the Ducati 900 Super Sport of the period.

It should of course be remembered that during the late 1970s and early 1980s Coburn & Hughes acted for both Ducati and Moto Guzzi in the British market. As proof of how inflation was sweeping the British economy at the time, the Le Mans II Black/Gold retailed for £2,999 in 1980 – a third more than the original Le Mans at its launch a mere four years earlier.

No Mark IIs were sold in the USA. Instead, a special USA-market model, the CX1000, was introduced in 1980 and sold until the end of 1981. This was basically a Mark II chassis with a 948cc SP engine.

Mark III

To counteract falling sales and introduce some worthwhile engineering changes, Moto Guzzi introduced the Mark III for the 1981 model year.

The Mark III was no tarted-up adaptation

Le Mans III – new bodywork, exhaust system and modified engine top end were just some of the changes.

The Le Mans Series

Le Mans III 1981

Engine	Air-cooled, ohv, transverse 90 degree V-twin, two valves per cylinder, one-piece crankshaft, one-piece crank-case, two-piece connecting-rods, plain bearing big ends
Bore	83mm
Stroke	78mm
Displacement	844.057cc
Compression ratio	9.8:1
Lubrication	Gear pump, wet sump
Ignition	Battery/coil, with Marelli distributor
Carburation	2 × Dell'Orto PHF 36 BS/BD
Gearbox	Five-speed, foot-change
Clutch	Twin driven plates, dry, car-type
Final drive	Shaft
Frame	Duplex cradle, removable bottom members
Suspension	Front, telescopic forks; rear, swinging-arm twin hydraulically damped shock absorbers
Brakes	Front, twin 300mm cast-iron Brembo discs with two-piston calipers; rear, single 242mm disc with two-piston Brembo caliper
Tyres	Front 100/90 V18; rear 110/90 V18

General specification

Wheelbase	1505mm (59.25in)
Dry weight	206kg (453lb)
Fuel capacity	25ltr (5.5gal)
Maximum power output	76bhp (crankshaft) at 7,700rpm
Top speed	135mph (217km/h) or 144mph (231km/h) with factory race kit

Coupe D'Endurance

During the early 1970s (*see* Chapter 12) both the factory and privateers campaigned the 750 Guzzi V-twins with considerable success in the long-distance races of the day. During the late 1970s, with the arrival of the Le Mans, the process was repeated.

In the 1977 FIM Coupe d'Endurance series, the Le Mans was the highest placed Guzzi in any of the rounds, ridden by the Spanish team of A. Perez Rubio and Carlos Morante at Barcelona.

It was during that same year that British competitors at last began to take the Guzzi V-twin seriously as a suitable mount for both endurance and short-circuit events. One of the first was Jim Wells, son of the well-known east London dealer Fred Wells. Jim, who shared with co-rider Tony Osbourne, developed a specially constructed home-built endurance racer using a heavily modified 750S3 engine housed in a one-off cantilever frame. Early gremlins included a series of punctures, a snapped crankshaft and oil breather problems. In fact it was not until the 1977 European Endurance Championship at Thruxton that they actually finished a race.

During the same year the Oxford Fairings team of Doug Lunn and John Goodall also campaigned Guzzis in long-distance races. The former rider (who was employed by Guzzi importers Coburn & Hughes in their Luton retail showroom) used the Oxford-sponsored bike – a race-kitted Le Mans I – in the four lap, 151-mile (243km) Isle of Man TT Formula 1 race, in which he came home in fourteenth position, averaging 86.99mph (139.97km/h).

The Oxford Fairings Le Mans was entirely stock, with the exception of the factory race kit (allowed in the rules). This kit comprised open Lafranconi exhausts, 40mm Dell'Orto carbs, racing camshaft and close ratio gears. The bike also had a new fairing (non Guzzi) and modified brake system. The latter saw the linked braking set-up ditched in favour of conventional hydraulics with a separate master cylinder. The Oxford Fairings bike was electronically timed (during the TT period) at just over 138mph (222km/h).

The cylinder barrels, heads and rocker covers, plus internal components for the valve gear internals were new on the Le Mans III.

of the previous two versions, instead it was very much a design in its own right. These changes were quite extensive, particularly to the engine.

Most noticeable were the new, square-finned cylinder heads and matching Nigusil cylinder barrels. Fundamentals such as the camshaft profile and valve sizes remained unchanged, even though the compression ratio was actually reduced (from 10.2 to 8:1). In the interests of improved low-speed running and torque, the power output was improved by a full 3bhp, whilst engine torque increased to 7.6kg/m at 6,200. This increase came about due to:

- Superior machine tooling giving improved operating tolerances.
- The use of aluminium rocker supports (which also reduced tappet noise).
- Improved air filtration and exhaust systems.

The latter was in fact the first from a European motorcycle to fully meet the stringent EEC regulation CEE 78.1015. The double-skinned exhaust header pipes and mufflers were now finished in sparkling chrome plate.

The fairing was entirely new and benefited from Guzzi's own wind tunnel test facilities. Although considerably smaller than the one fitted to the Mark II, it was much more aerodynamic. There was also a form of spoiler offering deflection of air current underneath the fuel tank and the top of the cylinder heads.

On the newly designed instrument console, pride of place went to a 100mm Veglia rev counter. This was flanked by a smaller diameter speedometer (also from Veglia) on the right, a voltmeter on the left, and rows of idiot lights below.

Together with either a red or silver paint job (including colour-coded fork bottom legs, the fuel tank had been enlarged to 25ltr (5.5 gal). The styling of both this and other bodywork reflected the new angular cylinder heads and

171

barrels. This gave the Mark III a more muscular, but attractive appearance.

Mark IV (1000)

Le Mans 1000 (Mark IV) was launched in late 1984. Technical changes not only included the larger 948.8cc (88 × 78mm) engine dimensions but other important improvements.

The valves were both increased in diameter by 3mm over the outgoing 850 engine, to 47mm (1.8in) inlet and 44mm (1.7in) exhaust. The compression ratio was increased to 10:1. Also specified were larger Dell'Orto carburettors (PHM 40mm) and new exhaust pipes of the same diameter.

The mufflers (still manufactured by Lafranconi – who were also based in Mandello del Lario) were different from the outgoing Mark III type. And both these and the header and balance pipes were finished in gloss-black chrome.

All these changes added up to an increase in power – 85bhp (at the crankshaft) – and maximum speed rising to 141mph (226.9 km/h), a 10mph (16 km/h) increase over the Mark III. With tuning this meant that 150mph (241km/h) was within reach.

Unfortunately just when this should have put Guzzi back on par with the opposition they made a serious blunder. This concerned the use of a 16in front wheel (the rear stayed at 18in). This followed a trend set by the Japanese. Perhaps it might just have worked for the latest ultra-quick steering Japanese fours, but on the long and narrow Guzzi it was an absolute disaster. And even though Guzzi finally saw sense and reverted to an 18in front wheel in 1987, the damage by then had been done, and the Le Mans never really recovered its former position as a serious sportster.

Various special editions were built, but sales remained slow, and it remained basically unchanged except for minor details and colour details. It was finally phased out of production during 1991 to make way for the forthcoming four valves per cylinder Daytona, which was launched at the Milan Show later that year.

Le Mans 1000 IV 1985

Engine	Air-cooled, ohv, transverse 90 degree V-twin, two valves per cylinder, one-piece crankshaft, one-piece crank-case, two-piece connecting-rods, plain bearing big ends
Bore	88mm
Stroke	78mm
Displacement	948.813cc
Compression ratio	10:1
Lubrication	Gear pump, wet sump
Ignition	Battery/coil, with Marelli distributor
Carburation	2 × Dell'Orto 40 ND/N6
Gearbox	Five-speed, foot-change
Clutch	Twin driven plates, dry, car-type
Final drive	Shaft
Frame	Duplex cradle, removable bottom members
Suspension	Front, telescopic forks; rear, swinging-arm twin hydraulically damped shock absorbers
Brakes	Front, twin 270mm cast-iron Brembo discs with two-piston callipers; rear, single 270mm disc with two-piston calliper
Tyres	Front 120/80 V16; rear 130/80 V18

General specification

Wheelbase	1500mm (59in)
Dry weight	215kg (474lb)
Fuel capacity	25ltr (5.5gal)
Maximum power output	86bhp at 7,500rpm
Top speed	141mph (230km/h) or 150mph (241km/h) with factory race kit

The Le Mans Series

Battle of the Twins

Twins racing began in the USA at the beginning of the 1980s. One of the most popular events at the annual Daytona Bike Week, Battle of the Twins (BOTT) was fiercely contested with home-grown Harley-Davidsons taking on Ducati, BMW, Triumph and Moto Guzzi. The first two competitors to enter Guzzis in BOTT events were John Treasauro (Le Mans), and the Californian Frank Mazur on the ex-Reno Leoni/Mike Baldwin 1970s Superbike Production class Le Mans-based machine.

The BOTT race on 9 March 1984, in the Heavyweight Modified section, saw racing history created when a woman, Sherry Frindus from Gainsville, Florida, scored a surprise victory. It was the first ever by a woman in an American Motorcycle Association (AMA) road race and on a Guzzi at that.

BOTT was introduced to British racing fans in 1983 via the *Motorcycle Enthusiast*-backed national series. The first Guzzi to make an appearance was a superb Le Mans ridden by its owner/builder, Richard Gamble, the same rider who had finished fourth in the 1977 Avon Tyres Production series. Gamble had been drawn back to racing simply because of the new twins series.

In 1984, a 750S3 V-twin made its début in classic racing. The rider, Mark Wellings, went on to achieve considerable success over the following years at Classic Racing Motorcycle Club (CRMC) events.

Another rider who made something of a return to racing was Roy Armstrong. A Guzzi dealer himself by now (Italsport Manchester), he was back in action with a virtually stock Le Mans 1000; notably at the BOTT Championship series during 1986 and 1987.

The British Twins series received a major boost for 1988 from the introduction of more sponsorship monies; *Motorcycle Enthusiast* being joined by Dunlop Tyres.

After three rounds in the 1988 series (Cadwell Park, Thruxton and Donington Park) Peter Warden was in the lead, riding the Clarke Brothers 920cc Guzzi. This was a pretty special bike with many tuning parts, including some from Dr John Wittner, the American tuner who was subsequently to play a major role in the birth of the Daytona model (*see* Chapter 14). Dr John's goodies included pistons, valve springs, connecting-rods and camshafts. Bob and Chris Clarke were the men behind Warden's machines. From the very beginning this was no standard model. Instead, in co-operation

Cologne International Motor Cycle Show, September 1986 and this 1000 Le Mans race bike had just won the German Twins racing series.

with Guzzi specialist Amadeo Castellani (*see* Chapter 14), the machine was subject to much work and special parts.

The first outing to Snetterton took place over two days and as each race progressed so Warden became more acquainted with the Guzzi's handling and he went on to score a fifth, a second, and two third places from four starts. This came against top class opposition including four-times TTF2 World Champion Tony Rutter and Tony Moran on Ducati V-twins.

After more tuning over the closed season, the Clarke Guzzi was put on the dyno by Castellani and put out 85bhp (at the rear wheel). This paid off, and after four rounds of the 1988 British BOTT series, Warden held a 13-point lead in the championship race. Warden was also leading the Norman Hyde and ACU Star 750cc Production series (the latter on a Suzuki GSX-R).

Then came disaster; whilst racing the Japanese bike at Cadwell Park, Warden suffered what was to turn out to be a fatal accident. As the series organizer, Gordon Anderson, was later to recall, Warden was a very special rider: 'He was one of the most likeable racers I ever met and one who showed a remarkable talent and smooth technique belying his three years racing experience'.

The next rider to race the Clarke Guzzi was Ian Cobby, winning many races and championships on the bike. After 1993 Cobby and the Clarke brothers switched to a Ducati, mainly because by this time the Ducati franchise had become a major part of the Chris Clarke Motorcycles business. Ducati's gain was Guzzi's loss.

The Le Mans Series

Roy Armstrong with his Le Mans 1000 at the national Battle of the Twins series in Scarborough, 1987.

However, the Mark IV engine was a competitive lump in the popular 1980s race series Battle of the Twins (BOTT) on both sides of the Atlantic. And some Mark IVs were successfully converted into competitive racers – usually with special frames and pukka racing components such as brakes and suspension.

But the days of the stock Le Mans in its original role as a production sports racing motorcycle were over.

Nonetheless, the name Le Mans still has an aura not shared in quite the same way by any of the other series production two valves per cylinder Guzzi V-twins, such was the impact of the original when it arrived in the mid-1970s.

14 The Modern Era

The Daytona Arrives

After the glorious days of the 1970s when a succession of sporting Guzzi transverse V-twins came on stream (V7 Sport, 750S, 750S3 and finally the Le Mans), the 1980s was a decade when the great Moto Guzzi marque stagnated, with some informed observers even predicting the demise of this once great name.

But survive it did, and every Guzzi enthusiast breathed a massive sigh of relief when at the Milan Show in November 1991, the factory unveiled its first truly new model for many years, the Daytona.

Definitive production Daytona as displayed at the Milan Show in November 1991.

175

The Modern Era

John Wittner – 'Dr John'

John Wittner, a former dentist, (more commonly known simply as 'Dr John'), from Philadelphia, USA, was the man who revitalized interest in the Guzzi marque (*see* page 179).

The Doctor John racing team had achieved early success by winning the American Motorcycle Association (AMA) Endurance Championship title in 1984 and 1985 with the first 1000cc Le Mans (*see* Chapter 13) to arrive in the USA. In 1987 a Dr John Guzzi V-twin ridden by Doug Brauneck claimed the USA Pro-Twins series title.

Alejandro de Tomaso, the owner of Guzzi at that time, was so impressed by these results that he gave Wittner one of two prototype 8-valve engines (originally constructed with street use in mind) that had been designed in the mid-1980s by veteran engineer Umberto Todero. Todero had been at the factory since the glory days of the 1950s and had previously helped with the design work on the original V7 back in the early 1960s. Todero also designed a V4 engine, but because of factory cutbacks it was never given the priority it deserved.

A specially constructed bike using Todero's engine with further development by Wittner and his team (including specially made camshafts), gained third place at the annual Twins event in March 1988, its racing début.

Further leader-board positions throughout the remainder of 1988 saw John Wittner invited to Italy early the following year with the exciting task of beginning work on a series production version for fast road work or racing use.

The prototype (with lighting equipment and other street-legal requirements) appeared on the Guzzi stand at the Milan Show in November 1989, but it was to be a full two years before the definitive production version was ready to go on sale.

Dr John Guzzi V-Twin

The 1991 bike utilized a rectangular steel space frame and a cantilever swinging arm similar to that of the Dr John racer. The styling, however, was completely new.

Wittner and his team at the Guzzi factory spent a great deal of time on the development work, which is why the project took longer then usual. However, at the time of its launch, attended by the author, the Daytona was heralded as a considerable advance. Not just the four valves per cylinder, single overhead camshaft (sohc) with toothed-belt drive, but the much more modern feel to the engine and chassis once under way. From the moment you leaned forward to take a grip of the Daytona with its low-mounted clip-ons and fired it up, right through to the light throttle and equally light clutch actions, the differences between the old and the new were instantly recognizable.

Privately built (German) Guzzi V-twin engine with belt-driven ohc and desmodromic valve operation on display at the Cologne Show in September 1986.

The Design

Using a half instead of the prototype's full fairing, the 992cc (90 × 78mm) 90 degree V-twin engine featured a belt drive to operate each cylinder's sohc. With 95bhp at 8,000rpm and

OPPOSITE: *Experimental V4 engine from the 1980s with near-horizontal twin shock rear suspension. This exciting project was cancelled due to financial constraints during the final years of the de Tomaso era.*

RIGHT: *The original 1000cc Daytona sports bike on display at the Milan Show, November 1989.*

The Modern Era

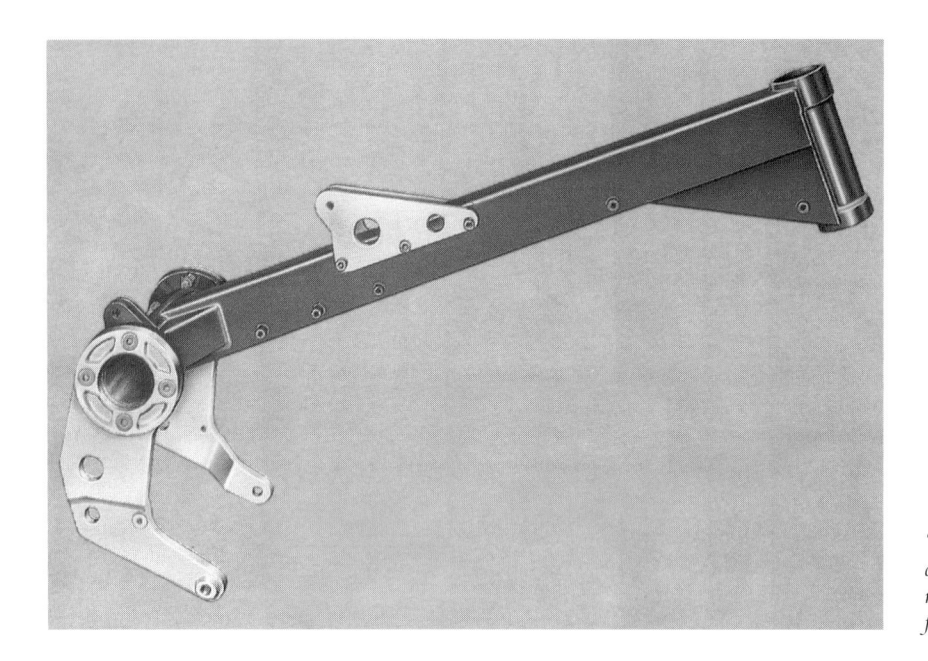

The production Daytona chassis utilized a rectangular steel spine frame.

Daytona 1000 1992

Engine	Air-cooled, sohc, transverse 90 degree V-twin, four valves per cylinder driven by aluminium gears and toothed belts, Nigusil cylinder lining, coil valve springs
Bore	90mm
Stroke	78mm
Displacement	992cc
Compression ratio	10:1
Lubrication	High volume pressure pump, wet sump
Ignition	Weber-Marelli digital electronic
Carburation	Weber-Marelli electronic fuel injection with dual injectors
Gearbox	Five-speed, straight tooth gears, foot-change
Clutch	Twin driven plates, dry with light flywheel
Final drive	Shaft
Frame	Rectangular steel spine using engine as a stressed member
Suspension	Front, Marzocchi telescopic forks; rear, chrome-molydenum steel swinging arm with koni single shock absorber, adjustable for pre-load, compression and rebound
Brakes	Front, twin 300mm drilled floating Brembo discs with four-piston calipers of different diameters; rear, single 260mm disc and floating two-piston caliper
Tyres	Front 120/70 XR17 tubeless radial; rear 160/60 ZR18 tubeless radial

General specification

Wheelbase	1470mm (57.8in)
Dry weight	205kg (452lb)
Fuel capacity	23ltr (5gal)
Maximum power output	95bhp at 8,000rpm★
Top speed	145mph (233km/h)

★Stage 1 (fast road) or Stage 2 (racing) performance kits available.

The Modern Era

> **Dr John**
>
> Even the most ardent Guzzisti could have been forgiven for doubting that the Mandello del Lario factory would ever get around to building its long-promised production version of the Dr John racing team's successful Battle of the Twins racer.
>
> After showing a prototype at the Milan Show in late 1989, these prayers were finally answered two years later, in November 1991 – the good news being that the Italian racing red Daytona 1000 was not only about to enter series production, but well worth the wait. It was supremely ironic that the man largely responsible for moving Guzzi into the modern era should be a former dentist (hence the Dr John title) from Philadelphia, USA. But that's exactly what happened.
>
> John Wittner, a lifelong motorcycle enthusiast, took up dentistry after training in engineering (and a stint of army service in Vietnam), only to throw it all in to go endurance racing with a group of like-minded individuals. He came into contact with the then Guzzi boss Alejandro de Tomaso about securing backing for an all-new racing chassis.
>
> The Dr John race team had its first major success in the US Endurance series in 1984, and again in 1985. Rider Doug Brauneck also won the US Pro-Twins title in 1987. De Tomaso was so impressed by these results that he gave Wittner a prototype eight-valve race engine designed by veteran engineer Umbero Todero. The Wittner racer scored a third placing whilst making a début appearance in the 1988 Daytona Twins event. Further success saw Wittner jetting off to Italy the following year to start work on a production version.
>
> The production bike utilized a rectangular steel spine frame and cantilever swinging arm similar to that of the Dr John race bike. The styling however, was all fresh and considerably changed from the 1989 Milan Show prototype, with the 992cc (90 × 78mm) four valves per cylinder engine fully visible below the sculptured half fairing. The engine employed belt drive to activate each cylinder's single ohc. In standard form the fuel-injection engine (Weber-Marelli) produced almost 100bhp, but factory tuning kits in Stage 1 or 2 (basically the former for fast road work, the latter for racing) added yet more potential.
>
> Compared to earlier versions of Guzzi's big V-twin theme, the Daytona was a considerable advance. Not just the four valves per cylinder sohc with belt drive, but the much more 'modern' feel once under way.
>
> Improvements since its launch, notably the introduction of a cush drive, improved build quality and suspension changes have seen Dr John's creation made even better. The Daytona has also been responsible for many of the improvements found on the later Guzzi series production models, notably the V10 Centauro, 1100 Sport Injection, the California EV and most recently the new V11. Yes, Moto Guzzi have a lot for which to thank Dr John.

maximum torque figures of 98mm at 6,000rpm, the original production model was reasonably powerful; fitting a factory Stage 1 (for fast road work) or Stage 2 kit (for racing use) made things even more interesting.

The throttle response was due to the Weber-Marelli electronic fuel injection with dual injectors, an Alfa-N system, an electric fuel pump with a pressure regulator, optimized digital control of the injection times, and a high-efficiency air filter. Not only this, but the Daytona was also unexpectedly quiet, both mechanically and through its twin exhausts (in standard, street-legal guise).

With a high peak rpm, at least compared to previous Guzzi vees, it was good that maximum torque was produced further down the scale at 6,000rpm. The abundance of low-rev and mid-range power made the stock Daytona a joy to ride. It also meant that there was a little more need to use the five-speed gearbox which, although it contained straight-cut instead of helical-cut cogs, was still a close relation to the assembly found in earlier Guzzi vees.

If the engine generally felt like a tuned version of previous transverse V-twin Guzzis, the chassis most certainly did not. At 205kg (452lb) dry, the Daytona was reasonably light, and with the combination of a 17in front and

The Modern Era

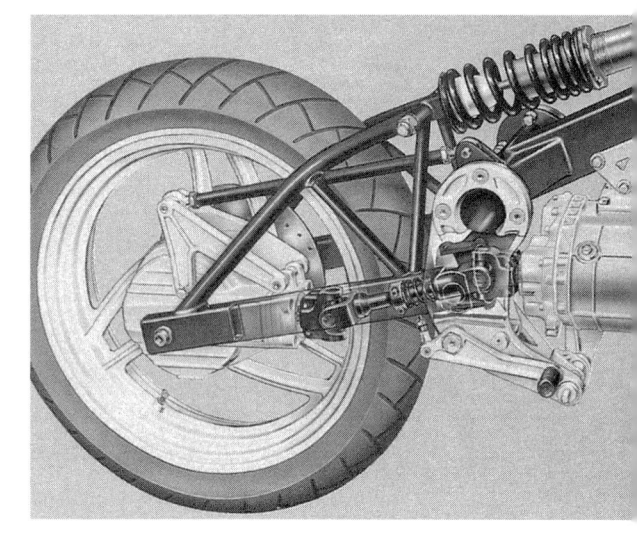

ABOVE: Cantilever rear end using a single Dutch Koni rear shock.

LEFT: Four valves per cylinder and ohc – the new Guzzi Daytona 1000 with rocker box removed to show valve gear.

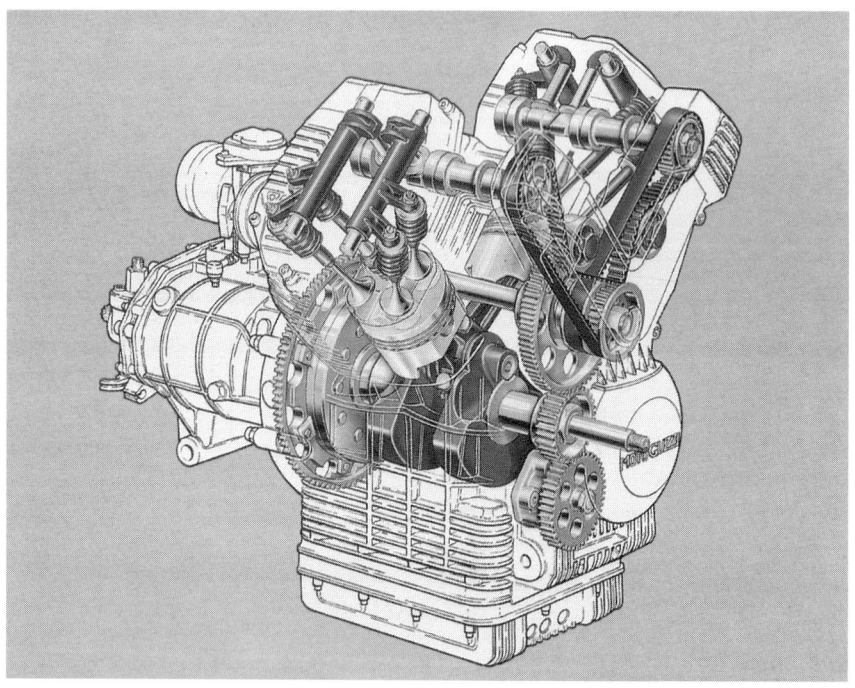

Cutaway drawing showing internal details of the Daytona's four valves per cylinder, belt-driven, ohc engine assembly.

The Modern Era

18in rear wheel, together with modern geometry, provided a much more sporting, 'flickable' feel than the slow-steering Guzzis of the 1970s and 1980s. This improved response was the more impressive because it had not taken place at the expense of straight-line stability, which was as good as ever. Much of this must have been thanks to Wittner's parallelogram swinging arm linkage, which all but cured the traditional shaft-drive torque reaction found on earlier examples of the transverse V-twin family.

Another departure from conventional Guzzi big twin practice was to be found in the braking department. Brembo brakes yes, but independent, without the traditional linked system. Suspension was taken care of by a pair of flex-free 41mm (1.6in) Marzocchi front forks and a multi-adjustable Dutch Koni rear shock where a key role was played by the strut's spring rate. This was critical because it acted as a counter to the dreaded shaft drive 'screwing' effect. Two springs were provided so that customers had a choice when tuning their suspension for the particular needs of the rider and road surfaces.

Daytona 1000 Dr John

In 1994, the limited edition Daytona 1000 Dr John made its bow. Finished in a distinctive black (including the wheels) and gold, it came with the Factory B race kit as standard, complete with carbon fibre Termignoni mufflers, although these were hardly street-legal and intended for track use only. The success of this machine (only 100 were built, but many more could have been sold) prompted Guzzi to build a more accessible high-performance version.

The limited edition Dr John Special with factory B race kit as standard, 1994.

Daytona RS

This duly made its entrance in June 1996. Compared with the standard Daytona, the RS engine was uprated to produce 102bhp at 8,400rpm and featured Carrillo connecting-rods, forged 10.5:1 pistons (previously 10:1), a full race camshaft, ram air intake and a larger airbox, whilst the M16 Weber-Marelli fuel-injection system sported a 54mm (2.12in) injector body with a higher pressure four-bar fuel regulator. Other details of the RS specification included:

- Fully floating 320mm (12.5in) Brembo racing front brake discs
- Fixed 282mm (11.1in) stainless steel rear disc
- White Power inverted front forks with 40mm (1.6in) stanchions
- White Power single rear shock absorber adjustable in compression, rebound and pre-load (shorter in length compared to assembly fitted to stock model).
- New swinging arm with elliptical-section tubes
- 17in wheel front and rear
- ZR rated tyres; front, 120/70; rear, 160/60
- New, lightweight, three-spoke hollow wheels

Aluminium timing gears replaced the chain and sprockets on the less expensive versions.

In fact the RS was really a pukka race bike but with dual seats, a homologated exhaust and airbox for the public highway. Here at last was a serious race bike straight from the factory. Previously, potential racers had to kit out their Daytona at considerable extra cost.

Daytona Racing 1000

Rather confusingly, the factory also constructed a batch of 100 Daytona Racing 1000 models. Built in early 1996, this motorcycle was very much a mixture of the RS and stock Daytona. This meant there were the old Guzzi-made cast alloy wheels, conventional Marzocchi 40mm (1.6in) front forks, a Ysasa battery (the new RS and other 1996 bikes featured a gel-filled no-maintenance battery). There

---

Raceco Daytona 1995

Engine	Air-cooled, 90 degree V-twin, four-stroke, four valves per cylinder with sohc driven by aluminium gears and two toothed belts
Bore	95mm
Stroke	82mm
Displacement	1162cc
Compression ratio	10.5:1
Lubrication	Gear pump
Ignition	Weber-Marelli digital electronic
Carburation	Weber-Marelli fuel injection, sequential with one injector per 54mm throttle body
Gearbox	Close ratio
Clutch	Double disc, dry
Final drive	Shaft
Frame	Standard Daytona lightened and modified (24 degree steering head angle)
Suspension	Front, White Power fork; rear, koni or White Power single shock
Brakes	Front, dual 320mm floating discs; rear, single 260mm disc
Tyres	Front 120/17; rear 180/17

General specification

Wheelbase	1442mm (56.8in)
Dry weight	173kg (385lb)
Fuel capacity	19ltr (4gal)
Maximum power output	125bhp*
Top speed	170mph (273km/h)*

*1997: 139bhp/180mph

Australian Magni Battle of the Twins racer, circa 1992.

Battle of the Twins 1000cc twin shock racer (built by Jim Blomley) at Aintree, early 1990s.

Mike Edwards with Jim Blomley's 1100cc Guzzi at Brands Hatch, October 1994.

Richard Wynn riding the final version of Jim Blomley's 1100cc Guzzi, Brands Hatch 1996.

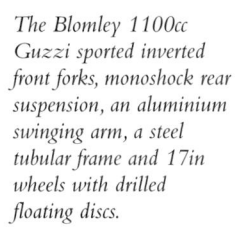

The Blomley 1100cc Guzzi sported inverted front forks, monoshock rear suspension, an aluminium swinging arm, a steel tubular frame and 17in wheels with drilled floating discs.

The Modern Era

Daytona RS 1997

Engine	Air-cooled, sohc, transverse 90 degree V-twin, four valves per cylinder driven by aluminium gears and toothed belts, Nigusil cylinder lining, coil valve springs		rear, steel swinging arm, oval section, single White Power shock absorber, adjustable for pre-load compression and rebound
Bore	90mm	Brakes	Front, twin 300mm drilled floating Brembo discs with four-piston calipers of different diameters;
Stroke	78mm		
Displacement	992cc		
Compression ratio	10.5:1		rear, single 260mm disc and floating two-piston caliper
Lubrication	High volume pressure pump, wet sump		
		Tyres	Front 120/70 XR17 tubeless radial;
Ignition	Weber-Marelli digital electronic		
Carburation	Weber-Marelli electronic fuel injection with dual injectors		rear 160/60 ZR17 tubeless radial
		General specification	
Gearbox	Five-speed, straight tooth gears, foot-change	Wheelbase	1470mm (57.8in)
		Dry weight	223kg (491lb) – with battery
Clutch	Twin driven plates, dry with light flywheel	Fuel capacity	19ltr (4gal)
		Maximum power output	102bhp at 8,400rpm*
Final drive	Shaft		
Frame	Rectangular steel spine using engine as a stressed member	Top speed	149mph (240km/h)
Suspension	Front, White Power inverted telescopic forks;	*Race kit available boosting power to 120bhp	

were full 'C' kit engine performance parts, a P8 computer and the old gearbox with its ten-spring clutch. From late 1996 onwards, the machines featured a much improved gearbox and a lighter eight-spring clutch.

The Daytona Racing 1000 was a generation behind the Daytona RS. Certainly for serious racing use, it would cost a lot of money to bring a Daytona Racing 1000 up to full RS specification. However, as with most small production batch models, it will probably become a collector's item in years to come,

Daytona 1100 Sport

Besides the four valves per cylinder Daytona, the other Guzzi of the 1990s to see racing use was the 1100 Sport. First announced at the end of 1993, it did not enter production for another year. Once it was available, however, it proved well worth the wait, being probably the best Guzzi two valves per cylinder V-twin sports bike since the Le Mans Mark 1 of the mid-1970s (see Chapter 13).

Actually, the 1100 Sport was a smart move on Guzzi's part, utilizing as it did the Daytona-based chassis and one of the new big-bore 2-valve 1064cc engines originally conceived for the top-selling California touring bike. It featured the backbone frame and full-floating shaft drive of the Daytona, powered by an engine that was the result of the firm's wide-ranging experience garnered with the 2-valve 90 degree V-twin over the previous three decades.

The Design

Many of the best features from the Daytona were to be found, including the four-piston

The Blomley 1100cc Guzzi in April 1998 with…

…and without the streamlining.

Guy Etherington with the final version of Jim Blomley's 1100 Guzzi V-twin, Cadwell Park, summer 1999.

Interesting one-off turbocharged dohc Guzzi V-twin with very special twin-port cylinder heads, aluminium frame, inverted front forks and six-piston front brake calipers, circa 1997.

Another view of the unique dohc twin-port head Guzzi V-twin. Note the location of the centre spark plug.

The Modern Era

gold Brembo calipers, a single rear 282mm (11in) disc with a two-piston floating caliper, braided hoses, a stainless steel exhaust system, 17in front and 18in rear wheels shod with tubeless radial tyres, and 41mm (1.6in) Marzocchi MIR front forks. New features were as follows:

- New design for the fuel tank with the capacity decreased from 23 to 20ltr (5 to 4.4gal)
- Seat
- Fairing (with 'ram' air intakes)
- Light alloy footrest mounts
- 40mm Dell'Orto carburettors (replacing the Daytona's fuel-injection system)
- Electronic inductive Marelli Digiplex 2S ignition
- A new, lighter frame (still of chrome-moly steel construction) with the front sub-frame incorporated
- A more compact rear shock absorber, adjustable for compression and rebound

The engine of the 1100 Sport was clearly based on the then current 1100 California, but there were some notable differences:

- Higher compression 10.5:1 pistons forged in special non-deforming alloy
- Special lightweight clutch, flywheel, and pressure plates
- Stronger and lighter crankshaft
- Stronger connecting-rods (also fitted to post-1994 California engines)

1100 Sport Injection

Even though the 1100 Sport had been well received, Guzzi, with a new management team in place, didn't want to be seen resting on their laurels and so in June 1996 an updated version was put into production.

Known as the 1100 Sport Injection, it benefited greatly, as had the touring California model before it, by switching from carburettors to the highly successful Weber-Marelli

1100 Sport Carburettor 1994

Engine	Air-cooled, ohv, transverse 90 degree V-twin, two valves per cylinder, one-piece crankshaft, one-piece crank-case, two-piece connecting-rods, plain bearing big ends	Suspension	Front, telescopic forks; rear, cantilever swinging arm, single shock absorber
		Brakes	Front, twin 320mm semi-floating discs with four-piston calipers; rear, single 260mm disc with two-piston caliper
Bore	92mm		
Stroke	80mm		
Displacement	1064cc	Tyres	Front 120/70 ZR17; rear 160/60 ZR18
Compression ratio	10.5:1		
Lubrication	Gear pump, wet sump	**General specification**	
Ignition	Magnetti Marelli Digiplex electronic	Wheelbase	1475mm (58in)
		Dry weight	210kg (463lb)
Carburation	2 × Dell'Orto PHM 40ND/NS	Fuel capacity	N/A
Gearbox	Five-speed, foot-change	Maximum power output	90bhp at 7,800rpm
Clutch	Twin driven plates, dry, car-type		
Final drive	Shaft	Top speed	148mph (238km/h) or 158mph (254km/h) with factory race kit
Frame	Rectangular steel space frame with detachable sub-frame		

The Modern Era

The Raceco/Three Cross Effort

Amedeo Castellani was born of Italian parents in London on 16 January 1956. The family moved back to Italy in 1968, where one year later, the 13-year-old Amedeo rode his first motorcycle, a 50cc Moto Guzzi Dingo.

Although his parents were to stay in Rome, Castellani returned to the UK in 1974 where he worked as a photographer. In 1981 he bought a brand-new Guzzi V50 – a move that was to change his life. A few months later the V50 was replaced by an SP1000.

Subsequently he quit his job as a photographer, setting up instead as a self-employed motorcycle mechanic specializing in Guzzis. He became the workshop manager at Moto Mecca, the Guzzi spares specialist, while they were still based in London. This lasted until Christmas 1985, when he became involved in Team MCN with Howard Lees and Anthony Ainslie, travelling around Europe to various 24-hour events as one of the team's engineers.

Castellani then returned to specializing in Guzzi's, setting up the Raceco business in Isleworth. In 1989, he went to work in Australia for Ted Stolarski and, with a Daytona prototype with carburettors, competed successfully at Daytona USA in the spring of 1990. Later that year he returned to Britain and his Guzzi business, which relocated to Hounslow before moving to Surbiton in 1992 where it was to remain until Christmas 1996, when Raceco moved out of the London area to rural Suffolk.

From 1987 until 1992 Raceco provided tuning expertize to Clarke Racing and their riders Peter Warden and later Ian Cobby. Then from the 1993 season came a highly successful joint venture with British Guzzi importers, Three Cross.

The Three Cross/Raceco Daytona racer began life as an ex-demonstrator with 8,500 miles (13,676km) on the clock. In its first year with Torquil Ross-Martin as rider it weighed 225kg (496lb) and produced 90bhp. By the time it was last raced in 1997 by Ian Cobby it weighed 175kg (386lb) and produced a staggering 140bhp! Besides Ross-Martin and Cobby, other riders to race the bike were Richard Defango (early 1994), Rick Lewenden (late 1994) and the Australian Grand Prix star Paul 'Angry Ant' Lewis in 1995.

The Three Cross/Raceco Daytona finally bowed out in 1997, having won every race it competed in and more than often setting pole in qualifying into the bargain. What a record!

Ian Cobby Clarke Guzzi Twins racer at the Italian Owners Club Cadwell weekend, July 1992.

A later version of the Clarke Guzzi with an aluminium frame and monoshock rear suspension.

The Modern Era

1100 Sport Injection 1995

Engine	Air-cooled, ohv, transverse, 90 degree V-twin, two valves per cylinder, one-piece crankshaft, one-piece crank-case, two-piece connecting-rods, plain bearing big ends	Suspension	Front, telescopic inverted (upside-down) forks; rear, cantilever swinging arm, single shock absorber
Bore	92mm	Brakes	Front, twin 320mm semi-floating discs with four-piston calipers; rear, single 260mm disc with two-piston caliper
Stroke	80mm		
Displacement	1064cc	Tyres	Front 120/70 ZR17; rear 160/60 ZR18
Compression ratio	10.5:1		
Lubrication	Gear pump, wet sump	**General specification**	
Ignition	Weber-Marelli electronic digital	Wheelbase	1475mm (58in)
Carburation	Weber-Marelli electronic injection	Dry weight	210kg (463lb)
		Fuel capacity	N/A
Gearbox	Five-speed, foot-change	Maximum power output	90bhp at 7,800rpm
Clutch	Twin driven plates, dry, car-type		
Final drive	Shaft	Top speed	148mph (238km/h) or 158mph (254km/h) with factory race kit
Frame	Rectangular steel space frame with detachable sub-frame		

fuel-injection system, found on not just the California, but also the Daytona and the brand-new V10 Centauro (essentially a naked retro-type bike with the four valves per cylinder Daytona engine assembly).

Instantly noticeable was the change from conventional to new inverted (upside-down) front forks (as per the new Daytona RS), three-spoke Marchesini-made wheels. In fact, except for semi-floating front discs and Pirelli Dragon GT tyres, everything was the same as the Daytona RS.

A Tester's Opinion

Certainly the new injected 1100 Sport was well thought of by the press of the day. *Motor Cycle News* tester Kevin Ash having this to say:

> The bike is superbly stable and encourages you to really lay it far over, when the tyres dig in and hold it accurately on line....The first clue comes with lighter, smoother throttle action, which no longer demands two fistfuls of twistgrip to get fully open. But more importantly, throttle response had also been upgraded. The old bike misfired and gasped at lower revs and made itself difficult unless you were nailing it. The injected machine runs smoothly from tick-over right up to the red line at 8,000rpm.

Daytona 1100 Sport Corsa

The final variant of the 1100 Sport (still injection) arrived in February 1998 in the shape of the limited edition (200 only) Corsa models. Available in either red or yellow, the Corsa had an all-black engine assembly (except for polished rocker covers), which had an almost overbearing effect on the bike's appearance. Unique features of the model included a silver 'Limited Edition' plate on the top yoke; Termignoni carbon fibre silencers and Dutch White Power suspension. In Great Britain (July 1998) the 1100 Sport Corsa cost £8,495 – a £500 premium over the stock bike.

Index

Aeberhard, Alex 18
Aermacchi 69, 146, 153
Agostini, Duilio 38, 110, 111, 138
Agusta, Count Domenico 104
Aintree circuit 183
AJS 72, 89, 111, 114, 119
    Porcupine 53
Alberti, Raffaele 18, 94, 134, 135
Albi circuit 52, 94
Alfa Romeo 25, 78
Ambrosini, Dario 60, 67, 91, 92, 94
Amm, Ray 104, 106
Anderson, Fergus 25, 48, 52, 53, 63, 68, 72, 83–93, 95, 102, 104–15, 138
Armstrong, Ian 165
Armstrong, Roy 163, 165, 168, 174
Ascari, Alberto 35
Ash, Kevin 188
Assen circuit 105
Austrian Grand Prix 72
Avus circuit 14

Baldwin, Mike 156
Balzarotti, Ferdinando 38, 87
Bandini, Terzo 16, 43
Bandirola, Carlo 106
Barnes, Trevor 70, 71
Barret, E.A. 65
Barrington, Manliff 28, 30, 31, 60, 74, 77, 87
Battista, Emilio 108
Beer, Gunter 72
Belgian Grand Prix 71, 84
Benelli 9, 28, 60, 87, 91, 111, 122, 156
Bianchi 14, 25, 81, 144, 149, 153
Blomley, Jim 183, 185
BMW 112, 173
    R75 156
    R90S 156
Bonelli, Dr Gerardo 120
Boreham circuit 65

Bourne, Arthur 76, 77
Brambilla, Ernesto 156
Brambilla, Vittorio 143, 156
Brands Hatch circuit 66, 70, 122, 154, 183
Brauneck, Doug 176
Brett, Jack 106, 119
Brough circuit 62, 70
Brusi, Riccardo 16
Bryen, Keith 120
BSA 70, 71, 114
    Gold Star 32, 69
    Rocket 3 156
Bultaco 72
Burney, J.G. (Gordon) 25, 26, 44, 45

Cadwell Park circuit 18, 173, 185
Campbell, Keith 112, 117, 119, 132
Cann, Maurice 31, 61, 63–5, 72, 78, 87, 88, 90, 103
Carcano, Ing. Giulio Cesare 39, 64, 88, 117, 122–5, 142, 153
Carena, Gino 156, 157
Cass, Kevin 72
Castellani, Amedeo 173, 187
Cavanna, Luigi 134, 136, 137
Cavendini, Mario 12
Cerato, Guido 35
Clark, John 119
Cobby, Ian 187
Colnago, Giuseppe 120
Columbo, Richardo 111
Cooley, Wes 156
Cotton 25, 68
    Telstar 69
Croft circuit 165
Crystal Palace circuit 70, 72

Dal Toe, Giuseppe 145
Dale, Dickie 65, 106, 110, 111, 116, 120, 131, 138–41
Davies, Pete (P.K.) 165
Daytona circuit 173

189

Index

De Tomaso, Alejandro 179
Defango, Richard 187
Diener, Les 62
DKW, 18, 46 54, 103, 105, 106, 112
Ducati 9, 156, 173
    750 SS 164
    900 SS 156, 164
Duke, Geoff 70, 92, 117
Dutch TT 67, 72, 85, 105

Edwards, Mike 183
Ennett, Derek 117
Etherington, Guy 185
Excelsior 31

Faenza circuit 41
FB Mondial 9, 65, 91, 104, 105, 120, 132, 142
Fenwick, Ted 70
Fiera circuit 38
Findlay, Jack 158
Finzi, Aldo 12
Finzi, Gino 12
Floreffe circuit 103, 108, 112
Fogarty, Carl 168
Fogarty, George 168
Foster, Bob 49, 90
Francisci, Bruno 38
French Grand Prix 52, 94, 111
Fumagalli, Carlo 17

Gamble, Richard 165, 168, 173
Gatti, Valentino 13
Gazzola, Luciano 156
Geminiani, Sante 91, 94
Genoa circuit 55
German Grand Prix 67, 98, 115
Ghersi, Mario 25
Ghersi, Pietro 14, 23–25
Gianni, Ing. Carlo 79
Gilera 9, 53, 79, 106, 112, 117, 118, 120, 123, 124, 126, 132
    Saturno 35, 41, 86, 142
Gira d'Italia 13
Graham, Les 89, 104
Guthrie, Jimmy 27, 46

Guzzi, Carlo 9–11, 20, 23, 26, 43, 55, 56, 73, 122, 146, 149

Haas, Werner 97, 98, 104
Handley, Wal 25
Hartle, John 119
Hinton, Harry 64
Hockenheim circuit 83, 103
Honda 54, 57, 72, 120, 122, 156
    CB750 163

Imola circuit 108, 117, 119, 158
Isle of Man TT 13, 23–31, 34, 44–7, 49, 60, 62, 77, 78, 85, 90, 92, 93, 102, 103, 107, 109, 111, 115, 119, 130, 131, 156
Italian Grand Prix 67, 84, 111, 116, 123, 129

Jawa 72

Kavanah, Ken 106, 108, 111, 115, 129, 138, 139
Kawasaki 164
    Mach 3 156
    Z1 156
    Z900 156
Kidson, John 68, 69, 72

Lario circuit 14
Laverda 54, 156, 164
    Jota 164, 165
Leoni, Gianni 91, 92, 94, 135
Levieux, Davide 156
Lewenden, Rick 187
Lewis, Paul 187
Liberati, Libero 117
Lomas, Bill 71, 98, 111, 112, 114–7, 122, 131, 132, 139, 141, 142
Lorenzetti, Enrico 35, 41, 64, 65, 80, 89, 92, 95, 98, 104, 105, 116, 141
Lunn, Doug 165
Lurani, Count Giovanni (Johnny) 146

Magi, Renato 94
Magni 183
Mandolini, Giuseppe 120
Marcartino, Prof. Arnoldo 149

Index

Martin, Leon 67
Maserati 25
Mastellari, Claudio 94
McIntyre, Bob 119
Mellors, E.A. (Ted) 28, 46
Mentasi, Guido 14, 15
Mettet circuit 84, 89, 95, 110
Micucci, Ing. Antonio 73
Milani–Taranto 21, 35, 38
Modena circuit 117
Montanari, Alano 103
Montjuich Park circuit 106
Montlhéry circuit 111, 135, 138–141
Monza circuit 14, 15, 43, 65, 94, 95, 111, 116, 123, 129, 130, 134, 135, 143, 144–6
Moretti, Amilcare 16, 43
Moto Guzzi models (multi-cylinders)
    150 V-twin 87
    250 parallel twin 31, 73–8
    500 across-the-frame four 19, 20
    500 in-line four 17, 41, 79–84
    500 three-cylinder (racer) 19, 54–6
    500 three-cylinder (roadster) 54
    500 V-twin 18, 41–53, 76, 87, 94
    750S 157, 159, 160, 175
    750S3 157, 160, 164, 175
    850 T3 162, 164
    1100 Sport 179, 184–6
    1100 Sport Corsa 188
    California EV 179, 184
    Daytona 158, 175–88
    GT850 153, 156
    Le Mans 153, 156, 160, 163, 164, 168–75, 184
    SP1000 166, 168, 187
    V10 Centauro 179
    V1000 168
    V50 187
    V7 700 142–3, 148, 168
    V7 750 143
    V7 Sport 154, 156, 158, 175
    V8 9, 41, 84, 118, 119–23, 141
    VII 179
Moto Guzzi models (singles)
    4VSS 15
    4VTT 15
    250 dohc GP 99, 100
    310 GP 90, 103
    317 GT 102, 104
    350 GP 89, 96, 101, 105–22, 141
    500 GP 112–4, 118–20
    Airone 11
    Albatross 59–72
    Astore 11
    Corsa 2V 12, 13, 17–21
    Dondolino 35–40
    Falcone 11
    Gambalunga 39–41, 63
    Gambalunghino 86–91, 94, 96–101, 103
    GP Prototype 10, 15, 16
    GT 11, 17, 56, 76
    GT 16, 11
    GT2VT 17
    GTC 11, 32, 33–6
    GTS 11
    GTV 11
    GTW 11
    Guzzino 134
    Motoleggera 134
    Normale 8, 11
    P175 11
    P250 11
    Tipo Faenza 41
    Tipo S 11
    Tipo Sport 10, 11, 14, 15
    TT250 22–24
    V 11
MV Agusta 9, 53, 65, 79, 94, 105, 111, 112, 117, 118, 123, 124

Neilson, Cook 156
New Imperial 25, 31
Norton 41, 46, 53, 70, 72, 79, 92, 104, 106, 119, 126
    Manx 38, 120
    Commando 156
Nott, Ernie 27
NSU 46, 97, 98, 105, 106, 111
    Rennmax 66, 70, 78, 103
Nuovolari, Tazio 14

Ospedaletti circuit 80, 96, 103

191

Index

Pagani, Alberto 72, 145
Pagani, Nello 14, 18, 143
Panella, Alfredo 16
Parilla 87, 149
Parodi, Angelo 149
Parodi, Emanuele 9, 10, 149
Parodi, Enrico 103, 112, 149
Parodi, Giorgio 9, 10, 12, 23, 26, 79, 139, 149
Paton 153
Patrignani, Roberto 143
Pike, Roland 31
Pinza, Sergio 38
Pridmore, Reg 156
Prini, Ugo 16
Prini, Vitorio 25
Provini, Tarquinio 65

Ravelli, Givanni 9
Remor, Pietro 79
Rex-Acme 25
Riva, Raimondo 156, 157, 164
Robb, Tommy 69
Ross-Martin, Torquil 187
Rous, Charlie 122
Royal Enfield 111
Rudge 27, 31
Ruffo, Bruno 51, 67, 87, 90, 93, 104, 135
Rumi 149

Salmaggi, Ing. Giuseppe 35
Salzburgring circuit 17
San Remo circuit 41, 67, 96, 103
Sandford, Cecil 105
Sandri, Guglielmo 18, 58
Scala, Bruno 168
Scarborough circuit 65, 72
Sear, John 165, 168
Serafina, Dorini 35
Sertum 149
Silverstone circuit 69
Simpson, J.H. 45
Slater, Roger 165
Snetterton circuit 69, 163
Solitude circuit 67, 115

Spa Francorchamps circuit 84
Sprayston, Ken 67
Stolarski, Ted 187
Surtees, John 115, 119, 132
Suzuki 72, 120
   GS1000 163
Swiss Grand Prix 21, 35, 45, 52, 57, 87

Taglioni, Ing. Fabio 56
Taruffi, Piero 146, 147
Tenni, Omobono 21, 25, 30, 44–6, 48, 78, 133–6
Thomas, Ernie 87
Thruxton circuit 170
Todero, Umberto 176, 179
Tonkin, Steve 168
Tonti, Ing. Lino 142, 153, 154
Triumph 54, 173
   Trident 156

Ulster Grand Prix 30, 64, 66, 67, 72, 87, 90, 111, 115

Varzi, Achille 21, 25, 78
Velocette, 66 111, 114
   KTT 67
Venturi, Remo 65, 143, 144
Visioli, Erminio 14

Walsh, Alan 154
Warden, Peter 173, 187
Wellings, Mark 161, 162, 173
West Raynham circuit 162
Wheeler, Arthur 66–72, 94, 105
Williams, Charlie 156
Wilson, George 92
Winterburn, Roger 165
Wittner, John 173, 176–181
Woods, Stanley 25–30, 44–9, 77, 87, 129, 130, 146, 156
Woods, Tommy 87
Wynn, Richard 183

Yamaha 72, 120

Zolder circuit 157